WITHDRAWN

The Two-Party Line

The Two-Party Line

Conversations in the Field

JANE C. GOODALE

with
ANN CHOWNING

ROWMAN & LITTLEFIELD PUBLISHERS, INC.
Lanham • Boulder • New York • London

ROWMAN & LITTLEFIELD PUBLISHERS, INC.

Published in the United States of America
by Rowman & Littlefield Publishers, Inc.
4720 Boston Way, Lanham, Maryland 20706

3 Henrietta Street
London WC2E 8LU, England

British Cataloging in Publication Information Available

Library of Congress Cataloging-in-Publication Data

Goodale, Jane C. (Jane Carter), 1926–
The two-party line : conversations in the field / Jane C. Goodale
with Ann Chowning.
p.   cm.
Includes bibliographical references and index.
1. Ethnology—Papua New Guinea—West New Britain Province—Field
work. 2. Women ethnologists—Papua New Guinea—West New Britain
Province—Correspondence. 3. Women ethnologists—Papua New Guinea
—West New Britain Province—Attitudes. 4. Kaulong (Papua New Guinea
people)—Social life and customs. 5. Sengseng (Papua New Guinea people)
—Social life and customs. 6. West New Britain Province (Papua New
Guinea)—Social life and customs. I. Chowning, Ann. II. Title.
GN671.N5G66   1996   305.8'009953—dc20   96–15066   CIP

ISBN 0–8476–8263–3 (cloth : alk. paper)
ISBN 0–8476–8264–1 (pbk. : alk. paper)

Printed in the United States of America

⊖™ The paper used in this publication meets the minimum requirements of
American National Standard for Information Sciences—Permanence of
Paper for Printed Library Materials, ANSI Z39.48–1984.

Contents

Illustrations

*Photographs by Jane Goodale except where noted * by Ann Chowning. Map with permission of the University of Washington Press.*

Acknowledgments

Without Ann Chowning there would be no second party to gossip with through these letters and quite possibly there would have been no field experience for me. So thank you, Ann, for your voice at the end of the two-party line. Readers should understand, however, that I alone am responsible for the supplementary comments, the introduction, and all of the postscripts including the final one.

To the many people of Umbi and Dulago (those who are mentioned by name in these letters and those who go unnamed), we first thank you—for putting up with us (two very strange people with sometimes incomprehensible habits and values), for patiently teaching us so much, and for allowing us to share in your lives. We have not obscured your names, rather, we have made them known in America and elsewhere, as you wished.

To all of the representatives of the Department of Native Affairs in Port Moresby, Rabaul, and especially the Kiaps and the Yun brothers (proprietors of the trade store) in Kandrian whose multifaceted support, friendship, and hospitality we enjoyed, we extend our heartfelt thanks. We would have had a very different and difficult experience without you. We hope you will overlook our occasional outbursts of frustration.

To the National Institute of Mental Health, Columbia University, and particularly to the National Science Foundation and the National Geographic Society, we acknowledge with gratitude your financial and photographic support and advice.

To the many unknown and known reviewers of this manuscript (in particular, Deborah Gewertz, Nancy McDowell, Philip Kilbride, Mary des Chene, Carol MacCormack, and students at Bryn Mawr College), your critical and insightful readings have given me much to think about, and your suggestions have enormously improved the book.

And, finally, I dedicate this book to my late mother, Susan Bainbridge Goodale, whose care packages meant so much to us in the field, who saved every letter I ever wrote, and who contributed the title.

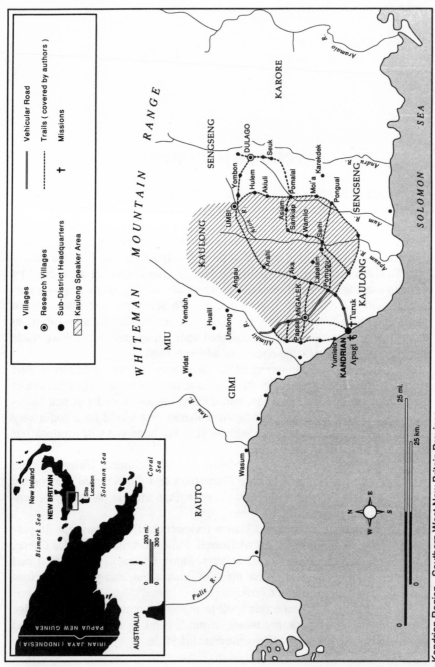

Kandrian Region - Southern West New Britain Province

Chapter 1

Introduction: Setting up the Two-Party Line

> July 1962—Umbi
> Dear Ann: Thanks for your note [telling me where she had settled]. I don't know whether the policeman will take this note to you or whether he has already seen you. If not, an Umbi-ite will carry it. All goes well here....

> Aug. 1962—Dulago
> Dear Jane: It's raining steadily and there's not a sign of life around so it seems a good time for letters...

So began the "the two-party line" of written communication established by me and my colleague, Ann, while conducting simultaneous ethnographic fieldwork in the interior forests of Southwest New Britain in the then Territory of Papua and New Guinea.

The Two-Party Line

Many years ago as a sophomore student at Radcliffe (now Harvard) University, I learned about an activity called ethnographic fieldwork carried out by anthropologists in foreign cultures. Returning home from this fieldwork, they wrote with apparent authority about how these other people went about their business of living. I spent the first two years of my undergraduate honors tutorial reading these ethnographic monographs, most of them later to be known as "classic," being descriptions of Andaman Islanders (Radcliffe-Brown [1922] 1967), Iroquois Confederacies (Louis Henry Morgan 1851), Trobriand Islanders (Malinowski 1922), Arunta of Central Australia (Spencer 1927), Crow Indians (Lowie 1935), Nuer of the Sudan (Evans-Pritchard 1940), and even the

Tribes of the Rif of North Africa written by my tutor himself (C. S. Coon 1931)—to name only a few. I learned rather quickly that how the information was gathered was rarely given by the author with the sole exception of Malinowski (1922), who described rather well in a preface how fieldwork should be done and expressed some of the loneliness and difficulties he encountered in the Trobriand Islands.

Cultural/Social anthropology was taught, (in the 1940s and 1950s) as a science, but its method, although guided by the scientific model, seemed to apply only to description and classification (ethnography) and comparison (ethnology) of social and cultural phenomena. Drawing on this comparative method, the ethnographer, and others who had never themselves been in the field, constructed theories concerning the evolution and nature of human society and culture. Field methodology—how the data were collected—largely remained a mystery to me and to most of my contemporaries. I believe that my professors considered such to be rather like equally foolish instructions of how to be a guest at a cocktail party. I was, in due time, sent forth by my mentors to do my initiatory fieldwork among the Aboriginal peoples (the Tiwi) of Melville Island, North Australia, in 1954 (see Goodale 1971). Ann, also a student at the University of Pennsylvania, had a different experience in that she was actually sent off in 1953 to attend a field school where she gained experience in ethnographic data collection.

None of my professors at the University of Pennsylvania, where I was enrolled as a graduate student (in the 1950s), seemed able to tell me anything more than just "to go there, live with the people, and learn what you have to learn." I count two Australians, W. E. H. "Bill" Stanner and W. E. "Bill" Harney, among the exceptions to the "dive in and learn to swim or drown" school of ethnographic advisors. Stanner, then a member of the Department of Anthropology at the Research School of Pacific Studies, Australian National University in Canberra, gave me initial advice before I reached Melville Island which concerned note-taking, questioning, culture-shock symptoms and remedies, and proper behavior (for a woman!) in the field. The legendary Bill Harney, a self-taught observer of the human condition including, but not limited to, the Aboriginal peoples of Australia, and a comember of the team engaged in fieldwork among the Tiwi, graciously completed the first phase of my education in methodology. He taught me through words and by deed all that I needed to know at that time about gaining respect and rapport and most importantly, how to learn a culture experientially through participation and observation. The post-Ph.D. phase of my education was largely self-taught and occurred during the fieldwork that forms the basis of this volume.

The year of my initiation, 1954, was also the year that saw the publication of *Return to Laughter*, the first of now dozens of books written by anthropologists (for example, Briggs 1970, Dumont 1978, Hayano 1990, Maybury-Lewis 1965, Mead 1977, Powdermaker 1966, Rabinow 1977, Read 1965, and Riesman 1977) describing their own experiences in the field. Laura Bohannon (1954), using the pseudonym Elenore Smith Bowen, wrote *Return To Laughter* as a fictionalized account of her (and her husband's) fieldwork experiences in Africa. This lively account remains a best-seller today. In this fictional work Bohannon is able to convey some of the excitement of learning why people are doing what they do, and some of the sadness as well as the joys of sharing the lives of others while trying to maintain one's own cultural identity with its acquired sense of what is right and proper. But this work, like those which follow, serve only to relate a reflexive view of what fieldwork really *is*, both in content and as a learning process. What is written *about* are the selected experiences that the author believes will convey the image of fieldwork he or she wishes to share with the reader. Most of the accounts were written about the author's first (and often most memorable?) field experience, but the related experiences were written down at a time when the author was a well-established professional scholar and teacher. There is a mixture of voices in these accounts. By quoting from notebooks and diaries, the voice of a novice is heard but all too soon these words are overlaid by commentary and discussion from the more mature voice of the professional reflecting on the experience many years later.

The voice *from* the field is rarely published. Mead's (1977) *Letters from the Field 1925-1975* is composed of letters written over her professional lifetime to friends, colleagues, and family, and we may assume the experiences were differently edited for the different recipients (as our two voices were in the text that follows). Malinowski's (1967) posthumously published *Diary in the Strict Sense of the Term*, written during his Trobriand researches, is surely a voice speaking from the field but one that was intended only for his own eyes and ears. The diary is so inwardly focused on the author's mental and physical health, challenged by his loneliness, that we can rarely hear his telling of the experiences he shared with the Trobriand Islanders and others, through which he learned so much about their culture and social life. Many of us who read this work felt a sense of betrayal that the reality of his fieldwork experience was in some ways quite at odds with the ideal he espoused some years later in the preface to *Argonauts* (1922). Just who had been betrayed, the author or the readers, was the subject of some debate for years following the publication. In the same way, some readers will feel betrayed as they read this account, because in these letters to each other, Ann and I chatted a great deal more about our own working conditions than about the anthropological aspects of the research in which we were involved. In the final postscript (chapter 9) I reflect on why, perhaps, this was so.

In 1965 I began to teach fieldwork methods as part of a required course in ethnography for majors at Bryn Mawr College. It was a difficult topic to teach. With very little literature, I resorted to anecdotal accounts of my life in the field, illustrating different methodological truths and realities, as nearly every fieldworker has done for their students since before Malinowski's time. To give them additional material I hired two students in my ethnography class to type up the written messages I exchanged with my co-fieldworker Ann Chowning, during the first and second periods (1962, 1963, and 1964) of joint fieldwork among the Kaulong and Sengseng people inhabiting the interior of southwestern New Britain, itself a large island lying east of the larger island of New Guinea. The students in that class urged me to publish these written messages to give others the same sense of "being really in the field with us" as they had received. It has taken me a very long time to feel comfortable in doing this, as these notes give an unedited and quite truthful version of a particularly difficult research assignment that we gave to ourselves.

Since that early beginning, the teaching of ethnographic fieldwork methodology has become an accepted part of most anthropological curricula, although even today it is not an integral part of the training offered in all anthropology departments to undergraduate or even to graduate students. Where formerly there were no textbooks, today there are many. See, for example, Agar (1980), Crane and Angrosino, (1974), Denzin and Lincoln (1994), Ellen (1984), and Pelto and Pelto (1978). More often, it seems, ethnographic method is included as part of a theoretical course where it is critiqued primarily for its result—the interpretation of culture (see Geertz 1973, Clifford and Marcus 1986) at the same time the work is examined for its essence, which in my view, is the *process* of learning *experientially*.

Some recent publications have begun to address the experiential aspect of the fieldwork process. In a volume edited by DeVita (1990), titled *The Humbled Anthropologist*, the contributors tell of particular experiences they had in the field that, they came to realize *only later*, contained a valuable lesson concerning a significant cultural point. In *Fieldnotes*, edited by Sanjek (1990), contributors confess that insights which have found their way into their monographs are sometimes nowhere to be found in their field notebooks. Rather, these insights (often appearing only while in the process of analyzing the data and writing the monograph) came from their own experiential data bank; what Sanjek (1990:5) calls *headnotes*, a term he attributes to Ottenberg.

The Two-Party Line is my attempt to convey the process Ann and I went through in building up our experiential data banks and field notebooks. However, ethnographic insights are very rarely reported in our letters to each other. *The Two-Party Line* is *not* an ethnographic monograph full of interesting facts about the Kaulong and Sengseng, their meaning, or analysis. The reader will read and learn more about the ethnographers than about the people we studied. It is intended primarily to show that the *process of cultural data gathering* is, at best, an unpredictable and serendipitous affair. It will demonstrate that learning a *totally unfamiliar* second culture is similar to learning one's primary (natal) culture—experiential and not experimental—in that control of the learning environment is largely in the hands of others; rarely, if ever, in the hands of the learner. Does this make it unscientific and methodless? I do not believe it does any more than scientific observations of astronomical phenomena or animal studies are seen to be methodless. Rather the difficulty comes in creating a written description of this process for readers who are unfamiliar with (or unaware of) their own cultural learning process. I believe that the process can, in part, be seen through the immediate writings of the fieldworker, without the filter of retrospection that selects only for known significance of the data. Other data remains unrecognized in the fieldworker's mind-bank, perhaps only to appear at some future time as having some explanatory significance in describing cultural phenomena.

There are many kinds of fieldwork documents: the notes one takes while interviewing or observing, the notes written up in the evening as one dutifully types everything in duplicate (an ideal never reached by us!), and the personal diary where presumably the part of the experience that the author wants to keep private is written. I never kept such a document since I felt everything I experienced should be part of my written fieldnotes, although some of them went only into my mental data bank. Then there are the letters one writes to others outside the field location, describing and explaining the experience, but inevitably filtered by what the writer wishes the reader to know, and how much shared experience the reader has with the writer. I wrote such letters to family members and fellow anthropologists. Readers of this volume will quickly realize that there is a significant stylistic difference between letters to family (and others who expected reports from us) and those I scribbled to Ann (which often crossed hers to me). In the former we attempt to describe and explain, while in the latter we seek merely to share and thus involve the other in the immediate experiences. In the former, there was an attempt to write in whole sentences, while in the latter there was often no need. Ann's and my letters are more similar to gossip over the back fence, than to carefully composed and selected information transmitted to those who could not share our experience with us in its entirety.

The Two-Party Line should be listened to rather than read, for had we possessed other more direct means of verbal communication, there would have been no need to write them. It is important to know that the two voices heard here are those of friends who happen also to be women. We both took our graduate training at the University of Pennsylvania, and for both of us this was our second or, in Ann's case, fourth field experience. Like a diary, these letters became our emotional dumping ground wherein we verbally expressed and shared our frustrations and joys of discovery, engendered by our attempts to understand, and in turn to be understood by, the people with whom we chose to live, and from whom we would learn. Like most ethnographers, we have found that fieldwork involves a process of confronting one's own cultural identity, and that the greater the challenge is to one's own cultural values, the more one is forced to the realization of the important part those values play in the formation of one's own cultural identity. In these letters the perceptive reader will come to learn, in much the same way as we the fieldworkers learned, the quality and quantity of cultural "baggage" each of us brought to the study and how we handled it. In the concluding chapter I reflect on the voices being those of women.

Because I wish to avoid the filter of retrospection, I have left the letters as they were written, however taking the liberty of correcting my notorious bad spelling and of eliminating names where they might cause embarrassment to others. Repetition, a part of the tedium and stress of fieldwork, has *not* been edited out, with one exception. Since nearly every letter contains reference to our logistical concerns in trying to coordinate our efforts getting supplies (money and mail) from Kandrian several day's walk away, I have here cut out some of these references. I have also added to the letters, both in brackets within the text and in the chapter postscripts, some retrospective explanations in order to clarify, translate, and explain terms and events for readers unfamiliar with the local Papua New Guinea scene.

To cover those times when we traveled together into and out from the field sites, or when we took turns making visits to each other, once each month (and for the initial period in 1962 where letters were not routinely preserved), I include some letters written to outsiders, chiefly my family. We made very few exits and entries during the whole period because of the difficult logistics and terrain. We depended on the monthly visits to each other for rest and recreation, during which we could escape some of the tension of maintaining working cross-cultural relationships, exchange notebooks, discuss interesting findings and puzzles in our data, and come to know each other's immediate environment. Our two communities, although speaking distinct (but closely related) languages, were culturally very similar so that these monthly visits were mentally stimulating as well as emotionally relaxing—but hardly completely refreshing.

The letters are presented chronologically in order to preserve the dynamics of the experiential process and to provide the only narrative structure to the story. It is important to realize, however, that this is a story without a plot. The time frame of ethnographic fieldwork (also called the ethnographic present) has been compared to a strip of film on the editor's cutting floor—an arbitrary slice of time in the total life story of *both* the ethnographer and the people with whom she lived in order to learn.

Why Did We Go There? What Did We Seek?

In 1962 Ann Chowning and I conceived a joint fieldwork project to take place in the interior of southwestern New Britain in the then Territory of New Guinea administered by the Australian Government under a United Nations Charter (now a part of the Nation of Papua New Guinea). The fact that Ann already spoke two Austronesian languages and had conducted prior field studies in two coastal communities in New Guinea was a positive factor in our decision to look for an *inland* Austronesian-speaking people. We anticipated luck in finding two distinct locations in which to carry out separate but coordinated research. We hoped to find an area where the people still practiced much of their precolonial, pre-Christian way of life and rituals. Our findings would then compare with published accounts of Austronesian speakers from the coastal regions where, it seemed, little remained of pre-Christian practices.

Our hopes of finding such an ideal location was encouraged when Ann heard of a talk in New York given by Thomas Gilliard, who had led an expedition a few years earlier for the Natural History Museum (New York) in search of Birds-of-Paradise, which were previously (and are today) unreported for New Britain. Gilliard chose to travel into the interior of southwestern New Britain to hunt for these birds in the then largely unexplored foothills of the Whiteman Mountains. His findings (Gilliard 1961) persuaded us that this area had indeed received little, if any, attention by European colonists, Christian missionaries, or Japanese or Allied armies during World War II.

Because so little information about this region was available, we sought and received funds from the National Institute of Mental Health and Columbia University for a short exploratory trip for ourselves, lasting from July 16 to September 8, 1962. On this trip we surveyed a number of communities in the region known as the Passismanua, located north and inland from the Administrative Headquarters at Kandrian (see map). During this preliminary period of fieldwork, we did indeed find two *inland* localities, inhabited by Austronesian speakers. I settled in Umbi with Kaulong-speaking people and Ann in Dulago with Sengseng-speaking people. How we did this is narrated in chapter 2 following.

Returning to Bryn Mawr and Barnard Colleges to teach for the next academic year, we set about immediately to apply to the National Science Foundation for funds to enable us to return for a more extensive period of fifteen months during our academic leaves in 1963 and 1964. Our initial objectives were to make the first, and therefore holistic, ethnographic description of the culture of the Kaulong and Sengseng. This would include their social, economic, and religious organization, beliefs, and practices and the relationships between these institutions. We were both interested in the dynamics of small groups, attitudes toward the self and others (ethnocentrism), differences between the *ideal* and *actual* social behavior in various contexts, and in the relation of their non-Christian religious system to their world view and personality. I particularly wished to gather additional data on the extensive hunting and gathering carried out to supplement the garden produce and on the woman's world view, two topics carried over from my earlier Australian researches. Ann particularly wanted to focus on the Austronesian languages and their comparative aspects, on folklore and religion, and on patterns of insanity (having experienced an attack from a person running amok in a previous field trip). In addition, both of us were interested in learning more about the rather unusual (for Melanesians) practices, reported by others and verified in our initial visit, of hunting with twenty-foot blowguns rather than the bows and arrows common elsewhere, the strangulation of widows upon death of the husband, the head-binding of infants, and cognatic descent—a form of kinship thought at that time to be very aberrant for Melanesia.

Through a joint affiliation with the University of Pennsylvania Museum, we were successful in receiving adequate funds from the National Science Foundation to return. In addition, we received extensive photographic support from the National Geographic Society. In June 1963 we returned to our respective communities (Umbi and Dulago) and remained there through July 1964.

It is during this period, June 1962 through July 1964, that these letters were written. Later each of us returned to this region for continuing investigation of our respective linguistic groups. In 1967 and 1968 I returned for fifteen months to Kaulong and again for a final three month period during the summer of 1974, while Ann returned to Sengseng in 1966, and again in 1980 and 1981. For these later trips I chose the Kaulong community of Angelek for comparison with my first community of Umbi. Ann returned briefly to her first village, Dulago, and for comparative data, visited other inland and coastal Sengseng communities. Our published results and interpretations covering in-depth various aspects of the Sengseng and Kaulong cultures are based on the *totality* of field experience and data collected during *all* these periods. An annotated bibliography of our collected writings on Kaulong and Sengseng is appended so that those who wish may learn the extent to which we ever came to understand the people we had came so far to live with in order to learn the knowledge we sought.

The Region

A brief colonial history of this southwestern part of New Britain includes German occupation of New Guinea and New Britain, which began in the late nineteenth century and ended with their defeat in the First World War. During this time their territorial capital was in Rabaul on the eastern end of the island and most of their pacification and development activities (mainly establishing coconut plantations) were confined to the volcanic and fertile eastern region and extended westward along the volcanic northern coastal region.

The southwestern coastal region near Kandrian, being of raised limestone karst origin, offered little for human habitation or agricultural development for either Melanesians or colonial developers. The relatively infrequent German patrols in the south kept close to the coastal regions and only few communities were encouraged to try growing coconuts for the external market. Australian patrols, conducted by colonial officers during the period between the two world wars, generally followed the German pattern in this south coastal region, with a few patrols penetrating the interior for more than a few miles. Most pacification and Christian mission efforts were also confined to the coast and offshore islands. World War II itself barely affected the interior regions, but a few members of the inland population experienced the war firsthand while working on other island plantations caught by the Japanese invasion. These men were subsequently repatriated as the Allies regained control over the Melanesian Islands.

Kandrian was established as an administrative patrol post just before the outbreak of the Second World War, during which it was abandoned to be reestablished in 1951. By 1962, when we first arrived, Kandrian was a headquarters base headed by an assistant district officer (ADO) and his staff: patrol officer(s) (collectively referred to in our letters with the *Tok Pisin* term, *Kiap*), agricultural officer(s), malaria-control officer(s), a police detachment (and prison), and a medical team run by a European medical assistant. In addition, there was a branch trade store of Chin Cheu's (Rabaul), and a school with a number of elementary grades up to grade six, which was utilized almost exclusively by the coastal (but not inland) population. A Catholic Mission was built at Turuk on a bluff above Kandrian where the nuns ran an elementary school. The Church of England Mission was located on Apugi, one of the offshore islands. The two missions equitably strove to share and not compete for converts while we were there. The Church of England mainly sought to extend its influence along the coast and offshore islands while the Catholic Church attempted conversions in the interior. In the nine months between our initial visit in 1962 and our return in 1963, however, both missions attempted to extend their spheres of influence into the remote Kaulong and Sengseng areas where we were located. They had minimal success but caused us some concern as expressed in these letters.

During our fieldwork, Kandrian was served by Trans-Australia Airways (TAA) with a twice-weekly service—one each way—Rabaul to Lae and Lae to Rabaul. The grass airstrip, located on a bluff above Kandrian, was frequently closed during the monsoon rains of April through September, as the entire area received an average of over 250 inches of annual rainfall. A short tractor road ran up to the airfield from Kandrian and to the first village a few miles inland. From there to our respective village locations there were only footpaths connecting the inland communities.

The underlying limestone of the region is carved and pitted by the heavy rainfall running off into numerous streams and rivers which, during the rainy season, flood and during the dry season may go completely underground flowing through porus limesone channels.The ground itself is full of potholes and underground caverns. The terrain was described on an early map as being gently undulating near the coast but extremely rugged as one approaches the impenetrable Whiteman Mountain range in whose southern foothills our respective communities were located. The soil is shallow and the forest cover is continuous, much of it of virgin growth. The population was (and remains) extremely sparse. Estimates at the time of our study were about a thousand Kaulong, and about three hundred Sengseng. The linguistically related Miu and Karore constituted a few hundred more.

The ethnographic aspect of our fieldwork was, of course, the major part but not the whole of the experience. Our physical survival depended on some contact with the outside world, and the closest point of contact was located at Kandrian, some four or five days of difficult walk away from our communities.

Each of us set up a household in our respective communities. In 1962 I lived in an eight-foot by eight-foot bark hut while Ann found a empty house. The following year saw the building of a separate house for each of us and minimally furnishing it with facilities for sitting, writing, sleeping, cooking, eating, storage, washing, and mental escape (mainly through reading). We hired young men from the local community as assistants to help us in the running of the household and to be linguistic teachers and often trail guides.

Maintaining this household required hiring carriers from our respective communities to make the round trip to Kandrian for (in decreasing order of importance) mail, money (shillings), meat, and other tinned food items. These supplemented fresh vegetables, fruit, and meat that we were able to purchase locally. We tried (sometimes desperately) to coordinate these trips at alternate two-week intervals so that each community would be responsible for only one trip a month and yet permit each of us to receive and send mail every two weeks. This ideal was never met. For our carrier volunteers these trips meant a minimum of five days away from their own affairs and sometimes no amount of pay could be seen to compensate for this obviously onerous task. For all of us the necessity to maintain this contact, for our mental and physical well-being, was one of the greatest tension producers of the entire experience.

Our dependent relationship with expatriates (nonnatives) in Kandrian, principally the administrators (Kiaps) and proprietors of Chin Cheu's trade store, often made us feel that we were operating with yet one or two more foreign cultures, with their own set of mutually unpredictable and incomprehensible values and behavior. I mention them by name in the text and collectively in the acknowledgments. While we seem to be mostly frustrated by them in these letters, in truth we couldn't have done it without their generous support and sincere friendship, albeit at a distance most of the time.

Although our major funding was through the National Science Foundation, it was the National Geographic Society that elicited more frequent correspondence. Prior to returning in 1963 we contracted with them to take pictures in the hopes that an article would result. On their side they provided us with cameras, film, and frequent advice. On our side we attempted to make a photographic essay of our experiences worthy of their publication. For the ultimately successful result see Goodale (1966). The relative importance and the attempt at mutual understanding of this endeavor are additional aspects of our work brought to light in these letters.

The people of Umbi and Dulago and adjacent communities put up with a lot by agreeing to let us live in their midst and to ask interminable questions. They shared their lives, triumphs, and sorrows. They patiently taught us to speak their language, and then how to see the world through their eyes. As in any human relationship there were moments when our different values clashed and threatened the ties holding us together. But as we grew to know each other the bonds became stronger. Today, I wonder if they ever wonder what has happened to us over the intervening years as much as we wonder about them. This is their story as much as it is ours.

Postscript

Just as there are two basic modes, the deductive and the inductive, of scientific inquiry and in the writing of murder mysteries, so too are there two kinds of readers. If you, the reader, enjoy engaging in the inductive process of discovering for yourself what is revealed about fieldwork and the ethnographers, in this exchange of letters, then read on and experience with us the always unique process of gaining ethnographic understanding through participant-observation (or what my colleague Philip Kilbride [1990] calls interactive ethnography). But, if you, the reader, prefer to know who the murderer is before reading of the murder itself, of knowing the answer before the question (as in deductive reasoning), then I invite you to turn now to chapter 9, The Final Postscript, wherein I reflect on certain aspects of our fifteen months of field experience that I believe are implicitly revealed in the letters, and about ethnographic methodology itself. Readers may well come to additional as well as different conclusions. If they do, then I will have succeeded in my goal of focusing attention on the voice and experience of the ethnographer in the ethnographic endeavor and process.

Chapter 2

My Feet Decided Which Village

[In June 1962 and prior to our descending on Kandrian, we made obligatory visits to colleagues in Sydney and Canberra, informing them of our plans. Ann left for New Britain before I did in order to make a brief visit to Lakalai, the New Britain community where she had previously worked, and we separately visited officials and colleagues in Port Moresby. I took a detour by going to visit a colleague (Nancy Bowers) in the Highlands of New Guinea and then in early July left Mount Hagen on a DC-3 cargo plane that made nine stops in nine hours on its way to Rabaul. At the next to last stop, Hoskins on the north coast of New Britain, Ann joined me.]

Kandrian July 1962
Dear Family,
 This will be a very quick and rather illegible letter for reasons given below: 1) the electricity has just been turned out for the evening. 2) Ann and I are going into the hills tomorrow and life has therefore been very busy since I picked her up at the Hoskins airstrip Thursday. Friday we shopped madly in Rabaul, had dinner with friends of hers and Saturday we caught the weekly plane to Kandrian. This is a delightful spot. Beautiful, complete with the nicest people (9 European families) and a natural limestone freshwater swimming pool, a tennis court and a Chinese trade store. We feel most happy about this being the base of operations. We have been staying with the ADO (Assistant District Officer) Dave Stevens and his wife Mary and have been royally taken care of by them.
 Our plans are as follows—tomorrow (and for 10-12 days), we go on a patrol with the Patrol Officer, Dave Goodger, who will take us through four dif-

ferent language areas and help us select our villages. Then he will see us set up and leave us to our own. It looks as though we will be able to get two groups, linguistically separate, but geographically close, and it all sounds most interesting. We will stay in the bush for 4-5 weeks, coming out early in September and taking the plane from here to Port Moresby Sept. 8. Mail and important messages can reach me while in the bush as we will be sending down for supplies periodically. If you wish to get in touch fast—telegraph or mark "urgent." The address is just Kandrian, New Britain. I will send another letter back with David, the Patrol Officer, when he leaves us and let you know further.

This trip gets better and better every day. Hastily, Love, Jane

Umbi, July 1962
Dear Family,

If this letter ever gets to you and is still legible I believe it will be one of the miracles of the year. If it does, please preserve it as it will be my diary of the last six days.

Tues. July 17—We (Ann, Patrol.Officer David Goodger, Malaria Control Officer Frank Roben, six native police, David's dog Roger, and I) left Kandrian by tractor for the interior. After 1 hour reached the village of Seilwa after nearly capsizing in ditches several times. Abandoned the tractor and picked up 45 carriers and walked inland over a good road. Found sneakers very slippery on mud. Passed through villages of Pomugu, and Lapalam and reached Aka at 3 p.m. Ann and I were given the *haus kiap* (government rest house) for the night with a *limbum* [a palm] floor and fairly watertight roof. Dave and Frank are under canvas. Rain began at 4:30 p.m. and continued all night. A few words of Kaulong (language) were collected.

Wednesday July 18—Rain continued until 10 a.m. Off at 11 a.m. Tried my spiked boots which gave great security, but also blisters in 1 hour. I changed to my spiked (golf) shoes, but ended the trek with one shoe and one sneaker. Found it impossible to walk without spikes, but even with tape on my heels the blisters were irritated—very slow going. Off the road after passing Maum onto a very rugged track going up and down steep ridges which are very muddy, rocky and "rooty." Reached Arihi at 4 p.m. No *haus kiap* here so all of us are under canvas flies. Ours is on a platform of logs 4 feet above the ground—precarious. Lovely village of 8 houses. The mission invaded 2 months ago so it is out for us. Very friendly people.

Thurs. July 19—Rain hard all day. Stayed at Arihi and mostly inside and washed muddy clothes which were dried at night over our pressure lamp. Invited Dave and Frank over for "tea" and to bed early.

Friday July 20—Off at 9 a.m with 48 carriers with our destination the village of Umbi. The distance is unknown. The trail goes through uninhabited country and is a very, very, very rugged native unimproved track with steep pitches up and down, along fallen trees over pits, through bogs in mud calf deep, slippery, rocky and treacherous. Personally this will be a day I'll never forget. In spite of heavily taped heels, walking became painful at 10 a.m. I considered going barefoot, but was advised against it due to extreme slipperiness and limestone (filled with sharp slivers of flint). I trailed behind at half pace walking on my toes entirely with Frank keeping me company and police bringing up the rear. At 2 p.m. I caught up to Dave, Ann and carriers and sat down and had a cigarette for 5 minutes. Went on as there was no place to stop. My wind and muscles were OK, but feet extremely sore. At 3:30, on top of a ridge, I sat for 2 minutes as I was very tired now too. No food since 7 a.m., but carried canteen, thank goodness. Frank kept 100 yards ahead of me never letting me catch up to him (if he had, I would probably have quit!—he knew it and I knew it). At 5 p.m. a native with a lighted pressure lamp sent back from Umbi met us as darkness growing. I finally reached Umbi at 6 p.m., 2 hours and 15 minutes behind the others. Hot coffee, cookies and shoes off and then dinner. Then soaked feet in hot water and disinfectant and applied antibiotic powder and put on gauze and to bed at 9 p.m. We are under canvas and have log beds.

Sat. July 21—Decided (!!!) I am to stay at Umbi for next 6 weeks. This *is* one of the two villages suggested for us. Ann will go to Seagit, 1/2 day's walk away. These villages are in two different linguistic groups. My feet decided which village I should take, but I think the only other method of deciding would have been to flip a coin. The patrol is stopping here today and overseeing a house being built for me on a slight rise 100 yards above the village. Umbi consists of 10 houses on a flat ridge above the river (Ason), and is surrounded by higher ridges on all sides. The exact geographical location of the village is unknown, but it is approximately 25 miles inland. Altitude is also unknown. Dense tropical rain forest all around. The patrol leaving tomorrow, leaving one policeman to make sure my house is finished and I'm settled in. Paid for house at 7 p.m.—30 workers, 3 sticks of tobacco apiece (total value US $18.00). Borrowed cards from the police and we four had a farewell bridge game til 10 p.m. Very pleasant—I'll be sorry to see them leave. We couldn't have had nicer company.

Sunday July 22—Reprieve from abandonment. It rained all night and all day very hard and the river is too high for patrol to cross. It rained too hard to do anything! Resorted and repacked all gear—still under canvas. I made out list for supplies to come up later and decided to write this all down and give to Dave to mail when he gets to Kandrian. Feet still sore, but not infected and are healing. Played bridge again in the evening.

Monday July 23—It's sunny! River going down and patrol leaving soon. We will have fortnightly mail service and I will keep you informed. Love, Jane

[Because of insufficient postage put on in Kandrian, this letter went to the dead-letter office in Port Moresby and then back to Kandrian where it was eventually mailed, with the correct postage, on 20 August 1962 to U.S.A.]

[Ann sent me a note within a few days, telling me that she was settled in Dulago, rather than Seagit.]

Patrol Members at Umbi

Umbi July, 1962

Dear Ann,

Thanks for your note. I don't know whether the policeman will take this or whether he has already seen you. If not, an Umbi-ite will carry it. All goes well here. The area in front of my palace has been cleared providing both a good view of the village and observations on jungle clearing! My walks are all lined with *putput* [a decorative plant, a croton] from Kandrian and my house made even more rain proof. All this is one way to get tobacco—but it's all been on their own initiative and certainly improves the outlook.

I don't know whether my Pidgin (*Tok Pisin*) or Kaulong is improving faster (or indeed if either are).

The jawless young man who we met in Kandrian is the best teacher of Kaulong here—he speaks slowly and will give me verb conjugations one by one as well as sensible translations. He is also my second houseboy (Debli)! And I'm very glad I agreed to have two. The Luluai's brother-in-law (Sekiali) is impossible as a linguistic informant. He mumbles both in Kaulong and Pidgin! And he is impatient and begging—like the Luluai [government appointed headman], he's out for what he can get! But I don't want to fire him yet until I get the politics straight. Neither of the two belong here and this has made some problems with their food supplying. However, I've been well supplied with *good* bananas, yams, *kaukau* (sweet potato), cabbage, and today—a flying fox [fruit bat] and I've upped their pay so they can buy food also and they don't appear to be starving.

[We thought, initially, that our household help, coming from the village, would be able to obtain their own food, and would not have to be supplied food by us, which would necessitate the importation of additional "cargo" (supplies), carried in by them.]

The population of Umbi has doubled today! There must be some reason I know not what (yet!). The "new ones" were all here the first day and I haven't seen them since.

I will certainly let you know if the tape recorder comes up. For I would very much like you to give me some hints and advise on what Kaulong [language] I have gathered. I too am finding the recording (of the language) difficult but not the pronunciation. I have not yet found tone to be phonemic [meaningful]. The grammar has me at times quite confused. I think I have it then I don't! I suspect some of my problem is Pidgin translations. My speaking Pidgin is limited but understandable. My understanding [of Pidgin] is vastly improving. But Kaulong is slow going.

My movements about the place have been strictly limited due to 1) the rain, and 2) my feet! My blisters are healing but now they have big scabs on them and I don't want to take any chance with shoes and bare feet are out until the second big toe heals. I do consider myself extremely lucky that no infection set in—it's just a question of time, but the inactivity is getting me down! How are your feet?

Little by little the material culture is being revealed. Beautiful shields, blowgun, and feathered darts. The feathered headdress we saw together plus an old fashioned *laplap* (loin cloth) made of cassowary (large flightless bird) bones? *[sic]* These last I bought from the Tultul (Government appointed #2 headman) on request by him. But I'm going slow on collecting in general until I know more about the problems of transport and import/export. But my tongue is hanging out. Any advice on import [export]? Are feathers out in general and/or just bird of paradise?

I think the Tultul (Kasli—with-one-eye) will take this letter to you. He has some unfinished *dinau* [debts-exchange] in Dulago. He asked me to write a *pas* [letter] to you about it. I told him as best I could that we had nothing to do with Kiap business—settling of problems etc. He has been the third person who has asked me to record names of others who have not "paid up" etc. to give to the Kiap. If you could explain to him again in your better Pidgin our position it would help. (I think he understood my explanation but another statement from you would reinforce it). Of course the information that is revealed by these requests is most interesting. The Tultul, by the way, is a different kettle of fish from the Luluai and holds considerable power here although another man yet is the "big man" [the person locally considered to be of greatest influence].

Are you cold? Since I am I suspect you are too. Next year three sweaters and woolly P.J.s [pajamas]! Love Jane

Umbi—July 1962
Dear Family,

I expect the "native express" any day now bringing me my cargo (food and such things as pliers and an umbrella which I forgot) and mail. So I want to have this ready to go back. The mail service up here is astounding. Yesterday I received 4 letters via Pomilo [Pomalal]), where Dave and Frank stopped overnight after depositing Ann across the river at Dulago. Today, I received a letter forwarded by Ann. With such efficient mail service, I really feel quite in touch with the outside world. I hesitated greatly about sending you my last rather gruesome report of the trip up here as I could see you imagining all sorts of worse things happening—so I hasten to report that 1) my feet are almost like new by now, and 2) I am most happily ensconced in Umbi.

My house is my castle—set up on poles with a split log floor (which I haven't fallen through yet!). The walls are of moss covered bark, the roof of leaves (and watertight!). Inside I have a built in work table and pole bed (the air mattress most useful) and I sleep like a log! On the verandah I have a folding table and chair and here I hold court most of the day (being unable to walk about much). I have a wash house with a borrowed government shower bucket and next to it, on the edge of the hill the necessary "small house" (latrine).

The only other house on this slight hill above the village is occupied by my *two* assistants—Sekiali—the 'cook,' and Debli—the 'washboy.' Both actually do everything from mending and/or improving on the house to teaching me Kaulong (the language). I'm being spoiled. They make my bed (i.e. air the sleeping bag) hang up my clothes—in fact if I want to do anything for myself I have to do it at night (my only free time).

The rest of the village have also been most friendly. However, including my two boys, there are only four who speak Pidgin (*Tok Pisin*). My Pidgin, I think is improving—at least I can understand most of it now and they seem to understand me. I now can pick out a few words in Kaulong and can give greetings, farewells to visitors. I'm collecting quite a vocabulary, but one needs more than words alone to understand and speak a language. The women and children are delightful, but as none of them talk Pidgin, we are reduced to smiles and giggles and half translations. I'm trying hard now, just to learn names and attach them to faces. I've counted roughly 50 men, women and children here, but people keep coming in and leaving which makes it confusing. I'm working principally on the language, leaving cultural information alone until either my Pidgin or my Kaulong improves, but little bits of information float in—just enough to tantalize me.

I've been eating very well. I've bought a huge bunch of bananas (10 shillings) yams, and sweet-potatoes (two different vegetables), native cabbage (more like chard), sugar cane (delicious) and coconuts and even a piece of pig which was killed the 1st day I was here alone for some important, but unknown to me, reason. My tinned (canned) meat, fruit and cheese and crackers and dry soup fill out my menu. And although my cook is hardly skilled on a primus, he is most willing and everything is edible, only he cooks too much—I keep cutting the proportion in half and hope by next week we'll reach normal proportions. Paying for the food has been a most fascinating procedure. The two village officials decided I "was being cheated," so now they are to price the food before I pay. This was all right by me, but yesterday Kahamei (the chief) priced one big and one small yam at 3 shillings and then after I paid, said the small one was no good and he would take it. I said, all right, you pay me 1 shilling quite jokingly and to my surprise, this morning he did. And tonight one of my boys bought a coconut from me. I was ready to give it to him, but out came a shilling and I've decided it's just as well to keep things straight. I only pay the two boys 10 shillings ($1) a week, but expect to give them a bonus when we all go to Kandrian in 5 weeks time. From the way they talk, I think the entire village is to accompany me to Kandrian.

Life in the tropical rain forest is fascinating. I've decided that next year I must either take up insects or botany as a hobby. Of the two, I think insects would be most rewarding. Sitting on my porch at night with the pressure lamp burning, all kinds of moths, locusts, beetles (some 4 inches long) come visiting me. The mosquitoes are not bad at all—in fact I've only seen a few. Frank (the malaria control man) said that during the rainy season they are all washed away and I can believe it. It has rained every day, but the sun has also peeped out for an hour or two every day—just enough to dry my clothes. But I doubt that I will come home with much tan. It will be all I can do just to avoid mildew! The temperature has been delightful—if anything rather cool. One needs

A Portion of the Villiage of Umbi

a sweater at night and often in the afternoons. Since I only have one, this presents a problem for I know if I have it washed it will never dry. But this sort of problem is just the reason for a preliminary trip. I already have a long list of things to bring next year and things to leave behind.

Continued on Sunday—Yesterday the outside of my house was worked on. An area of about 30 by 50 feet was cleared of all trees and bush directly in front. The paths were lined with a plant called "putput" (like box) and I even have a small stone wall along one path. It's all quite charming and my view is enlarged. All this was no idea of mine, but rather that of Kasli (the assistant headman) who of the two government appointed officials is by far the best and the most likable.

Continued on Monday—Rain. Hard. All day. A dreary and cold day. I am now most envious of the small native houses built on the ground with fires between beds. They look so cozy in the rain—the smoke filtering through the leaves of the roofs and mingling with the heavy mist and rain. The scene of rain, tropical jungle and mist shrouded mountains looks just like oriental prints—I wish I could draw well enough to depict it. I'm trying to get pictures but the light is so dim. I was sold a flying fox (fruit bat) today (my favorite Aboriginal food in Australia) and found (I must admit to my surprise) that I still find it most delectable particularly after canned meat. Mail going...Love Jane

Dulago, Aug. 1962
Dear Jane

It's raining steadily and there's not a sign of life around, so it seems a good time for letters. I haven't tried to get over yet for one main and a couple of secondary reasons. The main one is my knee, which I guess really started to bother me after we left Umbi. I walked to Hutkihyu last week and it was so painful (though quite a short trip) that I decided not to try Umbi for a while, and to rule out Seagit altogether. In any case, my present plan is to come to Umbi on Monday, August 20, given good weather and no unforeseen events that might keep me in the village, and otherwise as soon thereafter as possible.

I've collected over 1000 words but am far from figuring out either the phonemes (especially the vowels) or the grammar. People here are very willing to dictate, but no one speaks Pidgin well enough to translate accurately or, for that matter, to understand my questions. Still, I continue to think that it's very simple grammatically, probably as much so as Lakalai [a north coast New Britain language], and I don't think we need anticipate any real trouble with learning it.

Don't say anything about this in your village (enough Luluais are in on the act already), but we had a splendid fight here a couple of days ago (with fists and clubs actually used, and spears at least brandished, and a fair amount of bloodshed) involving the Luluai and his next-door neighbor, which resulted in the expulsion from the village of an obnoxious but bright boy, the son of the Luluai of Hutkihyu, who had forcibly attached himself to my household. All very exciting, and I hope I've improved my relations with the Luluai here by refusing to interfere. He killed a pig the other day, and I had my first fresh meat in three weeks as a consequence. The food supply here should hold up all right, though I'm constantly having to throw out things that rot before I can use them, but I expect (when we exit) to be completely out of such essentials as soap, matches, and coffee before I leave, so you can expect (when we exit) to be joined in Pomalal by a cold and dirty waif. Incidentally, the route that Dave has planned for us seems to involve no house Kiaps [rest houses], but I suppose someone will provide shelter. (Our sleeping bags are not water-proof.)

My luck with mechanical devices continues. Can't get the shower bucket to work at all, and the primus started acting up at the end of the first week and is barely faltering along. The pressure lamp leaks fantastically, but otherwise is still holding up, though it has its balky nights.

My ringworm seems cured, except possibly for a spot on the scalp which I can't see. The athlete's foot is hopeless; I might just as well wait till I leave before trying to do anything about it, since it's impossible to keep my feet dry here. [My] cold seems finally to be clearing up, but I'm sneezing occasionally and nervously waiting a new one. And how are *you*? If you're healthy, why don't you come see me? I'll presumably have to come over to your place to pick up the tape recorder, and I'm not anxious to make two trips.

Policeman just arrived (night of Tues.) with Dave's request for the patrol boxes back.

[Patrol boxes are metal cases, designed to be slung from a pole carried on the shoulders by two men. We had been loaned some by the
Kiaps. In our houses they were our only storage containers.]

Horrors! I barely abstracted some of your books from the package Mary Stevens sent, but I'll bring them over when I come. News of tape recorder sounds so poor that I will come over, and probably well before Monday, possibly Friday. I suggest that you send down with your patrol boxes any books both of us have finished; I've only got one such here. I've been out of bananas for days, which curdles my view of the universe, but otherwise all goes well. See you soon, I trust. Love, Ann

[Ann's letter crossed one I sent to her, a frequent occurrence.]

Umbi Aug. 1962

Dear Ann

I should have waited a day, but it got to the point when I didn't know when the cargo would arrive. I'm slightly confused as to whether the policeman will accompany your cargo. He is here tonight and if I understand it he is in-structed to go to Dulago only if I request it for some reason. All the tobacco came here (minus 122 sticks as pay along the road as far as Hulem for both of us and 24 sticks Hulem-Umbi for me).

[Tobacco sticks were at this time made up especially for trade in
Papua New Guinea. One stick equaled in value one shilling—
approximately 20 cents in the U.S. The preferred way of smoking

this was shredded and rolled into newsprint making a cigarette, or cigar. Therefore, it was necessary not only to carry stick tobacco for payment of goods and services, but also newsprint. Some people in our region had no use for Australian money, but would accept stick tobacco and "paper" in exchange for food or as pay for a service.]

I'm sending half on to you (2.5 layers + 19 sticks) with this note plus 1/2 the reading matter supplied by Owen Henney [teacher at Kandrian]. We'd better keep Stevens' [books] separate. As far as I can tell all the rest of the cargo here is mine. I haven't had time to check thoroughly so if you find you're lacking something let me know and if on checking tomorrow I find a surplus I'll send it over. The policeman (a jolly Sepik man) reports he left [Kandrian] Saturday but was held up by rain for 2 days (as we can well believe.)

If you are having trouble with the [Kaulong] pronoun *he,* you ought to have seen me this a.m. trying to get [the pronouns] *me* and *you* straightened out. I'd say [in Pidgin] give me the Kaulong for *mi lukim* [I see it] and Sekiali would give the phrase for *yu lukim* [you see it]. Ah me—we finally both retreated into our respective homes, he to sleep and me to ponder. He has volunteered to carry this to you so I'll try with Debli tomorrow.

The river has been no problem in spite of the steady rain. Only a "big" rain makes it difficult or impossible so if you decide you can stand getting wet, or you can't stand Dulago any longer come on over. No word about [tape] recorder. My house faces the wind and rain too but at least it has a view! Love, J. (PS. Please send sleeping bag cover back which has the books inside.)

[We had purchased a very expensive $500 tape recorder encased in aluminum and "lightweight"—the first of a new breed of "portable" tape recorders. It never worked for us once we had left the states and we left it with some volunteer technicians from the Australian Broadcasting Commission, but they never succeeded in repairing whatever was wrong.]

Umbi—Aug. 1962

Dear Family,

I got as far as the date last night when my porch was invaded by the night residents of Umbi who decided to sing—soon they decided to have an impromptu *singsing* down in the village so down we all went. The two young girls who were in residence for the night (aged 8 and 14) put on their dancing grass *purpur* (skirts) and two young men put bandages on their ankles (in lieu of feathers) and made paper hats (in lieu of cassowary feathers) and they sang while the girls danced bouncing their *purpur* bustles up and down. A slight drizzle didn't stop them. Kahamei (the *Luluai*—headman) said he'd talk to everyone to come in and have a proper singsing a week from tomorrow on one condition that I join the women. ("They have plenty *purpur*," he said.) The steps are not difficult—sort of like the Rockettes chorus line. Of course rain may stop the whole affair or the population may not be large enough.

This whole business of the village having a small daily population is very interesting. These people have only had villages for four years. Previously they made what some Patrol Officers called "rude" shelters by their gardens which are widely spaced over the mountains. The village plan was fostered by the Government in order to make censusing easier. Over each village they put a Luluai and, if necessary appointed assistant officers—Tultuls. It is quite obvious that the adjustment is not yet complete as families come in for a day or two then off to their old homes for 5-6 days. Rarely is everyone here. I suspect only when the patrols are sent in. This will make a rather fascinating study from the point of view of social and political organization (for next year).

I have not yet been out to the gardens for if it is not actually raining it surely will be (raining) within the hour. Also I've decided really my one job this year is the language. It is slowly progressing. I know many words and can understand a few simple sentences and say even fewer (without consulting notes). Recently, the women and children, who only speak Kaulong, have been "chatting" with me. Making me repeat sentences and words, most of which I know *not* the meaning. However my tongue is getting the feel of the sounds and I feel this is most valuable. After all this is how they teach *their* kids to talk. Also the language they use to their kids is more on my level!

If it were not for having the job of the language, life would be quite dull. As it is, it's either very quiet or very busy—nothing in between. I get up between 6:30 and 7(!) and after dressing sing out to the cook who makes coffee and opens a tin of fruit. Breakfast can sometimes be quite hectic for as soon as I appear on the porch, visitors call. One day I drank coffee, held sick call, and bought a huge fruit bat (live) all at the same time. The morning is vocabulary time with Debli—unless kids are around. Lunch at noon of coffee, cheese and cucumbers or peanut butter and crackers. Afternoon—language, shower and watch any activities going on, write notes etc. 4 p.m. is when anyone comes in, if they plan to, and is a time of buying yams, bananas, *bega* (P. aibika—a native green), etc. and my porch becomes full again. 5:30 dinner—a yam or sweet potato or *bega* cooked in bark on the fire, a tin of meat, tea (because the coffee is running low) and sometimes fruit if I have any room left. I suspect one reason the boys cook so much is that they get what's left. It's OK as long as the supplies last as once a tin is open it must be "et"—no place to keep it. So far I've been very lucky in keeping unwelcome guests out of my food. Only a very small rat (who looked so much like a field mouse I couldn't bear to shoo him away) came to nibble on my sweet potatoes and half a dozen cockroaches— always away from the food. The other flying friends are only interesting (the large beetle hasn't been back).

(Continued Sunday) Three new gals came in last night (late teens) and the village social life began to hum, i.e. the young boys are drifting in. Again a *singsing*, this time on my front porch—the whole house itself began to *yik* (K. dance) and long about 10 p.m. I joined in (without *purpur*). My house is rapidly becoming the social club of Umbi, a place where both sexes can meet on neutral ground and all can look out over the village at what or whoever is down there.

This is the way it should be, but I need a bigger house. Next year's house is going to take some designing—somehow I've got to figure out how to put a fire inside a house which is built above the ground! I need a fire not only for warmth, but also for cooking. My little pressure stove has gone on the blink and I haven't been able to fix it. This is not totally disastrous for the boys' house is 20 feet away and they can cook my food over and in their fire, but they are distressed for working the stove gave them not only fun but prestige.

(Continued Wednesday) The contact with the outside world has just appeared, i.e., a police messenger, thus providing outgoing mail service and also bringing your letter of July 28th—two and a half weeks isn't bad considering all the possible delaying points. The police man also brought a note from Ann saying to expect her over this weekend. This is good for the "not unexpected mental fatigue" has set in and I need some stimulation. It is also a cheery note that I found the vital instrument to make my stove work again and *all* the household is happier.

Nothing seems to happen here, but I suspect a great deal does underneath the language barrier. Ann reports she had a knock-down-drag-out fight in Dulago. There was a death in Yambon (halfway between us) on Tuesday. My shower bucket refused to "shower" yesterday and "poured" instead. (It *can* be exciting if you don't expect it!) I've been learning lots of cat's-cradles and reading lots of books. As I said earlier this state of mind [culture shock] is not unexpected—it is a disease, which is most common among anthropologists during their first 4 months of total isolation. Fortunately we've been supplied with heaps of paperback books of all kinds, by the good people of Kandrian. For this (disease) reading is the only medicine (aside from inter-visits)—a good thick juicy steak would help too. But I have had some fresh meat—delicious wild piglet—three times and I've literally been swamped with bananas and cucumbers. Love to you all, Jane

Umbi August 1962
Dear Family,
　　Your three letters of around the 1st of August just arrived. Mail has been delayed due to rain. The planes can't land to pick up or deliver and it is therefore questionable whether WE will be able to leave Kandrian on the 8th as we planned. However, if we do get out—we are going to Moresby for 3 days, then to Sydney. As yet we haven't made reservations further—I'll wire you our arrival date.

Rain has also upset our local exodus route over the (so called) "good" road to Kandrian as it crosses the river Apaum (Ason) twice. Here at Umbi, near the source, the river was impassable for 3 days. Yesterday a few courageous souls made it across, but the second crossing is in the middle of the river and all say it is not, nor will it be, crossable by next week, even if we don't have another big rain—which is asking too much. So it looks as if I'll have to go back over that "blankity blank" track to Arihi and I've just suggested the same to Ann.

Most of the past week has been spent making plans for next year, including a house (5 rooms), a garden, a pig and the same two boys. I've really been pleased as all of the plans were made by the Luluai and the boys, including the plan of the house which if it turns out half as nice as they say it will be, it will be a palace. It will be built before I get here and the garden planted and the pig fattened! Of course I've learned to expect the unexpected both the good and bad—but so far all has turned out for the best...Love, Jane

[Somehow the exit trip is unrecorded. What I do recall was the last 8 miles along the shadeless tractor road under a merciless sun. I became quite ill and took shelter under a village tree and waited till nearly dark to continue the trip. I was violently ill and had little sleep that night, and elected to stay in Kandrian while Ann went to Rabaul to close accounts and make official visits. I joined her on the plane to Lae two days later quite recovered.]

Interlude

[We arrived back in the States with only a weekend to meet the deadline for applications to the National Science Foundation. We submitted a joint proposal entitled Ethnography of Southwest New Britain. Early in January we received word of the award of a grant (GS 77) and began making plans for our return. I sent a letter to Debli, which was delivered and read to him, saying that it was time for him to take some people to Kandrian and pick up tools at Chin Cheu's store and a number of bags of rice to feed the workers (payment for which I had previously arranged), and begin the construction of my house as soon as the Good Weather time arrived.

Soon after, we received an invitation to come to Washington to discuss our prospective trip with the National Geographic Society (NGS). The upshot of this visit was that the NGS loaned us two cameras apiece, and offered advice based on their preview of our slides, in return for giving them a first crack at a "story" for their magazine if (and this was always a big IF) the pictures were of sufficient quality. We sent them some of the slides taken in 1962 and received the following letter on the eve of our departure.]

Washington DC May 1963
Dear Misses Goodale and Chowning;
    ...Truthfully, ladies, these eight rolls are pretty weak...
    In an effort to help you, I am going to list a few basic suggestions... Consider each photographic opportunity as a completely new challenge. Suppose, for example, that on your march into the interior of New Britain you come to a stream which must be forded. The fording supplies the situation. Now, what opportunities are there for pictures? There is the approach to the river from the side you are on. There is the actual splashing through the water from the same side (looking over the backs of the bearers, etc.). There is the coming out of the water on the other side, facing the bearers. There is the look back on the scene

from the far side. There are the close-ups of the natives—and yourselves—as you make your way though the water. These include full length pictures of individuals; tight groups of individuals; very tight close-ups of faces and expressions as the effort is made.

Now, how to handle this photographically. In this fording situation there are at least seven distinct opportunities and approaches, as listed above. Each one of these opportunities must be treated separately, as though this is the one chance to make a picture. For example, the general view from the near bank. You wait until some of the bearers are in the water, then you shoot the picture from the best vantage point you can find. If the meter says the exposure is 1/100th second at f 4, shoot the scene at this exposure, then again at 1/100th at f 3.5 and again at f 5.6 and with even more widely bracketed exposures if the light is tricky.

You have just begun on the fording. Now move to what you think is the next best position for a good general view—a scene setter for this exposure. Do the same general run of exposure all over again. When you are satisfied there are no more good camera angles from the near bank, move into the crossing stage, once again trying several angles and working them over completely with respect to exposures and shutter speeds. . .

[As Ann and I read this we chuckled mightily as we pictured the reality of our "marches" where we never saw the carriers from morning (when they were sent off) till night (when we caught up and paid them). When we splashed or slipped and fell into the river, or crossed over slippery single- and multiple-log bridges always with terror, we were hardly in a position to stop even once. Furthermore, due to our habit of falling flat on our faces climbing down and up the steep slopes, we felt it safer to entrust our delicate instruments (cameras and tape recorders) to the more sure-footed carriers; we did not tell the NGS this.]

[The NGS letter concluded:] Mr. Roberts recently sent you a couple of ammunition boxes. These should help you keep your film and equipment dry, particularly the cameras. Be careful when opening the ammo boxes. They can ruin fingers and fingernails. As far as film is concerned, do not worry about the weather, particularly the humidity. The important thing is not to leave the film in the camera any longer than absolutely necessary after exposure. Please try to ship film as often as convenient. The very best of luck and please keep us informed as best as possible on your progress—not only photographically, but geographically. Best, B. Gilka.

[We began our shopping in the U.S., but also devised a reverse of the usual Los Angeles/Sydney/Port Moresby route to Papua New Guinea. Our route involved a three day flight from Fiji with stopovers in Port Vila (Vanuatu), Honiara (Guadalcanal), and Rabaul (New Britain). Here we would first complete our local shopping, and follow it with a trip to Australia for items not available in Rabaul or Port Moresby. It was also most important for us to visit our anthropological coleagues in Australia, informing them of our research plans. Following this we would return to Kandrian and begin our second trek inland.]

Port Vila, June 1963

Dear Family,

Will mail this when I can. We arrived here early afternoon after having delayed the plane's departure 1/2 hour from Fiji due to our having too much luggage. After paying $120 for overweight luggage, we were informed that it was either our duffels or less than minimum fuel. We naturally agreed that fuel was more important so our duffels are still in Fiji. The money was returned and we were given a promise that they (our duffles) will come next week.

The plane we are on is a 12 passenger Heron with a crew of 3, a Capt. and Co-pilot and a "if you want anything just yell 'Charlie'." The plane is about 4 feet wide and Charlie 2 feet wide, but somehow he managed to negotiate the aisle with lemon squash, coffee and eventually a box lunch of unrecognizable and relatively tasteless English tea sandwiches and cakes. Today's flight was all over water but we've been promised scenery tomorrow to photograph. We window shopped (in Port Vila) this afternoon, but as this hotel is singularly lacking in visible management, we have been unable to get cash to buy anything...

Honiara June 1963

Up before dawn today to find it pouring rain. However the plane did take off between showers. The pilot somehow found Esperito Santo under the clouds and landed for a brief while. The clouds were heavy all the way which made it rather exciting...We hit the right islands (after three hours) and flew up the [Solomon Island] chain and finally got some of the promised scenery. Honiara is a lovely garden spot. Tomorrow's flight to Rabaul leaves at 6 a.m. so it's early to bed, but as the hotel is humming with everyone from miles around who came into town to pick up the weekly mail, we may be up a bit.

Rabaul, June 1963

Today's hop was the most fascinating perhaps because it wasn't cloudy and we were really island hopping from Guadalcanal to Bougainville, via the St. Georges Islands. (We were also on a much bigger 20-passenger plane.) Aside from being treated to beautiful full-circle rainbows, we flew over two active volcanoes which were most impressive (on Bougainville.) We were met (at Rabaul) by the DO (District Officer) of West New Britain District and deposited at the Cosmo (Cosmopolitan) hotel. We had a very busy and profitable day: banking, buying patrol boxes (from an ex-New Yorker who makes them!). Changing plane tickets as we can't fit in our desire to get to the highlands (of New Guinea) so am pushing everything up a day and a half so that we can have another day back here right at the end to buy that toothpaste etc. that we forgot. We also found that BP (Burns Philip), who is "Mr. Establishment" here tradewise, has a boat leaving this Friday p.m. for Kandrian so we can ship all our supplies by boat and save large amounts (we are really in luck as this boat goes every 5 to 8 weeks). Spent the rest of the afternoon setting up magazine and newspaper subscriptions plus a monthly shipment of six assorted paperbacks each, and window shopping in preparation for the assault on furniture, pots and pans, and gourmet canned tidbits tomorrow. Collapsed at 4 when Ann's friend, Margaret Kelly, wife of the ADO (Assistant District Officer) Bill Kelly, came in for a beer and an invitation to dinner tomorrow and an offer of 2 chairs and "all the paperback books (they've read) in the last 9 months" and a holiday with them next November or Early December before they go on leave.

Lae, June 1963

I am here in Lae, en route to Moresby and Sydney but alone! Speaking about the hazards of fieldwork—at 1 a.m. last night, after we returned from a farewell dinner party, Ann stumbled in her room getting undressed and dislocated her knee cap. I roused the manager out of his bed who raised a doctor out of her bed, who replaced the knee cap and carted Ann off to the hospital for x-rays and a cast! What a beginning. So I'm off alone to Australia to complete the shopping and make the official calls to colleagues [in Sydney and Canberra] as fast as possible. The Dr. says Ann will be able to walk with her cast so hopefully we'll go down to Kandrian on the 29th as scheduled but Ann will probably be delayed going inland for a while. So we'll just have to play it by ear for a while.

Sydney June 1963

I am sitting here [in the Metropolitan Hotel] huddled over what they laughingly call a radiator and attempting to keep the blood circulating. The rate at which I've been spending money these past two weeks is frightening. It's perhaps fortunate that pounds and shillings have no real value for me. I've been getting good stuff, because it's going to go through some really tough times...

This afternoon I descended on the Anthropology Department at University of Sydney—sat through a seminar, had a round of beer with them afterwards, and wrangled an invite to a brawl tomorrow night at the Chairman's house. They promise to get me on the plane to Canberra (early) Saturday a.m.—a promise which I view with some misgivings, but at least the evening should be entertaining and I could hardly refuse.

The Administration (Department of Native Affairs) in Port Moresby was most cooperative and I had a very nice and successful visit with them. I have been unofficially appointed a weather observer and they are supposed to meet me with the proper equipment in Lae when I change planes on Tuesday or Thurs. on the way (back) to Rabaul. I don't know what I'll get but at least a rain gage and a thermometer.

Rabaul June 1963

Dear Jane,

When I got your cable [from Canberra] I started off full speed for the TAA to change my reservations [to come back a day early from Moresby] and halfway there decided the hell with it. I could not stand two more unnecessary days in Rabaul. I'm really fed up with the place, as you can imagine, though last night I did finally disregard the doctor (who hasn't appeared since I left the hospital), and went out to Kokopo [to visit the Kellys]. So I'm going to Moresby tomorrow, back on Thursday.

I got a copy of *Playboy* for Bill [Kelly], (the one that got the publisher arrested as reported in this week's *Time*), so if you got one, give it to Hicks [District Officer]. I guess he does like to meet planes, though I haven't seen him either or anyone, though I did get a call from some coy (no name) type that I assume is the one for whom I didn't get the record, who had gone to meet the Moresby plane on the 12th and when I wasn't on it, assumed I wasn't here. I just stood him up by going out to the Kellys, so if you meet anyone who's pretty annoyed with me, he has reason.

I engaged Hancock for the Customs Agent. He says the film [from the NGS] should be addressed to us in Kandrian c/o him (R.W. Hancock, Customs Agent Malaguna Road) in Rabaul—this to avoid bother on further postage to Kandrian. I also did my alien registration. I've done no further inquiry on the film or duffle bags [off-loaded in Fiji].

Have a few more suggestions on things to get like hookworm medicine and stuff to preserve eggs with. We can do that on Friday.

Thanks for taking care of so many things in Moresby and elsewhere. I hope my trip, non-milk-run, will be less wearing than yours, but anything for a change. I'm leaving a parcel of stationery and my small bag c/o you just because I didn't want to take them to Moresby and haven't had time to do anything else.

I fear this is pretty incoherent—not much sleep last night, and tomorrow's plane pickup is at 5 A.M. Gaa! See you Thursday. With apologies, and love
Ann.

Rabaul, June 1963
Dear Family;
The trip back was exhausting. Left Canberra Monday noon and arrived Rabaul at 5 p.m. Tuesday with only catnaps on the planes. In Lae (at the airport) I met another American who brought my rain gauge [turned out to be a large bucket] and thermometers and his boss, to meet me even on his day off and then stood chatting until the Rabaul Local was finally called. Then off on this still fascinating but rugged flight (particularly with no sleep). However, gradually I'm getting to know people on the various outposts. The plantation owners at Jacquinot Bay [Southeastern New Britain] (who on my last trip through invited me, on first sight, to stay and visit with them) were sure I'd come this time to take them up on their offer. I did get to chat with Dave Steven (at Kandrian) this time and he reports my house is almost finished—in no way resembles the plan—but it's the best rest house in the district—which [he added] isn't saying much.

Ann has gone to Moresby for a few days for a change of scene. Her knee is still in a mammoth cast but won't be for long and it hasn't bothered her hardly at all. She figures if she straps (her knee) well and we take it easy, even if it doubles the time of the journey, she will be able to do it. I sincerely hope so. Love Jane

Umbi July 1963
Dear Family,

Arrived here two hours ago after a trip that bore slight resemblance to last year's (trek) except for the length of time. Five days with a day of rest on Sunday. The weather was perfect until today when we had slight rain most of the way with the resulting mud underfoot. We came the "easy" way and it *was* just that, in comparison with the other route. Even Ann managed to limp her way along with a stiff but painless knee, and carrying Roo (a small kitten acquired in Rabaul) in her shoulder bag. Using a pair of nail scissors, the only instrument we could find, I spent several hours cutting off Ann's cast the night before we left Kandrian.

The trip for me was without problems. We took a trail which crossed the Ason much closer to the mouth, and then led up to Pomalal. We spent two days on this segment and then spent a day together at Pomalal before splitting up, with Ann going to the Northeast to Dulago, and me going northwest to Umbi. We were accompanied by a most cheerful policeman who added considerably by his own presence and by performing his duties of handling the carriers of which we needed an unheard of total of 48 men, women and children. And even at that, our tables and chairs are still in Kandrian along with a few other odd items, but they are scheduled to come up in a few days, along with any mail that has come in.

It was good to get home—They've built me a virtual palace six rooms and about 10 feet [a slight exaggeration] off the ground. All greeted me and I do feel they are happy to have me back. Love Jane

Umbi July 63
Dear Ann,

"Reports" [rumors] are that the cargo will come tomorrow, so I'll start this note today (I'm at loose ends anyway waiting for tea to come and rain to stop!) *If* it wasn't for your knee—I'd insist you come here first to see *mang dango* [my house]. It's quite palatial with one exception—my bedroom, which (with my oversized bed, one patrol box and misc. tape recorder, radio and camera) is full up! I'm hoping that when they build me a raised bed so I can fit everything under it, I'll have room for a table and chair. But aside from this, I have an adjoining room *waswas* [bath], both of these at the extreme rear (of the house). Then comes a cargo room and a kitchen, then the front room with Debli and Ningbi's [my new assistant] room off it. The whole thing is to me immense and raised up off the ground enough so that I can almost stand, and under the house is the fire and a place where all can, and do, gather. At the moment there are no interior built-in tables due to the lack of nails, so we haven't unpacked the stove yet and all cooking is done quite adequately over the fire [underneath the house].

Due to the fact that the river is low, I've eaten fresh fish three nights in a row and is it delicious! These are good sized fish and fat and sweet (Now won't you come?)

One of my pressure lamps doesn't work due to a faulty pump, but otherwise all seems in shape and we are gradually settling in.

The C of E (Church of England) is here, two of them [Solomon Island Brethren], ensconced in a solid looking house as far away from me as the village is but to the other side. Since I will have to live with them, I've merely ignored them and they generally leave me alone and at the moment only gather the kids for 1/2 hour at 7 A.M. and 6 P.M. As far as I can tell they are teaching them to count and, as the Tultul said, "They talk nothing but the kids like it." So—?

[After purposely selecting communities where the missions had not yet been established, it was a great disappointment for us to hear while in Kandrian from the C of E Father (with a distinctly proud tone in his voice) that he had recently sent "brethren" to Umbi.]

The village seems to have grown or rather more who *lain* (census) here, actually *are* here, but I expect them to melt away next week when the novelty wears off.

The only thing which seems to have come up in my garden is half a dozen carrots so we replanted all sorts of things. Ningbi, whose been away at work most of his life and whose Pidgin is good, says everything should come up even in the rainy season. But I'll have to get some onions. Ningbi is a nice fellow who doesn't mind working, in fact like Debli, it's hard to find enough to keep them busy.

There is a large new garden right next to the village and I look down on it from my room. This makes superficial observation of garden activity a snap. It also is a pleasant view.

Sunday, 3 P.M.

The (remaining) cargo has arrived and suddenly my house is too small! I paid 7 men 16 shillings apiece. This covers 4 days carrying (2 days down to Kandrian with patrol boxes and 2 days back with cargo at a rate of 4 shillings per day). In addition I was persuaded to pay 3 men 2 shillings apiece for canoe charge on the coast. This charge was presented after I agreed to the other price and for the sake of future good will among carriers I paid it. Thus the total as far as Umbi, is 118 shillings. Debhe, who will carry the mail to you, is instructed to carry back 59 shillings. (I'm very low on both money and tobacco. If you want to send some (but *not* all of this) in tobacco, it's O.K.

I have to send someone to Kandrian this coming Friday to get nails and other oddments. So if you have any letters going get them to me by Wednesday night. It's a two day trip and if we want to make the Sat. mail they must go on Thursday. I will probably have a man-load and unless miracles happen, I may send my radio in. It worked perfectly and then in the middle of a word conked

Ningbi with a Freshwater Fish for Dinner

out last night! Just as I got the 2nd lamp to work! Such is life. But the tape recorder works! I'm going to try offering 8 shillings for mail and small cargo trip, but I don't think we should go over 10 (or 15?). What do you think?

Here are your cups. Do you have my frying pan?

Love to you and [the kitten] Roo. Jane

Dulago, July 63

Dear Jane,

I'll write this on the assumption that maybe someone will turn up with a trifle of furniture today or tomorrow. Though God knows where I'll put it; I can't move as it is. I wasn't fast enough to send one (letter) with your suitcase. I hope that it doesn't contain your best clothes. [It did.] I just asked [the Kiap] for any of my things except the large metal suitcase that those who took down the [loaned] patrol boxes could bring back, and this was the consequence. The carriers also report that the policeman to whom I gave the money to pay them abandoned them and went on without doing so. I'll soon be facing quite a shortage of shillings. As it is, without the expected newspapers, I'm almost out of paper [newsprint, in which the locals rolled the stick tobacco to make long cigarettes]. I do wonder about the Kandrian mail service.

Nothing has been done on my new house except the floor, which is a cool 6 feet above the floor [sic], and terrifying. People keep cutting posts and dumping them, but that's all. Eventually we'll have a housewarming with rice and all and a singsing [ceremonial singing] which would probably be a good time for you to come over if it's not too far in the future. I'll keep you posted. The shelves and bed in the old house had been removed, so I'm living all over the floor, which threatens to give way in various spots. I finally got a delegation from Yambon (but with no talk of building me a house there, and in fact they're contributing to this one) with much talk of how they want me (to live there). Anyway once this house is built I plan to alternate residence, going over there on Monday morning and coming back on Thursday night, which will give me three nights a week of sleeping in a tent. [This plan was later abandoned.]

You (or I) can't win [surviving a trek without physical problems]. No infections, though, despite all the scratches and one broken blister.

The food supply is excellent, and I was just brought three pigeon eggs, my first meat-like touch. The houseboy is rather less satisfactory: stupid beyond belief, demanding and actually from Katektek. Still there's no one likely in Dulago, though I may have made a mistake in not taking on Sanang.

We did have a singsing all night on Tuesday night, I've got some new kinship terms which thoroughly confuse my previous analysis and I just witnessed a very small curing rite (spitting charmed ginger). Nothing else of ethnographic interest. There are now several babies around, so I can observe them for the first time.

All I've missed so far is my metal cups and the tin of chocolates. I don't really care about the latter, but I do remember seeing them in Kandrian. Till later, love, Ann

PS. 59 shillings herewith. As I indicated I'm very low too, but we'll adjust later. I'll send another letter with the two policemen who are coming tomorrow. I paid these carriers for bringing my stuff, of course.

Dulago, July 1963

Dear Jane,

It occurs to me that I sent you twice as much money as you asked for, and if I'd had time to digest your note, I'd certainly have sent some of it in tobacco. I was somewhat distraught because of the sudden appearance of two policemen who announced that they were on "patrol" and were checking on house kiaps (Government rest houses). They then proceeded to order people from all the surrounding villages to get to work immediately on my house, along with various references to how I was living in a pig sty! (embarrassing, if true) and to what incompetent house builders they were. About all they seem to have accomplished today is to get some wall scaffolding set up, rather negated by the fact that they removed the already laid floors. I feel that they've antagonized the populace for miles around, and that I'd better keep out of it as strictly as possible. After all, the darn thing is a *haus kiap*. But what a mess!

Also just had another major hassle with the houseboy, who says he feels forced to buy all the food brought here which I don't buy, that he is shamed by having to cook in front of people (not really my fault; there's no room for the stove if I did want to use it), that I'd only given him 15/- last payday (and how much are you paying yours?), that he'd expected sugar in today's cargo, and so on. One more such session and out he goes; I've had it, and would of course never have taken him if he hadn't said he was from Yambon.

As you can see, I'm a mite annoyed. But it's nice to have all the cargo.

Just had a discussion with both the boy and the Luluai, and all seems to be well. I feel cheerier.

Your setup sounds magnificent. Mine will be very cramped by contrast, but I hope the height of the floor will help; I can use the space underneath as a verandah, if nothing else. My pigeon eggs sound pretty paltry compared to your fish, but they were awfully good—no little ones inside, as I'd fully expected.

I've played the radio very little so it may yet develop troubles. Second lamp went on the blink tonight, but the policeman got them both working.

Roo just had his first tussle with a pig. I live in constant fear of a large tusker here. He (Roo)'s delightful, but I wish he weren't so fearless. Right after the pig he tried to play with a dog.

As regards prices, I paid the ones who took my patrol boxes down and brought my extra gear up at a much higher rate—15/ shillings each way in fact, but I'm willing to try for something smaller if possible at this date. Certainly I wouldn't pay so much if they weren't carrying both ways. They did in fact bring back up a lot of stuff, so I could convincingly offer less for normal trips, much less for those with mail. We should be able to manage it for somewhere between 10 and 15 shillings. There seems to be a fair number of young men about. On the other hand, two of the four who went down for me last time were most pathetic about the sores they'd acquired in the process.

Herewith what I'd thought was my frying pan but am willing to concede may be yours.

For Christ's sake—a man just came to say that I should provide rice so they'll have the strength to build the house, because the taro is no good. They must have cooked a gross of the stuff yesterday. Oh, well, we'll see how it goes when the policemen leave. Love, Ann

Umbi, July 1963

Dear Ann,

Umbi has been like Grand Central Station today—first the policemen, whom I tried to impress with my house so they would go easy on the Umbi-ites for not finishing their *haus boi* (men's house). I don't know what the outcome is as I've kept away. Then came two "brothers" (Melanesian Brethren of the Church of England) to visit the resident brothers. The police and the four brothers are making one happy? household tonight and the sounds of their wireless is tantalizing. Then came a recruiter or two with your? two messengers. Confusion reigns supreme as you may imagine. I'm sending this pass with your? messengers, but hesitate sending the money (which you did over pay) having no official pass with them. I know you are short, but I will be sending two down to Kandrian toward the end of the week—probably Sat. They can pick up the Saturday's mail on Monday (as I remember there was no "delivery" on Saturday) and should be back here Tues. or Wed. Now, do you want to send someone with outgoing mail and instructions to pick up money (and chocolates) before Friday or if not, I'll send them over with the incoming mail next week.

(Continued after dinner)—On second thought (after talking to your boy whose name I've forgotten) I'll trust him to take the money and the chocolates. [He ate some of the chocolates en route.]

I tried the radio again tonight and it worked! *for ten minutes* and conked out again! so unless I get a full evening out of it before Saturday, I'll entrust it to Ningbi (#2 houseboy) to carry it down to Kandrian.

I am paying 10s [shillings] a week wages plus tobacco, but am also giving full meals including meat and biscuits etc. In fact I'm feeding at least one extra over and above us three each evening! (your boy and the Luluai tonight). It may seem excessive but last night the two boys bought a tin of mackerel from someone to share with me and they talk of paying me back for the rice when they get paid! And they also talk of helping to buy the food when their wages accumulate. In return I'm buying them shorts and blankets. I've given up figuring wages as such, but we have a happy workable arrangement and that is really all I care about. I've offered 10s for a Kandrian trip with cargo one way and it seems to be accepted. But it now appears two men and a boy will go so I plan to get more than originally planned. A duffel load at least. But I don't think (I) we can swing a mail trip in alternate weeks, but we shall see. I would think a trip every two weeks, i.e. one a month apiece, should suffice and if we add cargo lists every time it should see us through. What do you think?

I'm suffering from a sprained jaw from eating a very "strong" sugar (cane) this morning, but otherwise am in fine shape.

The police are taking two men to jail for not finishing the *haus boi* (men's house) and not building another house *in spite* of the fact that they have built my house, the "brother's" house and a *haus kiap* (rest house). However, Kasli, the Tultul, says, "*Em i gat gudpela kaikai long kalabus tru*" [they have good food in jail], and so does everyone else (agree)—I think they look forward to this "punishment."

The case which was sent up *did* contain all my good clothes! However, it gave me a good excuse to verbally express my anger at the Kiap [with the aim of disassociating myself from the Colonial Government]! However, they [the clothes] probably are safer here. I can air them and keep an eye on them. By the way, cooking the silica gel [drying crystals] in a saucepan over a fire works excellently [to restore its moisture absorbency ability.]

No more fish since the three meals last week, but hope springs eternal.

We have several quite sick people here, but no curing as far as I know. I'm also treating five bad [tropical skin] ulcers and innumerable incipient ones—far more than I saw last year.

I'm sending back £3 (3 pounds) which is what I recollect you over paid. Eventually, I'd like the container back. Love, Jane

Dulago, Wednesday
Dear Jane;

I didn't know the boy went to Umbi. He was supposed to be escorting a *kandere* (mother's brother), whose husband was calaboosed (jailed) from Hutkihyu by the policemen, back to their common home in Katektek. I should have taken the opportunity to get rid of him, but I'm always a moral coward in these matters. As I said, however, one more hassle about anything and that's the end. I'm paying him 20/- and a goodly part, but not all, of his food, though I plan to add heavily to the food ration after I send in my next order. I've already given him a blanket and mirror and he's asked for shorts. No suggestion on his part about sharing. I also pay 10/- weekly to the Luluai's wife for firewood, and a stick of tobacco for each 2 containers of water (to various). The other boy is simply a hanger-on whom I'm trying to get rid of—not from here, and no addition to the household.

I agree with you that one trip every two weeks should be sufficient. My next one will come as soon as my house is finished, since I'll have to get food for the *kaikai* (feast). This may be very soon—it looks as if the walls may be finished today, if the rain stops. I'm trying to figure out how to get some light inside the place at the moment, but studying this one (my old house) I suppose that the roof pitch can be modified or handled in some way to admit some light.

As I may have told you, I've played my radio so little that it may well be in the same condition as yours without my knowing.

I can't figure out how on earth to put together the table? footstool? that doesn't have a solid top, and feel that something may be missing. If you have one (3 joined legs?) I'd appreciate a diagram!

This *pas* [letter] is being sent primarily because I feel I'd better get some film out. I've also written one chatty "newsletter" to NGS full of inconsequential tidbits, but not typed yet—nowhere to put card table—or anything else.

There's a tiny lime tree on the edge of the village and I got 3 *mulis* (lime/lemons) yesterday (probably the month's supply; children were playing with the rest).

I just came across Roo eating a mouse. Isn't that impressive? It may well be his second; he was not very eager for his steak & tomatoes last night. He just pays me flying visits now.

Do you know about tooth-blackening names, new names given boys when their teeth are blackened? I assume you have them. Here they all end in -*git*, the name for the tooth blackener, and are called *ya-hi-da-git,* "name accompanying blackening."

The house builders all knocked off at 3. All the exterior walls but one small one beside the door are up, but I'll feel better when there's some stab at a roof. One of the builders tells me the whole thing will come down at the first wind, which isn't very reassuring. I should be able to get in three rooms, with a *haus 'waswas'* (bath house) underneath too, but I may lose that argument. My knee now bends to a 90 degree angle. Vast improvement. It hardly bothers me except at night when it's uncomfortable in almost any position.

This seems to be the only village in which no one was calaboosed (jailed). The Luluai's brother avoided it by telling the police that his house, in which they wanted to sleep, was unoccupied, though in fact two complete families use it, and hastily sending all the others off to the garden hut. He's nervous that they'll catch up with him, however, especially if they're returning next week as announced.

Roo just walked in feeling terribly proud and licking his chops, and is now having a complete bath. I suspect that it (the mouse) was his first.

The lad who's bringing this (a member of my favorite family) and named Paiyali, has volunteered to carry messages to Umbi or Kandrian whenever necessary. He took the patrol boxes down so I'm hopeful that he means it. Like one of his sisters, he always looks miserable; don't take it personally.

Thanks for the money. That was the right change. Love Ann.

Umbi, July 1963
Dear Ann;

Don't know when this will reach you. Ningbi arrived back yesterday afternoon reporting that the cargo was stranded at Aliwo. Remember the concrete bridge just this side of Aliwo? He says it's completely gone and the stream is flooded too much to get the cargo across. It may take some days for this stream to subside. Anyway, Ningbi swam across with my £30 of shillings (it's a wonder he didn't sink), and left the others to wait it out. He also came to report that

Ann and Roo on her Verandah in Dulago

in addition to my one patrol box and kerosene, the Kiap sent another Patrol case! What this contains—we'll only have to wait. But it does foul up my financial arrangement—which was as follows: for one case (with outgoing radio) and 1 tin Kerosene, I sent Ningbi as boss, plus two men and one wife. I didn't pay Ningbi extra, as he is a houseboy. I paid 10s apiece to the other three, plus 10s for buying food in Kandrian for them all, and 5 sticks of tobacco. Ningbi also reports that in the villages close to Kandrian they charge money for food for weary travelers. So we may have to take this into account. Ningbi just came in and said he thinks the other case contains papers and books—I gather our mail. He also says the Aliwo water takes a long time to go down and they will have to make a *diwai* (wooden) bridge before they can cross.

Kanegit died last Sunday. I did *not* go to the burial however as 1) it was reported to us at 3:30 p.m. 2) he died in place *matmat* (hamlet, burial place) 1 hour away, 3) all were going to sleep "with him" then *plantim* (bury him) Monday A.M. and this matmat has one house, 4) heavy rain, 5) the "vapors" (menstrual cramps) as we call them in Philly [Philadelphia]. Debli decided to stay with me and I got some interesting, if disjointed and conflicting information. But unless more happens in the future the whole (burial) thing can be summed up as "a man died and we ate pig." (It's quite a change from the Tiwi.) I'll get around to typing up my notes on these soon. However, information on *hangupim meri* (strangling widows) came quite unsolicited. I don't *think* they hung-up Kanegit's wife, but I haven't seen her and all but one family has come back to the village.

A young man, Gospo, went *menge* [insane] on Monday and I must admit frightened me when he marched into the house speaking belligerent Pidgin. I actually didn't recognize him. If he was in town I would have said he was drunk, wild-eyed and unsteady on his feet and marching (as he) walked. He ate unripe bananas without peeling them and marched around in the pouring rain. Half an hour later he reappeared at my door and asked for a razor (blade), which I gave him as it was quite obvious that he had recovered. No one did anything for or to him. He left shortly afterwards for his garden.

The rain and hunger (due to taro tabus assumed by many people due to the recent death of Kanegit) and the disinclination to go collecting food in the rain) has made everyone short tempered. Yesterday I bought a large amount of taro from the Luluai and then an argument between Debli, the Luluai, and another man resulted in a decision that the taro sticks also belonged to me, that Debli would plant them and the resulting taro would be ours. But the decision cost Debli 5 shillings to smooth the Luluai's feelings and Kahamei (the Luluai) paid the other man 5 shillings so that they could "all sit down peacefully together again."

> [Actually, after the first acquisition of taro with stalks, no similar offerings were made to me. Taro stalks are the most valuable part of the plant, since they hold the regeneration power and rarely are they offered for exchange purchase. Taro corms typically are not offered

for sale at all, but *given* as food. My household presented a heretofore unknown situation regarding food purchases.]

For two nights now my crayons have provided entertainment and diversion. Debli continues to show imagination and so does Ningbi, but the lack of imagination on the part of others is astonishing to me. Perhaps it has something to do with (lack of) acquaintance with anything resembling two dimensional pictures. Another thing that amazes me is the fact that no one does anything while held up by rain. They sleep, talk, sit, and if absolutely necessary, chop wood. The drawing at least, occupies my houseboys. I must admit I haven't done much either!

My emergency dental kit [a going away gift from my dentist] was put to use last night! I discovered a large part of one filling had disappeared! My first attempt at dentistry is not too successful as I still have rough edges and a depression, but it doesn't hurt, thank goodness. Tonight in peace and privacy, I'll try to build it up. [Attempt unsuccessful, but managed to survive without further dental problems for 16 months.] Wouldn't you know—this is the first filling I've ever lost, much less filled.

Two Arihi men have volunteered to collect the additional cargo and I have just paid them 10s apiece and 5s to buy food in Aliwo and Debli contributed 2 more shillings for food. It's getting expensive. Incidentally Ningbi reports Foldi [District Officer] was in Kandrian. I wonder if they will let us know when Kandrian is deserted by DNA (Department of Native Affairs).

Next day 10:30 p.m.—Large hassle over cargo pay ended with 15 carriers! But only paid a total of 53s, not counting for food and the initial 5 (men) have to pay me back accordingly! I surely hope they do (2 houseboys offered to help me pay!). Have long critical letters from both Gilka and Terry (NGS). Will send them over when I have time to digest them. Love, Jane

Next morning 7 a.m. P.S. Now being slightly more awake:

1. I've paid for my cargo and our mail at rate of £1 per patrol box and 10s for Kerosene as far as Umbi. I also bought a lovely sweet small *kundu* (drum) for £2/0/0.

2. I won't charge you for your half of the mail case to Umbi as you will have the problem of returning the patrol box!

3. I have *not* paid the men (from Yambon and Pomalal) who are taking this to you from Umbi. I did pay the Luluai from Pomalal for previous carrying charges which he said he didn't get (6/)—I was too exhausted to argue.

4. I think with the hassle of last night over the cargo we *must* offer standard rates. But I am willing to go as high as £1/10/0 per patrol box and I think I will have to pay per box and not man in the future.

5. I don't know what your plans are about sending down for cargo in the near future due to the river situation, but let me know. Here is my outgoing mail in hopes!

6. *If* you do send for cargo and only *if* you might have room, Chin Cheu (trade store at Kandrian) did not send as much rice as I thought I had ordered and we three would greatly appreciate another extra 2 lbs or so. He also didn't

send as many tins as I ordered (I'm minus 2 and Ningbi counted them in the store and verifies that it was Chin Cheu and not hungry carriers!).

7. Just got the bill for B.P.s [in Rabaul] food which we don't yet have! Could/would you write them for both of us as I don't have time. My food bill was for £15.0.0. I will also write them when I pay what I figure I owe, but we ought to register the fact that the food is missing. I suspect it may be in Kandrian where, as I strongly suspect the [missing] Air Cargo Package [containing film] (part of which is here for you) was. I had just written Ken [Weaver—NGS] to put a tracer on it and no planes as far as I know have landed since he received the letter.

8. The Tultul from Yambon says the water (river) is still too high to go this morning so I may add to this rambling note.

Dulago, July 1963
Dear Jane;

I don't really expect anyone to turn up with mail before tomorrow at the earliest, but I am hopeful mostly because I'm virtually out of cigarette paper. There's a great burst of activity going on right now, and if the rain holds off for most of the day, it's barely possible that the main part of the house (exclusive of *haus kuk* (cooking place) and *haus waswas* (bathing place) and probably the porch will be finished today. I hope they at least finish the roof so I can move some of the gear out of this house and have space to turn around. I expect to be thoroughly impoverished when it's done; I hope John Yun (of Chin Cheu's) really can supply shillings on demand.

I'm going mad with inactivity, but plan to rest the knee until the end of the month, when I'll probably start spending time in the gardens.

I hear you've had a death. How splendid for you (ethnographically, that is). I remember dreaming once after I'd left Lakalai in '54 that someone had died, and waking up feeling terribly guilty because I'd been so happy at having a chance to see a funeral. Everyone here is flourishing and I see no prospect of deaths, births, or even marriages, though we've had a couple of splendid family quarrels. There are advantages to living in an old village though; there are the graves and family trees to discuss, and I've found a disinterred shell, a broken ax, and a broken bark beater (have you seen them? unexpectedly elaborate) in poking around the grounds. [Pigs were responsible for the disinterment.] The local populace is rapidly dividing itself into cat-lovers and non-cat-lovers. I fear my cook is among the latter. The former have a delightful time with Roo, who is very active and totally fearless.

The Luluai of Yambon cross-questioned me about the letters I sent via you, and obviously suspects me of being instrumental in the jailing of various. Suspicious old beast (especially since this is the only village from which no one has been jailed so far, though they are fearful.) Unlike your people, these are most reluctant to go to jail.

What are your rainfall figures? I'm beginning to develop athlete's foot (soreness between toes), have a mysterious patch of something at the corner of my mouth, and am scraping the mold off camera cases. It really makes me feel at home.

What are you telling people your name is? I've been saying *Dien*, but evidently we're at cross purposes.

I take it that I was only to pay these carriers from Umbi to here? I hope I'll be sending people down early next week, but whether I can get your stuff or not depends on how many carriers I manage to rustle up.

Moved into new house today, though they haven't finished thatching it. What a relief! It really promises to be very nice.

I won't hold up this man by writing more. Situation in rain here is same as there! I'll let you know what I work out for carriers. Love, Ann

Umbi, July 63

Dear Ann

I have given these men two sticks [of tobacco] to carry this to you.

I am a bit rushed as two men have just come and said that they are going back to Dulago and will carry this to you—and that you are sending men down to Kandrian tomorrow. So here are some "passes" which should also go. If I have time I will package up some film to go also, but I don't know how long they can wait, or rather will wait. I am getting frightfully bored and am thinking that I will come to visit you sometime soon. Perhaps when the cargo arrives back I could come over and pick up my mail? How does this seem to you? If it is suitable let me know. We still have not had the big singsing here for Kanegit (who died) but it is supposed to come off when "*gudpela taim liklik*" (the weather is a little bit good). Evidently all come to it from Yambon, Arihi etc. Why don't you come too, if it is as complex as it sounds, two (people as) recorders would be advantageous!

I am being hovered over, and this makes making sense rather difficult. Nothing much has happened here except yesterday I went swimming for the first time and washed my hair—the swimming here is better than Pomalal, but all laughed at me because I kept going back again to "*waswas*" (bathe). I also ate my first large white wood grub—do they have witchity grubs here? It wasn't bad, but I don't think it will become my favorite food.

I have made very little headway with the language. How are you doing? The major problem is that too many people come into and under the house and sit and talk and I can get little concentrated work done either with informants or on writing up what little I have gotten. If I retreat into my room, everything seems to happen.

My other problem is to get people to stop posing for pictures. It completely discourages me from taking pictures to have vacant staring eyes looking directly at me.

It is obvious that I need "intellectual stimulation" so let me know when I can come and visit!

I hope your cargo doesn't get held up as long as mine. I am down to my last two pages of (cigarette) newspaper. Love, Jane

PS. I am paying 6d per pound for all [local] food as it seems to average out to what I was paying before and all buy it back at the same "scale." At the moment I have been swamped with *tapiok* (sweet manioc) and some of it has gone bad so I must curtail my purchases from other places, but it is extremely hard to say no, when someone has carried it all the way here.

PSS. Here is a package of film which only contains 5 films. Can you add some to it to make it look slightly more impressive? I've tied it with string, but the other tape is inside, and it should be fastened with the tape.

PSSS. Here are also some books some which I would love to send to Kandrian as we have both read them. Others which are for you. In spite of the boredom, I can get alone to read!

Postscript

Settling into a new field home is done very cautiously, as a cat does in turning around and around many times, kneading and molding its bed before it can curl up and sleep comfortably. Playing "guest" to our villager's "host" is very different when you are without a local Emily Post to help guide your proper behavior in given situations. Many mistakes are inevitable but you hope your hosts will forgive you the first time. But just as a child learns what to do by acting, then hearing parental approval or disapproval, so does the field-worker learn appropriate behavior, eventually.

During the time of our first two visits, the exact geographical location of Umbi and Dulago to each other and to Kandrian was known only approximately and relatively, and we depended solely on a map prepared for us by Dave Goodger based on his knowledge of the many main and minor foot paths through the dense forest cover. We searched in vain among all possible geographic sources for reliable maps that would correctly locate our little world of the Passismanua with that of the greater world from which we came. The National Geographic Society also searched in vain for a base map with which they could locate the events we reported on in our article (Goodale 1966a). The map that was published was a compilation of the Goodger map with my accounts of where we had walked, how far, in what direction, and how fast. In today's world of satellite-aided navigation it is much easier to make maps of such a heavily forested terrain hidden under dense cloud cover for the majority of time. In the early 1960s this was one of the few places on the face of the earth that had not been covered by aerial photography during World War II.

At the district level the Department of Native Affairs (DNA), under Australian Trust Territorial management (UN charter), was headed by a District Officer (DO), based in Rabaul at this time, and locally in Kandrian by an Assistant District Officer (ADO), a Patrol Officer (PO), and occasionally a Cadet Patrol Officer (CPO). These officers of the colonial administration (all called *Kiap* in Tok Pisin) had virtually total authority to oversee (by making annual or more frequent "patrols" throughout the district), maintain an annual census of all residents, keep the peace in the local communities, adjudicate disputes, establish laws, and impose penalties covering all aspects of the local residents' lives.

For example, in "our" area Kiaps had outlawed headbinding of infants, widow strangulation, and rain making; and had required them to establish graveyards in areas not used for habitation, to establish villages. It was required that all married couples build houses in such villages, and dig and maintain a pit-latrine for each house.

The village (as a whole) should build and maintain a house for the unmarried males (*haus boi*) and keep all such houses in good repair. In addition, Kiaps required all people with sicknesses or other medical problems to be taken to the nearest aid post for treatment. The common penalty for violation of these laws was time in the Kandrian jail (*kalabus* or calaboose) or, for the more serious crimes (such as murder), a court trial in Rabaul.

The Kiaps also had to take care of and assist visitors (who had obtained required entry and research permission from the DNA in the colonial administrative center in Port Moresby), which included anthropologists. The fact that all Kiaps had themselves received some anthropological training meant that they knew, and for the most part respected, the ethnographic method and its practitioners.

In addition to the Kiaps, there were other employees of the DNA, the *didimen* (agricultural development officers), *doktas* and *doktabois* (doctors and/or other medical officers, the latter being local men with medical training, who were in charge of the aid posts). Malaria control was under an expatriate resident in Kandrian who patrolled regularly with a team of locals, who sprayed DDT in village houses, and sometimes dispensed the currently prescribed malarial preventative to the populace. Other DNA personnel at Kandrian were the local (native) police detachment, who accompanied patrolling Kiaps and other personnel, and also made independent patrols carrying messages from Kandrian to persons or groups in the district and assisted the Kiaps in maintaining their laws.

The school, mission, and trade store were independent from the DNA administration. While occasionally we express our frustration with these officers of the colonial administration and independent establishments in Kandrian, it was a frustration which reflected more our total dependence on them for all communication outside of our own "two-party line," required for our material and nonmaterial support. We chose not to carry shortwave radios into the interior (with our "luck" with radios they probably would not have worked), and satellite communication systems were yet to be developed. Communication with each other and the outside world was essential for our mental as well as physical survival, as indeed was communication with the local population of Umbi and Dulago.

One of the laws established by the DNA was that the local people should carry the Kiap's cargo (material goods). For the first and second trips into the interior we utilized what may seem to be an enormous number of carriers to accompany us. In the first trip (1962) we had to provide for housing (tents) as well as cots, cooking gear, food, first-aid supplies and medicine, a few changes of clothes, plus incidentals. Our first houses were simply furnished (a table and a chair; we slept on floors or raised benches). We had a kerosene lamp for light, and a small kerosene primus stove. We each had a few enameled plates, a mug or two, knives, spoons, forks, and a can-opener, but little else. But we were only two of four expatriates for whom the cargo line had to carry supplies; there were also a small detatchment of local police (the number determined by the Kiap) whose housing, clothing, food, etc., also needed to be carried. Each patrol box was limited to 50 pounds in weight and carried by two men. A kerosene drum was a woman's load, carried on her head. Frequently, carriers would double up and trade off loads; there always seemed to be more carriers than loads!

For our much longer stay in 1963 and 1964, we planned for a few minimal creature comforts: two small tables to write on, two chairs (one comfortable) to sit on while writing, two stoves, two pressure lamps, two kerosene lamps and two drums of kerosene each (doubling was both a backup strategy and for use of visitors), a radio, two air mattresses (one for camping), a small tent, and food for a month plus some luxury (emergency) food, such as smoked oysters and canned pheasant. In addition, we had buckets to carry and store water in, some enameled ware (cups and plates), and a year's supply of medicines and bandages for our personal use and to treat the locals; not to mention the necessary tools of the ethnographic trade—the cameras, film, and accessories such as flashbulbs, blank notebooks, pens, tapes, and a (new) tape-recorder—and the always-essential supply of paperbacks to read, and most important for our hosts, stick tobacco, newspapers, and a supply of shillings. For this load, even 48 carriers were not enough!

The established pay for carriers was very low considering the enormous burden on them that this task imposed, not only physically, but also because it meant taking time away from their own working concerns. Resupplying ourselves and maintaining the communication link with the outside world throughout the 15 months of our second trip was never free from hassle—over timing, over payment, and over difficulties encountered en route, such as cuts, sore backs, hunger, floods, sorcerers, and the like. We gave voice to our continuing frustration in nearly every letter to each other, and tried as much as possible to minimize the number and size of the trips. We also continually renegotiated the price and ended up paying almost twice (sometimes more) than the going rate.

Language learning was essential and occupied a great deal of our time, particularly so because both communities were devoid of any competent *Tok Pisin* (Pidgin) speakers. Kaulong and Sengseng are grammatically fairly simple and closely related to each other and to Miu and Karore, spoken in communities adjacent to our regions (Chowning 1969). The vocabulary, however, is complex and contains many synonyms. It was some time before we found that lexical complexity correlates with marriage tabus which prohibit a newly wed person from using a word derived from, or similar to, the name of any in-law (affine), alive or dead (see chapter 7).

Fights, deaths, and other forms of confrontation are times when cultural rules are most apt to be expressed and thus they provide significant learning situations. Kanegit's death was the first in a series at Umbi attributed to sorcery, and Ann's and my good mood that it caused is not to be misunderstood as showing a singular lack of sympathy with the local people. For the insights it gave me, I was lucky (ethnographically speaking) that Umbi provided more of these *unpredictable* life events (birth, death, marriage, etc.) than did the smaller population at Dulago and so my study focused on these life course events more so than Ann's. Such is the nature of an inductive research "plan."

I have always regretted not recognizing, and therefore not seizing, the opportunity to follow through on my observation that the Umbi villagers were not able to perceive three dimensions in a two-dimensional picture. The moment passed almost immediately as I began to identify and explain to the viewers pictures in magazines and photographs that I had brought with me. The people of Umbi quickly became skilled picture readers and, because I never told them which way was "up," they also quickly learned to read the pictures from all four sides with equal facility. I continued to use their interest in magazine pictures to stimulate discussion of many comparative aspects of human life.

Finally, the initial excitement over the material culture rapidly disappeared as we found it nearly nonexistent aside from spears, blowguns, shields, and various ornaments made from pigs, and dogs teeth. Song, we *eventually* learned, was *the* culturally significant medium for self-expression. It was impossible to be in the village more than a few days without noting that Kaulong and Sengseng learn and love to sing almost before they learn to talk. People of all ages break into song at all hours of the day—as they walk to the gardens in the morning, or return at night, or sit on their house steps. *Singsings* (social/ceremonial events), we learned, are scheduled and hosted and begin at dusk and end at dawn (twelve hours in these latitudes) and are the most important sociocultural events in the region.

Jane and Kamanli at Umbi

Chapter 3

They Had a Big Ceremony Last Weekend

Dulago, Aug. 5

Dear Jane,

It's noon, and the last of the carriers just left for Kandrian, and naturally it's pouring. After all these nice days. Oh, well, it's such a relief to have them off at last that I feel quite cheerful. I am, however, a bit fed up with the same old faces, and would love to see you. I really don't know whether there will be a singsing with the *kaikai* (feast) or not, but it would be very nice if you could come over as soon as possible after you get this. At least you'd have a chance to meet everyone.

Dulago has expanded; 7 *mok* (married people's houses) now, and a total, though of course not simultaneous, population of 35. Hudeuk (my cook) has just been away for a week and left again, and I'm infinitely happier with his substitute, the boy who brought you my mail last time (and may bring you this, for all I know).

I was brought a beautiful possum last night, but listening to it being strangled (I watched as little as possible) and plucked while still alive was one of the most harrowing experiences I've been through in the field. (Complete with babies in pouch!) Roo (the kitten) was forbidden to eat any (for his own sake—general tabu on meat for all domestic animals), though I managed to smuggle him a bit, and a few hours later, after he had gone out and caught his own supper, I had to intervene to keep the village boys from taking it away from him so they could eat it themselves. I'd gotten the impression before that they regarded cats as a hunting dog, [whose purpose is] to catch rats for them to eat, and it turns out to be true.

My handy book on Papua New Guinea informs me that it is one of the three major administration policies to eradicate the native religions and introduce Christianity. I wish I'd known before. In any case, watch what you say to Dave *et al.*

Could I borrow your screwdriver? My knife is incapable of coping with the problem of door hinges (and I'm out of nails).

Next Morning

Do come as soon as possible, and stay as long as you can. I definitely need some mental stimulation, and we'll work on the language. Kasup (Paiyali's brother) wants to leave now, so we'll leave other discussion till later. See you soon, I hope (don't worry about waiting for when the cargo comes back—just come). As you can gather, your stuff missed my carriers. Oh well. Love, Ann

Umbi, August

Dear Ann,

I was down in the new *haus boi* (men's house) when your boys appeared with (your note) and looking at the beautiful weather today, I was all set to go back with them.

However, on my way back to my house to write you, the Tultul (village official) stopped me and told me that they were going to hold an inquest on Kanegit's poisoning death the end of the week. He says that it will be on Friday, but I don't exactly trust their holding to schedules so—much as I would love to take off for Dulago tomorrow—I think I'd better wait. It (the inquest) sounds most interesting. According to the Tultul, every man from all villages from Sankiap, Yambon, to Arihi, must come and wash their hands in special water from near Yambon, which is being brought over here. If one man does not come, he is the one who killed Kanegit. And they must all come at one time. The singsing won't be for a couple of weeks yet.

If the inquest is over on Friday, and the outcome is not going to provide more interesting information and activity, I will leave for Dulago on Saturday and stay over Sunday. I will pick up my mail at the same time so don't bother sending it over before—all can do without (news) paper for a while.

Of course if there is a big *pela* (type) rain on Saturday, expect me as soon afterwards as is possible.

All of a sudden some good ethnographic information is coming my way. I will try to get my notes typed up to date by Sat. and will bring you a copy then.

Love, Jane

PS. If men from Dulago are required to come to the inquest, why don't you come too? Just a thought, don't bother to answer, come if you can and or wish, and the above plan will be held to weather and inquest permitting.

PSS. My two screwdrivers are either too big or too small to work the screws we bought! I used a hammer on the screws and it worked OK.

Umbi, Aug.

Dear Family;

Our mail "service" has broken down recently due to numerous difficulties all coming at once: 1) rain in Kandrian so no mail plane for a month, and 2)

Ann's carriers taking a week to get to Kandrian due to stopping for "business" along the way. So already our idea of "regular" alternating biweekly trips has gone askew. We have had over a week of glorious sunny weather.

I made the first visiting trip to Dulago last weekend; left here with Debli, Kaliam (a friend), and 3 young lads who had been visiting here, carrying my cargo of one sleeping bag, one overnight case (knapsack), and a package of one fish and one eel (which my other houseboy spent the night catching) as a hostess present. We left shortly before 9 a.m. and after the first long (1 1/2 hour) climb up the mountain on the other side of the river, the trip was an easy one, but it took us a total of 5 hours. We stopped to try to catch a snake, for eating taro and bananas, to visit with a young couple in a garden and to eat *selemon* (a nut) with them, to visit with the women in Yambon, the intervening village, and then on to Dulago.

Dulago is a tiny village compared to Umbi, only 4 houses now but 2 more going up (Umbi has 15 now). It is an old village with large ficus trees in the center and coconuts and betel palms on the fringe, but in spite of these I like my views of the mountains on all sides even if Umbi is a new, rather raw looking clearing. Ann's house is as big as mine, however I think mine is more conveniently arranged. The visit was most successful. We both needed it and I got some good pointers on the grammar, but mostly it was just the relaxation and talking English that did the trick.

We took a lot of pictures of each other for the NGS and including trail walking as she accompanied me back as far as Yambon. Our companions were greatly amused when I insisted that Ann pause calf-deep in a mud hole while I took the "required" number of exposures. We were nearly convulsed too! But we had received a long lecture [see earlier] telling us how to take pictures of river crossings, all of which would be for us totally impossible to accomplish *and* cross the river too. So we did our best with the muddy trickle.

Dulago, August 1963
Dear Jane,
(Wednesday) Unfortunately I said something in the presence of several people, about being cross with and shamed by the Luluai's (village official) behavior, and Hudeuk informed me that I would end up with everyone refusing to carry cargo for me. In fact, he seemed to be saying that this would happen if I paid by the case rather than the carrier [an attempt to control the escalation of number of carriers per trip]. However, I have every intention of paying by the case. I'll just take a chance on that. But I've had to say that I'm no longer cross with the Luluai, so don't say anything at your end.

Hudeuk improved during the time I was in Yambon by going through all my patrol boxes, removing the money I had hidden (ostensibly to a safer, but in fact, to a much more conspicuous place), playing the radio (which he denies), and God knows what else. So yesterday we put up the front door only to find that he can easily come in through the front window. Hell! It would be nice to have someone I could trust! The front door, everyone agrees is a lousy job.

However, nothing can be done about this or the now totally exposed *haus waswas* (bath house) until I get some more nails. So I'm sending a note to John Yun asking him to give me some nails if there is room in your cargo. O.K.? (I just found my lunch pawpaw half missing.)

Now that I've seen the new Yambon, I'm very glad not to be there. In any case, they're likely to be fully occupied for sometime with clearing, building their own houses, etc., and I suspect I'll be a major inconvenience.

My people won't smoke [tobacco rolled in] magazines (and I refuse to give typing paper). Your pages [from magazines] are now decorating the men's house and Hudeuk is griping (about the now total lack of paper), though he's the one who led the refusal.

The pawpaws and limes (sent to you) were a present like.

I've just been patching up a woman whose husband slashed her with a knife.

The Tultul of Yambon was just here and says he and others are going to Kandrian to collect the Kiap. It sounds like a perfect opportunity to send out mail in the blank period between your next cargo and mine.

Thursday night—I am now a victim of nervous indigestion, and just when I was brought both a snake and a bandicoot. Word came in last night that my carriers were in Sailu (Suihi?) and needed relief. This morning several with Hudeuk went to meet them. The relief returned, bringing a bit of the cargo, but not the mail, and news from Hudeuk, that the Luluai had gone into my tobacco and our newspapers and was selling them in Pomalal. "Seen with own eyes," you understand. They're still two villages away. I will, of course, send your mail and some tobacco as soon as it comes.

The cargo carrying just in this direction is costing me at least £20, which means that I won't have enough money (shillings) to pay for the house and keep going all month. Furthermore, the carriers had to leave a bag of rice behind, and who knows what else. So I'm sending a couple of other people down next week with the Luluai of Hutkihyu to rectify all this. The list of goods sent (who's Eddie?) [John Yun's brother who had switched places as proprietors of Chin Cheu's Kandrian branch store] which I have received indicates that it's everything but delicacies. Wish that Rabaul stuff [ordered from BPs] would turn up. Still can't understand why they couldn't carry it all.

I'll never get to sleep tonight. The reason that I'm having to pay so much is that 13 men went, and it looks as if I'll have to pay each of them 15/- wholly apart from any further ruckus that may develop about food. They spent the money I'd given them for the trip down for *bilas* (dress-up items) so they'd look good for the Kiap, and now talk of starving on the road! After all this time, I'm not surprised.

I don't know yet what I'll say to the Luluai, but, regardless of what was said above don't feel any hesitation about saying what you think. Even more maddening is the fact that I've been trapped here for so long. There's a marriage payment business (Tultul to Luluai) in Yambon tomorrow that I'd love to see, but I don't dare not be here when the stuff arrives.

[Cargo (supply) management was almost as frustrating to us as it was for the carriers. For both carriers and anthropologist it forced an interruption of "normal" activities. In addition, it meant that we had to alter our working relationship from that of *friend* to that of either *employer* or *employee*.]

Friday morning—Because one old man was carrying on, I gave everyone (over the protests of some) £1.0.0 (this I figure covers the food money). Since Dave, damn it, sent our Rabaul gear [from BPs], requiring 2 carriers you owe me £2.0.0 for it. I'm sending some papers for Bessasparis (Patrol Officer) to return to Kandrian. Thanks to his sending this, of course, what I ordered for [my house completion] feast had to stay at Chin Cheu's. I'd sent a letter telling them definitely not to send the Rabaul stuff if it came, because there weren't enough carriers. Oh, well. These men have been given a stick (of tobacco) apiece from here to Umbi. Love, Ann.

Umbi August 16, 1963
Dear Ann;

(£2.0.0 enclosed.) Sorry about your nervous indigestion, at the moment I'm suffering from a splitting (nervous?) headache so may not make much sense—and me with fresh fish for dinner! After the cargo was unpacked I lay down and overheard (but not understood) a discussion on cargo with "£1.0.0" and "case" mentioned. I'd dearly love to have understood what they were saying! I'll let you know how I make out next week.

Fell into information on "business" [social/kin groups] a few days ago. Briefly—two names (info. from Ningbi): 1) *poididuan* or *bimeididuan* (two versions? of one recorded), or 2) what you say when you go to another place: *bimakokwal* (literally "place of my birth"). Translation of both was (in Pidgin) *bisnis* (kin group). If you go to a place where no one knows you, you give name of father. You get one kind of *bisnis* from father and *another kind* of *bisnis* from mother. Both are exogamous! Get land rights from both. A #1 boss of *bisnis* is *yiang numuru kuksun* (male first-born). The Luluai of Yambon is #1 of the business to which "everyone here, in Umbi, belongs." That's why he was witness to Kanegit's handwashing. Land rights are with business as a group. The illustration given referred to "when Kiap wants to buy land." Try as I could, I could get no individual names for different "businesses" and at the moment, doubt they have them (worse luck!).

(Later after eating fish.) Head is down to a dull roar after 4 Aspro and 1 Codral. Tultul has just arrived back after a trip west concerning the poisoning (sorcery)—the Luluai went east. All are to come again to wash hands Wednesday! Due to this business delaying government work, Kasli would like my carriers to leave here on Sunday. They will wait for Tuesday's plane and get both our mails, and be back Wednesday (they say! if no rain) but by Thurs. for certain. I trust you will send your outgoing mail with your carriers and so agreed to this change in schedule. (It was either this or wait until next weekend which I really can't unless I live on a diet of taro and tinned puddings [cakes]!)

Many thanks for generous loan of tobacco. You have made everyone very happy. I will return same to you later this coming week. L. Jane

PS. I will give whoever carries this 1 stick (tobacco) apiece. I think there will be two people [meaning don't pay them twice!].

Umbi, Wednesday night Aug. 21:

Dear Ann,

I expect the cargo tomorrow, but also a repeat performance of the handwashing [sorcery trial] with men from Sankiap, Agiuli, Hulem, Yambon, Arihi, as the first was not a true trial as the (rumor of a) "police patrol" was a more powerful threat. Anyway will send this and anything else in the way of mail with some returning to Yambon.

The *singsing* for Kanegit will not take place until after the Kiap has come and gone so will expect you anyway after Kiap and will let you know about the singsing as I know more.

My cargo train did not leave on Sunday as 1) rain, 2) no volunteers, and 3) a garden invading pig was killed and eaten by all. On Monday 4 volunteers appeared to carry 1 case and 1 drum of kerosene (10/- apiece) and after they left about 4 others trailed along "for the ride." I offered to contribute a bag of rice to the village only if they would volunteer to carry it free. Which they agreed was fair!

Am trying working out kin groups and it looks like kindreds, cognatic kin groups, rather than anything like double descent. Inheritance is both from MB [mother's brother] and F [father] per the dead man's [Kanegit's] inheritors. Would love to discuss Social Organization and kin terms with you when you come. I'm having a terrible time getting (kin) terms of reference.

Thurs.—continued—No cargo yet (as you may assume). Handwashing took place but still many missing. I'm getting more and more information on poisoning as this thing drags out and incidentally fights, murders, and scheduled wars. Who knows when I'll get it typed up.

The "locals" were given a lecture from visitors about not teaching me the language fast enough—so spent a most profitable afternoon with the women really working at it and now it helps. Have been having a feast of meat—a *blak bokis* (flying fox/fruit bat) last night and for breakfast, a delicious black cockatoo. Tonight was offered 2 *blak bokis* and bought only one for breakfast again. My house looks like a United Fruit (company) storage barn—full of bananas! I refused to buy some more which were brought from Sankiap and as they saw I was firm, they looked the bananas over and "discovered" they were extremely poor quality and since then all locals have repeated to me again and again that I was right to refuse. Something they have been very hesitant about saying while the seller was still about! So I hope they will continue to be on my side at the right time and back me up again. I'm usually too sorry (embarrassed) not to buy food when it comes a long way.

Friday night—Cargo came this afternoon and aside from paying an extra 10/ because the knapsack was filled with overflow cargo of mine, all financial arrangements worked as planned—great relief! Only minor complaint was that your £51.0.0 and my £20.0.0 in silver (coins), which Debli personally carried plus cargo, has made his back very sore! I sympathize with him. Everyone thinks you are very rich now. But I did say it was to pay for your house and they agreed you needed it all. I haven't counted yours—I didn't have the energy.

Here also are 90 sticks (of tobacco) I owe you. You really saved the day. Eddie ("John has gone to Kandrian" [surely Rabaul]) also sent some *Time* magazines some of which I'll send too. My first *Time* (subscription) came in today's mail so we'll be set in the future.

I seem to be financially minded in this note, but I've just reduced my price in half for taro, tapiok and bananas to 1/- per 4 pounds [weighed on a small scale we brought in with us] and all seem very happy. The advantage is with them now as they can buy twice as much for 1/- from me. We'll see what happens when I pay the new price out. Love, Jane

PS. Keep any books you've read over there—I'm swamped with reading matter and just never find much time to read. I'll let you know when, if ever, I run out, and will also send you what I finish.

[We had to order (import) shillings to use for payments for food, services, etc., as much as we had to import mail and minimal food supplements. I began to purchase from visiting people more food than was required by my own household in order that others in my community could purchase the same from me, should they not have food from their own gardens to eat. I became the local marketing middleperson.]

Dulago, August 20

Dear Jane,

In view of the weather, I can't believe that your carriers will keep to schedule, but I'll start this in case.

The big news is that on Saturday, after complaints by Kasup I gathered up my nerve and fired Hudeuk. The ensuing hours were fully as harrowing as I expected, and doubtless there'll be more trouble (he most unexpectedly reappeared here last night), but I'm delighted not to have to spend another year with someone I neither like nor trust. The reason was just an accumulation of little things, and you can tell, as I'm doing, that I was just *les long pasin belongen* [I've grown tired of his ways].

I've recently been getting a lot of cargo cult talk—and my policy is to say that it's *giaman* [nonsense]. Keep your ears open. It's referred to as *kivung* [a meeting], and the cult itself is apparently centered on the coast near or at Ablingi. Have they been talking to you about the airstrip they're planning to build here so they won't have to *hadwok long kago* [work hard carrying cargo]? I've just been stamping on the Luluai's aspirations in this direction. God knows why they think an airstrip is less work than carrying the cargo, but I strongly suspect that it's tied in with the cargo cult too.

We had a splendid little do this morning—chasing a man who had been given up for dead and then recovered (the idea seems to be on the order of punishing children for giving parents a fright) and I was handed a baby to hold while everyone rushed around with clubs and spears. That's a new hazard to explain to the Magazine. My letter from Terry (NGS) was gentle (except about exposures); he said a couple of my shots taken in route were "good" and another "fairly interesting."

I've managed to get nothing further on *bisnis* [kin groups]. The first terms you give are ones that here just mean "we're siblings," and ordinarily mean that the people concerned really have the same parents. The two versions you give are just with different subject pronouns: "they are siblings (*pohididuan*)" or "we are." The *kokwal* I suspect derives from the word for "to bear children" and the suffix indicating mutually doing something with someone else. The point is that I don't think either of your terms would distinguish siblings from more distant relatives.

I did get some interesting statements to the effect (apparently needs extensive checking) that you can play with a FaSiDa (father's sister's daughter) but not with a MoBrDa (mother's brother's daughter). Anyway there is certainly something peculiar about relations between a man and his Fa Sis and her children. This should be just your cup of tea.

Saturday—Got some fascinating stuff yesterday on something that punishes you if you swear a false oath on fire. It comes from checking the word for "true" in Chinnery's (1928) vocabulary for A Kinum. The word he gives is the Kaulong one, so check "true." I think it [descent] is probably cognatic too, but who knows? Love Ann

[Extract from Ann's letter to the NGS—August 1963]
The headman of my village seriously proposed to me today that the people of this area should build an airstrip so that they won't have to work so hard in carrying cargo for Jane and me. I'm not sure why he doesn't think that it would be equally hard work to build an airstrip. I suspect that the whole thing is tied in with a "cargo cult" which seems to be flourishing on the coast. He was asking me about it just before he mentioned the airstrip. Leaders of these cults teach that the dead ancestors will return by ship or plane, bringing with them all of the white man's goods of which the white man has wrongfully deprived the natives. I was told the other day that the coastal people tell others that if Americans ruled here, they would cut the throats of everyone involved in sorcery. [This can create a problem for the anthropologist.]

Umbi, Aug. 1963, Mon. Eve
Dear Ann
Will try to get this and some outgoing mail to you tomorrow (Tues.) or Wed. in the hopes that your "next week" means toward the end of the week.

Was intrigued to hear of your talk of a (cargo) cult. I too have been talked to about building an airstrip and have discouraged it by saying that it was fine except I had no money to buy a *balus* (plane) so they would be working [making] the *ples balus* (airfield) *long nating* (for nothing). I also said that if I indeed had the money, which I didn't, I'd buy a helicopter, and Ningbi knew what it was and agreed it'd be much less work. I also suggested they make the roads passable for horses, which they thought was a sensible idea. Haven't heard anything about it for over 3 weeks now, but will keep my ears open.

Our calaboosed man returned today with reports that the policeman is due a week from this coming Friday and the Kiap is walking behind him. The advance policeman is to see if everything is done before the Kiap gets here. The village is determined to keep an old *matmat* (hamlet/graveyard) as the village's burying ground rather than make a new one. Reason being that ancestors are buried there. I do hope that the Kiaps will recognize this as a reasonable desire and not make trouble, but somehow I doubt that they will. They have worked hard clearing up the selected *matmat* and making a good road to it and building a good house on it. I haven't seen it yet, but have been invited to do so before the Kiap—obviously so I'll say a good word.

I'm glad to hear that your household has straightened out and Paiyali is working for you. We have our ups and downs, but I do trust them both and Ningbi is an excellent informant. Longpapa (the second one who carried your money to you) himself told Debli that the reason you fired Hudeuk was because he played your wireless (radio). I told them what you said to say and they agreed you were right (to do so).

Today has been its usual Monday madness. Everyone in (the village) but no one working but *bunging* (gathering) in, and under, my house. It's impossible to get anything done. There are just too many people, pigs, dogs, and talk.

[Monday was designated by the Kiaps as the one day in the week that all able-bodied men and women must spend working on government-generated projects, such as the village (houses, latrines, and clearing), and the paths and roads and bridges linking villages. Typically, Monday also became a day for villagers to gather or visit other villages in order to settle debts and other important social matters.]

The language is progressing slowly and with small groups of women and children with one Pidgin speaker I can really get somewhere. The village is rarely if ever, completely deserted this year and I think it's because 1) gardens are closer, and 2) the (C of E) "school"—both working together. But normally, there are one to three women baby-sitting, and 7-8 children of various ages here every day and perhaps a young man or two. It makes the weekdays very pleasant and mostly profitable.

I have just contracted for two young lads to carry this mail to you. I have paid them 2/ apiece, which is enough I think. Naingli, the older one, speaks fair Pidgin; Lita, the one with the beautiful smile, understands only a little. They will wait if you desire to send a note back. Debli is just again complaining about his back due to (carrying) the money—however, I think it's because he wanted to go to Dulago and I want him to make a lockable door for the house tomorrow. He cut brush all day without a complaint.

Ningbi is just squeezing the last of the *mulis* (limes) into my tea. Have you any to spare? Would love to buy some from you—*dinau* (on credit) of course. Here are some films of mine to *bung wantaim long* (put together with) yours. If you are sending any (to the NGS for developing). I only have one large mailing box left. How are you doing. I have written for some more. I also wrote Terry and Gilka [NGS] a somewhat toned down version of what we thought of saying!

Love and will expect you sometime during early September. We'll see what happens with the Patrol if anything—Jane

PS. Just a note—but had a unique experience last night. The boy who went *longlong* (crazy) before, was "taken" again last night while sitting by my fire and talking to a few of us. It was absolutely fascinating to see the onset and the development of it. It was also incidentally hilarious as he insisted the tiny unripe bananas he was eating were *pekpek bilong dok* (dog's feces) and, as he only understands and speaks Pidgin while *ulu* [Kaulong for this type of illness], the ensuing dialogue was quite understandable in its entirety. However, Gospo has a sickness called *ulu*, quite distinct from *menge* where one will run, run, and run, and will fight. *Ulu's* do not fight, they just don't talk or behave normally, nor do they have any recollection of their illness. There is known to be another man subject to *ulu* at, or close to Asahi, while "*altogeta man long dispela hap*" (everyone here) they say, is subject to *menge*.

Dulago, Tuesday Aug.?
Dear Jane,

Since the men have not yet returned from Kandrian, I'm rather hoping that they'll be bringing the Saturday mail, if any, so I'll start this just in case. It's not that I'm anxious for mail at the moment, but I suspect that it will be a long time before we get it next. From the accounts of cargo of mine that's still at Kandrian (since it can't be anything I've ordered) I can only conclude that Dave is trying to send everything up, including my good clothes, last year's boots, etc. Pretty inhospitable, I must say, and pretty annoying.

I should warn you that I've told people that the leprechaun on the cover of one of the *Times* I'm returning is a *tamberan bilong narapela hap* (a spirit from another place). You may be getting requests to see it (though the photograph of the moon is the real attraction).

The semi-Sengseng-ness of Umbi becomes more and more evident. It's the only Kaulong village men from here aren't afraid of sorcery in—and Pomalal is supposed to be a hotbed of sorcerers—just the place for a *haus sik* (aid post).

Look in my dictionary notes for (kinship) reference terms, most of which start with *ed- (et-)* or *ve-, vi-* (designating female and male respectively).

Mother is *totni-n* (3rd pers. ref.) and Father *ve-tama-n* here and they're the ones I hear most frequently. [Eventually I found that the Kaulong terms for mother (*inu*) and father (*iok*) were unexpectedly different.]

Assuming that tabus there are the same as here, don't mention a baby's teeth unless you know that a ceremony involving the killing of a pig and putting of dog's teeth necklaces and *mokmok* (stone valuables) around the child's neck has been carried out. I mention this because I had violated it, and had noticed a startled reaction, but not enough to realize how serious it is (penalty is death for the child).

Managed to avoid my first lizard by giving it to Paiyali, who won't eat the snake that was part of the same meal. No eels for some time—just snakes and assorted rodents. It makes the tinned meat more attractive anyway. Your messengers just turned up. If it weren't for the rain, I'd have them wait for the expected carriers, but who knows [when]. I'm sure I won't be sending mail out this week and suggest that you send more over on the weekend. I've got plenty of film yet. Did write Terry but not Gilka. However, I must request some more flashbulbs.

I'm getting *nowhere* on corporate kin groups; it's really maddening. But a lot on individual kin behavior and doubtless all will come in time. Also haven't been able to get any stories. If you can get a name for them, let me know. At times I feel that I'm accomplishing very little, and then I have a fruitful session like this morning on babies—all because I asked the meaning of a word I'd overheard—and cheer up. However, without Hudeuk there is exactly one good Pidgin speaker in the village, so progress is bound to be slow.

A boy fell out of a tree yesterday and dislocated his knee and the women on the spot promptly and ruthlessly manipulated it back into place. So I guess I don't have to worry much (about mine).

I would have sent you some *mulis* (limes) with the last runners if Debli hadn't said he'd collect some for you at Kandrian. Herewith.

Report here is that *amok* (insanity) is brought on by eating mangos which had been eaten by a parrot and is cured by binding the person hand and foot and applying fire. Gaa!

Can't think of anything new. Still suspect the Kiap is not coming, but I've just learned to be very suspicious of all rumors of the sort. Love, Ann

Dulago, Friday A.M.
Dear Jane,
Could you possibly lend us [for house feast] at least one of your big pots to cook rice in? The rice-cooking is scheduled for Sunday. The pig is coming tomorrow, and we are desperately short of things to cook in. It would (or they would—anything would help) be returned promptly. If I were sure they were having a singsing as well, and at a specific time, I would invite you to come join in, and would be delighted to have you in any case, but who knows what will really happen when.

If you have any more mail, send it along. The Tultul of Seagit, who brought our last batch of mail, say Dave (who's apparently away at the moment) and swears that no patrols are planned for the near future. So there's a counter-rumor for you. Love Ann

Umbi September 1963
Dear Ann;
     I am sitting under a bark shelter in Ningbi's garden in the pouring rain when your lad came and the word was passed via "telegraph" to me. I'm determined to spend the day here, so Debli went back and got the pass and your lad and Ningbi will go back with him to give him the large saucepan. Bring it back when you come to visit. I keep *kaukau* (sweet potato) in it most of the time so it can be spared until we get another large eel! The other saucepans are fairly constantly in demand and use.
     It certainly is a relief to get away from the house and in spite of the rain, I am trying to take pictures, but I could swear at the 20 exposure rolls. Just as I ran out of film, Debli started singing (magic) into a taro leaf of water which was later poured over the taro and poured into holes in the garden. However he did it again and this time I was prepared. I only hope they come out.
     The Luluai's wife had a baby girl yesterday in a cave. It is said that if one has a baby in a garden the garden is completely abandoned, no matter what stage it is in. Thanks for your tip on baby teeth. It holds true here also.
     I do not think I will mention your counter rumor as to (Kiap) patrols as it may not be true for here, but only places who were in trouble last time and there is enough anxiety at the moment to confuse the issue would be unfortunate.
     My last carriers are expecting the police to come after them as Maum (village) has accused them of defecating in the *haus kiap* (government rest house). So the less I say of Kiaps and police the better.
     Your boy and Ningbi are ready to go so—let me know when you think you will visit—we are ready and waiting, come anytime. Love Jane
PS. Still haven't written any letters.

Dulago, September 5, 1963
Dear Jane,
     I'll start this in case you send over anyone with mail. Aren't you glad it isn't this time last year [when we made our exit hike]? I'd hate like hell to be traveling in this weather. And for the same reason (and because I'm all right on supplies, though the fruit is reduced wholly to peaches thanks to the fact that almost all my recent pawpaws have rotted before ripening), I'm not planning to send anyone to Kandrian until the 16th. I wish we could get mail at least, but I suspect that the rivers are pretty thoroughly flooded. I'll plan to come see you as soon as the carriers have left—weather permitting, on Tuesday the 17th— unless I hear to the contrary.

Did your policeman turn up and did you get the rumor about the two Americans en route to visit us being stranded at Utkumbu by the river? The latest decision is that it was just those down river people trying to fool the hillbillies. The latest returnee from calaboose that I've seen, says the Kiap doesn't expect to come for a couple of months.

The Tultul of Seagit (who brought our latest batch of mail) has virtually settled down here to act as an informant. His wife's from here, and so was his mother's family, and he's infinitely superior to anyone here. For the first time I'm really getting information on spirits as well as a wide variety of other topics. Mostly very brief data on each, but it gives a starting-point for all sorts of inquiry.

We had the [house] feast but not the singsing thanks to the weather. The latter is promised for *gudpela taim liklik* (fairly good weather). We did have dances for the baby's tooth ceremony, all in the rain, but I hope some pictures come out.

The Luluai just sold me a large bunch of bananas which everyone later told me will rot without ripening (and they seem to be right) and another small bunch which belonged to another man. Great!

Descent groups continue to defeat me. I try all kinds of attacks and come up with nothing or with leads that peter out. In a way, that makes it all the more likely that there are no unilinear descent groups. I don't think we could have missed them for so long. But in that case what on earth were those things that Chinnery [in an early anthropological report] describes—and more to the point, how on earth did he get them?

September 10 (I think)—Plans are still the same. All other things being equal, I'll be over a week from today (Tuesday). It's a good thing I haven't tried to send to Kandrian earlier—no one would have gone. The reason I'm not coming over sooner is that I'm trying to finish things to get in the outgoing mail. If you have any, send it along. Love, Ann

Umbi, September 9?, 1963
Dear Ann,

I'm completely deserted for the moment. One of the few times so far this year—and it's rather pleasant. A very small puppy however is keeping me company so I'm not really lonely. I hope to get this *pas* (letter) to you tomorrow. There is talk of holding the big singsing for the dead man (Kanegit) this coming weekend. Kasli (Tultul) has gone to find out exactly when (as far as he can) so I can tell you. (We are both invited to it.) It will be held at Angus, the hamlet we passed last year on the way to Arihi—about 1 hour away from here, and will go on all night. (They worried about me sleeping—where? and I told them not to worry—so it will be a long night.) They will kill 1 to 3 of the dead man's pigs in the morning and we are to feast afterwards. I would suggest that you come a day ahead if possible, so you (and I) can get a rest beforehand. They are all working a *banis* (fence) on the dead man's *ples* (hamlet) and when this is finished the women will feed taro to the selected pigs. This is what has to be done before the singsing and why no one is yet certain of the exact day it will come off. But do *come*—we can, or may be able to, take turns snoozing through the night.

I will be late this month in sending down for supplies—it should be this coming weekend, but naturally will wait till after the singsing, but bring any outgoing mail with you and the carriers will leave as soon as everyone has recovered. I'm practically out of food now but have saved a few choice items for your visit so you won't have to eat bully beef [one of the few food aversions Ann has]! I've had no fish since the one I brought over to you! Too much rain. I've also had no washing done for weeks and am truly grubby physically and mentally so am looking forward to seeing you and the singsing.

I'm no longer alone having been joined by the one really incongruous couple here. An old man with a young wife who are (it seems) eternally involved in the inevitable love triangles—the current 3rd man at the moment is Debli. It really is a most interesting case, but they are only appealing to me as a "case" and not people.

Your mail boy has just come—plus a most distracting problem of a mother dog with 5-day old pups which a man deposited under my house—the mother dog most upset and the puppies likewise. She is now removing them one by one to the nearby house thank goodness. Anyway—I still don't know yet when the singsing will take place. But if you want to take a chance come on Friday. If not—I'll expect you next Tuesday (assuming the singsing is over or not begun). If I hear today after your mail-boy has gone, anything more definite, I'll try to get word to you. I thought you had sent your mail down at least a week ago, so have *les* (been lazy) about writing letters so have still not got any to send down. I may by tomorrow—now having incentive to write some.

I too have had a time *not* getting any unilineal descent groups. But have planned another attack on them soon. In fact I now doubt that the linguistic grouping is all it's supposed to be. All on your side of the river use *edi* for sister (according to my Kaulong informants) but here they use *edok* (according to one informant), and I'm wondering whether Kaulong-Sengseng-Miu etc. are [distinct social] groups or not or are they descriptions? Oh well—will discuss later and will let you know about the singsing.

My version of the "two Americans" rumor was the people of Utkumbu wanted help in rebuilding the bridge so they could get to a tooth-blackening (male initiation) ceremony at Asahi—so they "sang out" for help with the rumor and the bridge was built "quick time!" I'm now waiting to see what happens when a real call for carriers comes again and no one appears! The policemen did not turn up. Nor is there talk of a Kiap coming.

It really seems like our supply trips are coinciding, but I guess that can't be helped. Maybe in good weather we can rearrange them bi-weekly again. Love, Jane

PS. In case I (we) don't exchange further word and if I don't see you Friday, I'll expect you Tues. But I will try to get word to you and if you could let me know if you will come to the singsing it will help in my planning. L. J.

Tuesday night

Dear Ann,

Just had a talk with Tultul about the singsing. It *will take* place Saturday-Sunday [Sept. 12-13] barring large natural disasters. It is to be a very private affair but you are welcome plus one *only* Dulago *boi bilong yu* (your cook). They were very anxious that I stress this so I hope you can tactfully suggest to who ever comes with you that only one can stay. We will provide carriers back if necessary.

The pigs are all portioned out (for distribution) already and no one except the dead man's brother, Kulpo, from Yambon, is coming to the singsing from elsewhere. As I said earlier today, come Friday. Things are already in preparation and who knows where we will be Saturday before the singsing proper. There is talk of a singsing tomorrow night—as a warm up? to be held at Angus too. I haven't tried the tape recorder in the last month, but certainly hope it works and the batteries will hold out! Oh yes, could you also bring one of your hurricane lamps (not tilly). I only have one. They asked to borrow the tilly, but I vetoed that idea. But an extra lamp would be most useful. You see, I'm assuming you will be tempted and will change your plans and come, but if you don't I won't take it amiss, but expect you Tuesday. But do let me know, so I will be here on Fri. if you decide to come.

[I certainly sound desperate in the paragraph above, trying to make certain some personal plans in an ever-changing scheduling by the locals. Of course they and we had different criteria for which we tried to plan. We always seem to be saying "but who knows?" to each other because we rarely did know what would happen even a few hours hence.]

PS. This (tobacco) tin belongs to Paiyali—he spoke for one a month ago. There is a months waiting period for my tobacco tins.

[Tobacco tins made excellent containers for lime, a necessary component when chewing betel (*areca* nut).]

Dulago, September 10

Dear Jane,

Yes, of course I'll come. Just keep me posted. The only real drawback is that I'm almost sure to have the curse (which hasn't started yet) but such is the fate of the female field worker.

I've just acquired two armbands which I wear on my forearms and the dangling ends get into everything. Also the one which the Luluai took off his own arm to give me is alive with tiny insects. Gaa!

You may be able to persuade men to go to Kandrian in the weather we've been having—after all, you're on the right side of the river, but there hasn't been a prayer over here. I was also virtually alone today—only some small boys and Paiyali, but, after I wrote you, got the first information on the local equivalent of masking (P. *tumbuan*; here called *kapuk*). They aren't real masks, but coconut leaves covering face and body and a headdress, which is probably why I couldn't get anything on it last year. [I wasn't to see a *tumbuan* singsing until I got to Angelek four years later.]

I know what you mean about grubbiness. Furthermore, I have to scrape mold off my tobacco (the poor quality wet kind) before handing it out. You obviously got the good stuff in your last shipment.

I now get fresh meat three or four times a week, and have had two pig legs in the past two weeks. Marmot (bush rodent) tonight. The meat supply is consequently holding out well, but my luck with pawpaws has been so bad that I'm not well off for canned fruit. But I trust that I'll be able to hold out.

My excellent informant has gone home, but will be back eventually. Apparently the Luluai of Seagit is constantly taking part of his line and starting a new village elsewhere, so it's probably just as well I'm not there (where Dave wanted to put me). It's the real stronghold of conservatism in this area, however.

(September 11)—Isn't this (good) weather magnificent? I've just finished scraping the mold off my camera cases and putting on leather dressing and putting out my moldy bedding to air. Paiyali is down at the stream with a mountain of dirty clothes. I'm trying to sun myself and write letters at the same time, but am interrupted by a constant stream of people with sores, including the same ones coming back with different sores.

We're waiting for a garden-invading pig to be brought from Hutkihyu to be killed here, presumably today, so there may be more pork in the offing. Because of my recent diet (marmot last night, bat today) it's temporarily tabu for me to go to the gardens.

[This was a tabu which I never heard of or experienced in Umbi— maybe because I didn't ask about it.]

Afternoon—Paiyali is very grateful for the [empty tobacco] tin. He's mentioned it to me several times. Weather permitting, I'll be over Friday, probably bringing a leg of pork or two with me. The pig was supposed to be killed today, but has gone bush. We may have a singsing over it beforehand, but who knows. If the weather does not permit Friday, I'll come Saturday morning. I'll tackle the question of who stays as soon as possible. Paiyali's going to Katektek to collect a *dinau* (debt), and the Luluai and his wife were coming primarily to sell you their *mulis* (limes), but I'll try to fend them off.

See you Friday, if possible. Love, Ann

Umbi Sept. 18, 1963
Dear Family:
They had a big ceremony over the weekend. The ceremony was in honor of a man who died recently. It was held at a place about an hour's walk up the mountain from here. I went up there last Thursday morning and from then until Saturday night I did not go to bed! The first day they built a small shelter of

leaves in which they made two benches of poles beside a fire. It was fortunate that they did as we had a heavy rain that afternoon. We cooked taro (which is like potato) and taro leaves (like spinach) for supper. About 10 that night, my two houseboys and two younger boys and two girls appeared to sing. No one else came but we seven sang and danced as we were supposed to do until the sun came up the next morning!

The next morning others arrived and the men went off to catch the three large pigs which they were to dance in front of that night and then kill for the feast. They tied the pigs to poles to carry up to the dance ground where they made individual beds for them and covered them with leaves so the sun would not hurt them. The rest of the day was spent cooking large amounts of taro for the night for no one would go to bed this night.

At 6 p.m. Ann arrived with some extra food, for by this time I was sick of taro, taro and more taro. Also I was about dead from lack of sleep. The singing and dancing this night was by everyone in the village and began about 11 p.m. and went on until dawn and some of them even sang until 11 a.m., but they moved away from where they had been, for the pigs were to be killed. About 3:30 a.m. I lay down on one of the benches by the fire and Ann curled up in a poncho under me and we both caught 40 winks until about 5 a.m.

After the pigs were killed, pieces were sold to everyone (I got four legs) and about noon we all staggered down the mountain. That afternoon the pieces of pigs were wrapped in ferns and bark and placed in an earth oven and covered with hot stones and leaves and mumu-ed (cooked) and that evening we (the combined households) ate the 1st leg and went to bed early. The next day we ate 2 more legs and slept and the next day we finished the last leg and began to feel alive again.

Love, Jane

Umbi, Wednesday September 1963

Dear Ann,

Cargo did arrive today with the usual complaints, but no real other problems. However the rice was not collected and Kahame says he will go down this Sat. to collect rice and will fetch and carry mail for us also. So if you want to answer your mail send it over by Friday. Terry (NGS) seems more pleased with my photos, so I'm cheered, but no advice on flash—so if Gilka's letter to you has any more info. pass it on.

I've *just* heard from Kahame, that the Tultul sold some of the rice I sent up [before my arrival in June] to prepay for the house! Such is life up here! I have given Kahame 2 sticks [of tobacco] and said you would pay him some more for the bag of mail. (I gave Naingli 2/ as he doesn't smoke), but I forgot Naingli's working for me anyway.

Went for a delightful swim this morning and slept 4 hours in the p.m. as I got 2 hours sleep last night due to a singsing *long nating* (for no reason) with a rat chorus (in my thatched roof) thrown in, going on until 4:30 a.m.

Just got the Tultul's side of the rice story and it seems Kahame sold some of another bag (of rice), so we shall "*wokim toktok*" (discuss) it.

We have another imminent death—a young mother with five children. Reports are that she just sleeps and cries and doesn't talk. She also is sick out in the bush so I haven't seen her and I am torn as to whether I should, or even could, give advice when not asked for—so I am doing nothing. This too is one of the "joys" of fieldwork. If she were here and I could see her and watch the medication, I would probably suggest medicine, but now I just don't know what I can, or should do. I shall probably do nothing unless specifically asked.

Belo and Kilok (my two recently adopted puppies) are most satisfactory. Overly affectionate, but we wish they would or could kill rats. How is Roo doing with your rats? (The rats are so small they eat the food off the traps, but don't trip them!) Love, Jane

PS. Dave (writes that he) would like his mail bag back and he is going on leave November 16th. He personally checked up on my wireless in Rabaul, which still wasn't ready!

Umbi, Tuesday, September 24?
Dear Ann,

Excuse the grubby page, but better you than *narapela* (someone else)! They say if the weather holds, the cargo will arrive tomorrow, but I'm not really expecting it until Thursday. Ningbi left for Talasea (at least that was his intent) and say's he'll be back this Sat. or next. He will call in for mail, if and when he gets back to Kandrian. Meanwhile, the young pass-carrier, Naingli, is helping us out but Debli is dissatisfied so we're switching to Kaliam (the lad who came to Dulago with me) on Sat. It's been a hell of a week. Mainly because everyone has been bush since the singsing and no food was coming in and this, with my dwindling supplies, has been a period of hunger. But I gather it is for everyone. Taro is in very short supply and wild yams, *pinatang* (caterpillar variety), are the chief staples for the few who wander back to Umbi for a night.

However, in my desperate state of depression, I started in again on my census information one rainy afternoon and suddenly whole new vistas opened up. Umbi is composed of at least 3 main "groups": Akimut (of which Angus is but one *bidanu* or matmat [graveyard or, here, also a hamlet]), Humumi and Parangin. The last two were friendly, but both fought Akimut. Now the organization of the village (Umbi) begins to make some sense and is probably why Umbi is so large. These groups, with one or two exceptions, are exogamous, but the majority of marriages are between these 3 groups. I haven't got a name yet for the group, only place names. Kaliam and Debli, my informants on this, began to rave about their place Parangin, which is "on top" to the north, so much that I made up my mind to visit it at the 1st opportunity and get away from dead Umbi. Today, we went and it was a thoroughly enjoyable day and instructive (incidentally, we also bought food from the *lapun meri* [old woman] who lives there permanently looking after 10 pigs). It was an easy uphill walk (1 1/2 to 2 hours). On the way we stopped at *bidanu* (hamlet) Olias to visit with Yiaragit (Saha) whose existence I doubted. He is one of the 2 old men "left to die at Angus" as reported by Gilliard (in his *National Geographic* article in 1961). The other man has died. He (Yiaragit) is a fascinating apparition. He's blind, minus nose and teeth, skin and bones, bald *and* wears *muruk* hair [*sic*] [cassowary plumes] fastened onto a band around his head and hanging down over (hiding) his eyes and face. He was made blind and lost his nose because he swore falsely with the [special poison-trial] water, that he did not kill another's pig. This was when he was Kasli's age [about 30-something]. He, however blind, planted gardens, worked fences, chopped wood etc. until a short while ago. Now he still gets his own water, and looks for firewood, but most of the wood and all his food is brought to him by passers-by (relatives). I hope to get a few sessions with him on the "good old days" but we shall see. He remembers the Gilliards fondly for their gifts of meat, tobacco and razors.

Once we reached Korepo's (the old woman's) house and were resting before getting the food we came for, Kasli and daughter appeared and I got more information about residence in past in matmats and much more on death and burial and shells. (Kasli is turning into my most valuable informant.) They say when the Kiap banned widow strangling he also banned skull collecting [and thus the important mortuary ceremony as well] and all the skulls were reburied. But I mentioned I'd like to see one as I had two (skulls) in my own place (i.e. at home)—we shall see. We have made plans for me to visit for overnights in Parangin in the future and certainly much more information comes to light when out of Umbi. My spirits are much improved by this excursion and my legs are slowly conditioning. How are your blisters! I heard from Kasli you had a rough trip home. My sympathies are with you. Love Jane

Dulago, Thurs. night

Dear Jane,

I feel greatly cheered, mail really does help. If you can get this film out with some of yours, fine; it's all I've taken since Sunday, but I hate to think of its sitting around for another month. If there is a spare crevice in anything that's coming back for you, I suddenly realize that I'm going to be desperately short of soap. With all the wet weather, I hadn't realized what normal consumption would be. I'm not writing to John myself in case it's too difficult for your carriers, but if they have room for two boxes (or even one), I would appreciate it if you would ask him to send it.

A bill for books addressed to you was enclosed from the parcel from the Magazine Shop addressed to me. It seems simplest to pay it myself and ask you to pay mine, since who knows which one it was intended for anyway. This is being brought over by someone from Yambon, as you probably realize. There's literally no one available here, what with my carriers, demands for workers at Pomalal, and everyone else off to Katektek. I'd go with them if it weren't that I feel I have to wait for the carriers. Must go answer letters. Love, Ann

PS. I'm surprised to hear of your food shortage; we're certainly experiencing nothing of the sort. And don't just sit there and starve; I'll always be glad to supply what I can. Paiyali told me last night though, that all the eels caught with my equipment are being eaten in the villages. I'm really not surprised.

Dulago, September 1963

Dear Jane,

The rumor is that your group has already left for Kandrian. I certainly hope it's true, but I won't count on it. Yesterday, I was infuriated by receiving requests for pay for my last trip from two different Luluais, one who said he'd fed my carriers taro (at Katektek, where they stayed for four days) and another who said his men had helped carry. I didn't give it. Hope to God this next one works out better. The feet really didn't bother me on the trip back, much to my surprise, but as I approached Yambon, I started to have stomach pains and by the time we left I was sick as a dog—diarrhea, nausea *et al.* I took to the bush three times on the road and finally staggered home well behind everyone else. I gather they thought the length of the trip had done me in, though I suspect the morning pork, but in any case they were all remarkably matter-of-fact about it (indeed uninterested), which saved me considerable embarrassment. The stomach is still a bit upset, but not badly. The right heel now has an enormous completely raw spot on it, but it feels less painful today, and doesn't seem infected. We had singsings for two nights after I got back, so that last night, when they went off to sing at Seagit, was my first good sleep. Paiyali went too, so I tried my thermos for breakfast coffee, and it worked splendidly. I may have to resort to it for daily use. He said he'd had a major quarrel while I was away with three of the married men (including one of his brothers) who object to his walking in this direction early in the morning to heat water for me. It's tabu for unmarried men to be near the *mok* (house where women sleep) early in the morning—suspicions of adultery. Always something isn't there?

[I had discovered that filling a thermos at dinnertime with boiling water eliminated waiting for my two helpers to light the primus for the first cup of coffee in the morning, which I could now enjoy in a few moments of peace and quiet before the day began.]

It seems likely that our major singsing in the cemetery with killing of the tusker [a male pig with tusks] will take place very shortly after my carriers return. I'll keep you posted, but hope you can come. It'll probably be our best opportunity to photograph and record in reasonable comfort.

You will doubtless be charmed to know that the picture of Mandy Rice-Davies on the cover of *Pix* [magazine] was identified by a boy here as you.

Tuesday—The Luluai talks of someone going to Umbi tomorrow to sell you some *mulis* (limes), so I'll write a little more just in case. My carriers finally left at 2 p.m. yesterday (after waiting for some pig to be cooked). I didn't even ask when they'd be back. By making a tremendous effort, I got the Lakalai and Tikal reports [previous researches] and hell's own amount of official correspondence done (splotch) this is the first pen I've had trouble with, but it's a real bother—by Sunday night. What a relief! I'd like to celebrate but I don't quite know how. I finally saw some taro planted, but with no ritual whatsoever. Plenty of interesting general data, though. Did you know that when the taro's leaves wave in the wind, it's dancing with joy over the arrival of its owner and saying, "Daddy's come!" (*tuwo me gut*)? Isn't that dear?

There wasn't a single woman (or girl) in the village last night. Most of them just left in the afternoon, and some are due back today.

An interesting situation here at the moment. Better not mention it in Umbi. The big tusker (pig) belonging to the Luluai and his brother, Mubudli, has been breaking into gardens, and the brothers have threatened to use sorcery against anyone who interferes with it. Furthermore, Mubudli has threatened his wife (and baby) with sorcery because she's criticized the pig's behavior. She's fled home to mother, who's advising divorce. The really interesting aspect is that no one seems to think that the brothers know any sorcery (but there's general fear of their tempers). Love, Ann

PS. Here bees (*selen*) do make honey: I was just brought the lot with wax and bees and all. It's delicious.

PSS. I'm finally typing up notes; I'll send some over with your carriers.

Umbi, Friday September 27?
Dear Ann,

Assuming someone will arrive today with your mail, I will try to scribble a note. I had a busy? day yesterday. On the spur of the moment at 8 A.M. I decided to join Debli to go to look at the sick woman in the bush and threw in my bag some Sulphatriads (tablets). We got to the 1st garden and the wailing informed us that we were too late. They insisted that they had already buried her (which I doubted) and I should return to Umbi. I tried complete silence (in reply) and it worked and eventually we took off for the matmat [hamlet grave site] where the old man (with a face mask of *muruk* [cassowary] feathers) lives. Arrived at 9:30 and observed the burial (in the hamlet house) with associated *in*activity until 4. Of course at the crucial moment when they finally got to put the body in the grave, I was (I think quite deliberately) lured away with "*yu go drinkim kokonas pastaim bihain yu kam bak na sindaun*" (you go drink coconut first then come back and sit down). (I'd sat in the house for 1 hour after the grave was completed just waiting for the crucial moment.) Of course when I did get back all but the dirt was in the grave. The whole thing is remarkably (I think) dull, lacking in ceremony or ritual and there was only a 5 minute ritual wailing by 5 women at the end. Only 1/2 the village bothered to come although she was a young mother and popular (the split is according to the old residence pattern). On top of the dullness of the affair—I, of course, had decided not to take my camera on the short trip of the morning. But aside from getting more shots of the old man, nothing of photographic uniqueness occurred. We sat and cooked and ate taro until 4:30—by this time word reached us that there was a white "Father" visiting the village. This I found was true on my return.

A young Australian C of E Priest from a mission 25 miles west of Kandrian came on patrol. We spent a pleasant evening last night chatting. He's off for a look at the river at the moment before going back to Arihi. He told of the cargo cult on the coast which reached his place. Supposedly started at Popi (Catholic) Mission and a man, Koriam (head of council) is supposed to have started it. Just a month ago, he (the Father) was given £15.0.0 "for the Church." [He says that] Dave also received large sums (of money) "for the Government" This was to buy "good graces" with the respective bodies. The cargo was supposed to arrive at the C of E mission with the visiting Bishop, but bad weather canceled the Bishop's visit. But they just sat down and waited until the news of the Bishop's not coming was verified. He also says *mokmok* [stone valuables] are used in hiring professional killers down there. They are given to an inland native and the victim designated. After the murder is completed, the murderer returns the *mokmok*. He also said the "brothers'" aim at the "school" here in Umbi is only to live and work with the people and run a school for ABCs only, if they wish, and only to anyone who wants to come. They are instructed to do *no* converting, to join village ceremonies if invited and make no effort at forcing any change. They will be here a year or so before a Papuan teacher takes over the school. This is heartening news to me. At least we aren't competing openly.

The Luluai just told me that he will probably wait and go down for the rice Monday, as the cargo carriers are tired and one of the men who will go has a swollen leg and he will wait for him. Sorry to rush you on the mail, but that's life. Love, Jane

PS. Do keep me posted on the singsing.

PSS. Thanks for offer of food. If we really get desperate again, I'll take you up, however, some visitors from Yambon have offered to bring food so we shall see. The whole problem seems to be this big garden which was hit by the taro sickness (a blight). The other gardens aren't ready yet. I think the hunger is why they are so anxious to make an extra trip for the rice and I'll certainly ask them to bring soap for you. I'm not getting anything but mail this trip as they are going FREE!

Dulago, September 30, (Monday)
Dear Jane,
Herewith one of your magazines which was addressed to me. (I've read it.) The Magazine Shop is clearly going to pieces. I know you've read some of the magazines that I'm telling Bruce (Malaria Control) to take to you, but you can pass them out. I don't want to reject any of them after he's been so kind as to bring them. Herewith also a few notes. Keep in mind that they're for the first two months (6 weeks last year, 3 weeks this year) and probably as untrustworthy as you'd expect.

Some people from here have gone down to Kandrian today (Luluai summoned by Dave; Kasup to buy things), so I've sent extra notes which say that Chin Cheu should send the soap and Dave my mail by them. However, the river may well be too flooded for them to cross, so that they may arrive after your team. We'll see what develops.

I'm dead for lack of sleep (so's Bruce) after staying up talking last night, and rather running out of conversation. But it has been a pleasant break.

With all the Luluais going down to Kandrian, I don't know when the pig will be killed. Nor does he, I suspect. I'll keep you posted, but in the meantime plan to come over whenever you like. Love, Ann

Postscript

Whether the Kaulong and Sengseng had unilineal (patrilineal, matrilineal) or cognatic descent groups was a major question for us to answer. In the 1960s determining the descent group structure was considered a primary task in ethnographic research. That Kaulong and Sengseng trace descent from both parents (cognatic) was fairly easy to figure out, but the existence of any functioning (corporate) social group based on this, and larger than the nuclear family (parents and children), was much harder to discover.

People could reside in any hamlet from which a male or female ancestor had come, and shifting of residence due to conflict was very common. Thus discovering that Umbi consisted of three cognatic descent "groups," each associated with a separate hamlet and region, was a major help to my understanding of their social organization, and explained the apparent lack of political cohesion of the village as a whole. Getting "one kind" of kin group from the father and another from the mother represented a distinction which was not made clear to me until 1968 during my fieldwork in Angelek! (See Goodale 1995.)

"Cargo cults" were a common form of nativistic, or nationalistic or cultural, revival in Melanesia. They were usually led by a charismatic person, in this case Koriam Urekit, who went on to win a seat in the House of Assembly in the first nationwide election held later in 1964. Many cargo cults had as their aim to overturn the present relationship of inequality between the European colonials and the colonized Melanesians and therefore were not looked upon with any favor by the Native Affairs Administration. European missionaries took varying positions.

The cargo-cult belief that ancestors would return all the wealth stolen from the locals by Europeans if certain procedures were carried out often led to abrupt and radical cultural change. Common features were attempts to provide landing strips for the ancestors' cargo planes, and to advocate giving up the "old ways" in preparation for the "new ways" to come. We did not expect such a cargo-cult movement would reach our remote locations. However, Ann's community had some trade relationships with Sengseng relatives who had moved to coastal locations, and who carried the message of the cult back to their relatives in Dulago. When I asked my Umbi informants about this "cargo" talk they laughed and said their ancestors were just bones, and therefore couldn't come back. What really was highlighted by this data was the different trading patterns of Dulago, which directly included some coastal people, from trading patterns of Umbi, which did not directly involve any coastal people.

Rumors and thefts began to be frequent and drove us both to distraction. While I watched a boy take fifteen minutes to steal a banana from in front of me I wondered why he didn't just ask. Much later I learned it is very rude in Kaulong to ask for something belonging to another. They believe that the owner ought to see your need and make the offer. It comes down to learning to respect the power (and wealth) of the owner, and the responsibility of an owner to respond appropriately. In Kaulong and Sengseng the owner has a choice of giving or not giving. By giving to another and by the other's acceptance, there is established an exchange relation, because now the receiver must make exchange gift at some later date, which itself must be reciprocated, and so on. Outside of the nuclear family, Kaulong and Sengseng exchange relationships establish and validate an individual's kin relationships throughout the Passismanua region and even beyond. Everybody must establish their own network of kin through the giving and receiving of items.

Rumors are similarly a power play, and bigmen (leaders) from other communities began trying to manipulate our headmen by spreading rumors concerning us. In the case of the "Americans" supposedly coming to visit Ann and me, we independently knew that none of our friends (anthropological colleagues) would venture into this very distant world just to visit, and therefore both of us countered by not sending any carriers down and won a few brownie points from our local friends by showing appropriate behavior. Most rumors are political plays and may be safely ignored, usually, unless they come from the Kiap. Understanding local politics came gradually and by trial and error as we were increasingly drawn into participation into the life of our village societies.

Knowing that we both would be besieged with requests for medical aid we returned with a substantial first-aid kit—containing, however, few prescription drugs, and those mostly for our own use. Burns, cuts, fevers, and colds were the usual cases we were asked to treat. We were careful not to present the European as the *only legitimate* medical system and, as the indigenous medical system was intact, we only treated when asked. Often multiple cures were tried.

Mondays in our villages were days when the Kiaps decreed that everyone should work on their village houses, clearing grass from the village area (making it a mud hole but free from debris, including pig feces) and fixing trails and bridges. But what these days really meant was that people would come from their gardens to their or another village to meet people, pay off or settle debts (large and small), resolve grievances, and plan future events. It was a great day for the anthropologist after six days of little or no human activity in the village itself.

Singsings where pigs are sacrificed were the most important events at which people from other hamlets gathered. They were held for a number of different occasions. Outsiders came armed with spears and shields and used these as percussion together with the drums as they sang throughout the twelve-hour night. In the morning the pigs were killed, butchered, and "given" to the outsiders as part of a pork trade exchange partnership—a highly political relationship. The singing may last for one to seven nights. Singers will sleep during the day while the anthropologist should stay awake to record whatever occurs! Once I had learned what to expect, I found I could manage a few catnaps. At this point in our research many new aspects of Kaulong and Sengseng life began to come into view.

Chapter 4

I Cried Instead with Amazing Results

Dulago, Oct., Friday

Dear Jane,

I hope you made out better (conversationally) with Bruce (malaria control officer—on patrol) than I did. I ran dry about halfway through his stay, and began to wonder if I'd gone bush (crazy). Still, it's an awfully long time to have to make continuous conversation with a total stranger, especially one who knows so little about the Territory. Did he tell you about his brother's and mother's deaths and his wife's operation?

Two of the men from here are just back from Ablingi (a coconut plantation on the coast), having heard (the cult leader) Koriam's latest word, which is that a *dinau* [debt] settling *kivung* [meeting] is to be held on Sunday here because they owe so many, or so they say. I suspect that these are the "native courts" referred to in patrol reports. Anyway, it will be interesting to see what goes on. Those who don't obey are supposed to go to jail at Ablingi, (where they will do time) "breaking coconuts" [to make copra].

Pigs have been rooting in the cemetery lately, and have uncovered portions of three burials, including at least one red-painted skull (I couldn't see enough of the second skull to be sure) and a couple of leg bones which indicate that their owners couldn't have been buried curled up. It's all I can do to keep my hands off them, as you can imagine. I did manage to handle the first skull and jaw, which were completely out of the grave. As it is, I rush out daily to see what may have been uncovered.

> [Burials were typically inside the main and sometimes only hamlet house, which then would be vacated and shut tight for a number of months, "until the stink is finished." It was felt necessary to protect the new grave from pigs, both wild and domestic (which are not

penned up), which is one reason for their resistance to the Kiap's law to have a separate and unprotected graveyard. Mortuary ceremonies involved digging up the skull and some long bones and painting the skull with red ochre, after which they were placed in the hamlet house. With contact, the Kiaps insisted that all these skulls be reburied, but pigs still unearthed them occasionally. Dulago was an old hamlet where many bodies were buried and reburied.]

I'm just back from a visit to our old man who's too old to move. He lives in an old-style (log) house, with his hair in long locks all over, but wasn't really very interesting. I also felt but didn't see a *masalai* (bush spirit), which went across my bare foot and startled the hell out of the boy walking behind me. It felt squashy for a snake—large toad, maybe?

Sunday—Your letter just arrived as I was needing to blow off steam. My present opinion is that cargo carrying might be all right if people at Kandrian would just follow my instructions. I asked the one man who was going down "nothing" [without plans] to bring back my order from Chin Cheu's—3 boxes of soap, a bag of nails, and 10 tins of fruit, so I could hold out till November if necessary and in a letter to Dave asked for the mail. Today the poor lad staggered in with the rucksack, loaded with all the stuff that apparently hadn't been in when I sent my previous order—10 tins of luncheon meat, puddings and cookies, 6 boxes of soap plus the rest of the order—and, to my bafflement, no mail at all except notes from Dave and Mary (finally thanking me for the present of paper dolls). Since he'd finally picked up help along the road, after he'd spent my advance payment at Kandrian, I shelled out an additional 5/- to the relief [person]. However, I have paid only 15/- a carrier since the first trip, plus staking them to rice at Kandrian when they're going down specifically for me. This load cost me s£1.0.0 (but no rice), but I have no intention of making a general practice of it if I can avoid it.

Everyone here is supposed to be off to Pomalal tomorrow to rebuild the *haus sik* [aid post]. Maybe I can at least pin down Paiyali to desperately needed work on vocabulary. I too feel that I'm accomplishing nothing, though the notebooks fill up at an appalling rate, hence my decision to begin typing up my notes.

I'd love to see you at any time, the sooner the better. There's no earthly reason why it need be a weekend. The Luluai stopped off at Pomalal with the *haus sik* [aid post] stuff, and goodness knows when he'll have his singsing (though if he doesn't hurry the rats will finish off the rice). I don't trust Bruce's information about the date of the [Dulago] singsing, having been present when he got it. But will discuss with you.

I'm more anti-Dave than anti-Kiap, but I too am fed up with this *haus sik* business, especially since no one in this area has any intention of going to Pomalal [for medical aid] while we're in the vicinity.

I threw my rat-traps down the privy during Hudeuk's reign because he was trying to requisition them for the *haus boi*—men's house—and I was afraid that Roo would get caught. The rats here are bad too, and getting increasingly

brazen. Roo managed to get all the way up into the Kanda [roof thatch] last night (and down again), but I don't think he'll ever manage to catch one up there. Bruce offered rat-killer, but the same problem applies. More later.
Love, Ann

Umbi, Oct. 10 '63
Dear Ann,

I'm writing this while waiting for events to happen—it's now 12:45 and the policeman was reported to be arriving today at 11 a.m. to take all able bodied to jail for failing to go to Pomalal [to help build the aid post]. Absolutely no one, including the Luluai, came in on Monday when the word was brought. The Luluai appeared at the *haus boi* [men's house] Tuesday and shouted (to whom I don't know as no one was there) for all to follow him! This a.m. he shouted from across the river that all were to come in at 11. So far only those who are known to be exempt from going due to age or dependent infants have appeared. Eight of the school kids have been here since Sunday without parents and *means of support*! The big bag of rice (I bought for them) as far as I know is still "stuck" at Arihi for lack of help in carrying it, and Tultul Kasli's "back is broken." The "report" (rumor) is that if they go to jail it will be for six months! How's that for an unexpected hitch in fieldwork plans! *If* this is true, no one but very young and very old would be left here and a few nursing mothers and obviously no carriers! Isn't it a delightful thought!

By the way there was no mail for us last Saturday either. Debli was asked by Dave to wait behind for it and there was nothing except a black umbrella which John got in and for some reason sent it up to either one of us—do you want it? I don't especially, but I guess it's hopeless to send it back. He also sent up some canned "sponges" (i.e. cakes) unasked for. I felt he was playing Marie Antoinette [i.e. "let them eat cake"]!

In fact I've got rather a hopeless feeling about everything but will come over as soon as I have the answers to some of the questions.

Friday, Oct. 11—Some answers have come in—other questions have arisen—this has been a week to forget. Full account I will unburden myself on you when I see you. As you can tell I'm slightly "something"—I wish I had brought tranquilizers with me or a bottle of booze! Anyway—I will be over Monday—weather and the state of the nation permitting. The rice arrived today carried by one Umbi-ite and four Arihi men (who of course had to be paid!) but Kasli also had to buy help so we two are going to sell some of the rice to the lazy Umbi-ites—the thought of revenge is sweet—the realization of it, sweeter we hope!

No Umbi-ites in jail yet and Arihi has "worked" out a plan for my cargo with some of the Umbi-ites so I may be able to get more cargo.

Will see you Monday—Kaliam and one *manki* [young boy] will be with me and if you can lay in a supply of taro I will be glad to buy it for them. Taro is a delicacy here! Love, Jane

Dulago, Friday October

Dear Jane,

It looks as if Plakli will be going to Umbi soon with tapioca (manioc) for you, and I'll try at least to send this (and other things if someone else goes). Latest word is that the Pomalal [work] group won't be back till Monday. Hell! I've just been struggling with caterpillars in the kerosene pump (complete with nests), an unexpected hazard. I believe I once asked what could possibly go wrong with kerosene pumps? Now I know.

Please return the kinship page (of notes) as soon as possible. I need it. Also, if you can spare some money when your carriers return, I'll repay it when mine return. (I'm optimistically assuming that both groups will depart.) Having received no fresh meat, I'm rapidly being reduced to the most unattractive (and smallest) cast-offs from Chin Cheu's. I'm overflowing with other food, though, since Paiyali has been sick (and bad-tempered) and off his feed for days.

Thanks to the rats, my house is beginning to leak. I'll probably be awash by the next rainy season. Assuming, of course, that this rainy season ever ends. Finally planted my seeds, and the Chinese cabbage and lettuce came up overnight, but no signs of tomatoes or watermelon yet.

[Besides keeping us awake at night with all their carousing, the house rats tended to break up the drying thatch, causing the roof to leak.]

Saturday—I just collected a genealogy in Sengseng (not all of it, because Paiyali turned up before we were finished) but the whole process cheered me immensely. It has some tie ins with Umbi too. It's Twaltwal's (he's the former Luluai of Malah, now living at Valngin) and his wife is a close enough relative (to Paiyali) so that he couldn't give me the part that ties in with her (your children will die if you say the names of your *tabu* [in-laws].

The ear (lobe) was traditionally pierced with the *leg* of a large insect here-called *magah* and called *phasmid* in English. They're about 6 inches long on the average, and everywhere I've worked they're the thing I'm gladdest I didn't have to eat.

Someone just announced that Kim Novak's eyes (in a magazine picture) looked like yours. I don't know; they never say these sweet things about me.

Monday. I'm feeling very pessimistic (since Paiyali is) about the chances of getting anyone to go (to Kandrian) on time, but we'll see. The annoying thing is that there are plenty of men around who haven't gone to Pomalal (to work on the *haus sik*), but they're all trying to be invisible.

Herewith some bananas, with which I'm overloaded; a little tobacco to keep your household going; and all the money I can spare. Two watermelon seeds only have sprouted; everything else looks fine. Love, Ann

Dulago, Wednesday, Oct.??

Dear Jane,

I've just finished getting more of Pahiok's genealogy (she's Paiyali's mother) and it has so many links with Umbi that I think it would be interesting if you brought your genealogies when you come next so we can compare notes. It turned up a second-cousin marriage (their mothers were children of siblings of opposite sex) and one to second-cousin-once removed (opposite sex all the way in this case). Also what looks like a case of bro-sis (marriage) exchange, certainly in fact, if not in intention.

Breadfruit's now ripe here. I hope you all have some as well. I don't really like it, except for the seeds, but it is a change.

I asked about *midan* (Kaulong), *mihidan* (Sengseng) [bigman or leader], here and didn't get at all the same picture. It sounds as if it's primarily an achieved position rather than an inherited one and to the degree that the wealth itself is inherited it doesn't seem to follow that simple a pattern. It's sons of a second brother in this village that hold the position.

[I had told Ann, when I visited, that in Umbi it seemed there was a direct line (father to son) of leaders of one of Umbi's hamlets through three generations. Ann's interpretation was the accurate one—it just happened that the firstborn sons of the founder of the Umbi hamlet were all achievers of high degree.]

I've developed what I gather is a whitlow. I thought it was just a hangnail, but got puzzled by the swelling, and finally stuck in a needle, only to be considerably startled by what came out. James' advice (our Medical Guide for first-aid in "remote" areas)—"to put the finger of a rubber glove in the abscess"—is certainly not very helpful.

Friday—Bad-tempered Mubudli returned last night, complete with wife and child, so we should have some excitement around here again. The pigs have now unearthed a pelvis, a tibia, a foot-bone, and assorted ribs. Also, I finally found out about the mysterious pole in the matmat. It's what the (exhumed) skull should be on (for mortuary rituals). I'm terribly tempted to remove the partially exposed skull, which is painted red, and set it up there.

Saturday, Oct. 12?—Thanks for sending over the reading matter. The umbrella is mine—ordered for me via air freight. John sent a note up with Kasup saying he'd sent it via Debli. Both mine are buggered up. So please bring it with you when you come. I also got the mysterious sponges [cake], but assumed it was because when I asked for assorted puddings last time, I got 3 *large* and 3 *small* plum puddings!

Your situation sounds ferocious; let's hope it doesn't turn out as threatened. Few of these things do. I'm fed up with having all my best informants away, but Paiyali yesterday really settled down to being an informant.

I'm feeling a great need for a change of scene. If things are really bad, we might consider a small *wokabaut* (trip) if there's anyone to carry [our gear]. However, I'll be delighted to see you. We'll sit down and commiserate or go finish digging up the cemetery [which of course we never would do].
Love, Ann

Umbi, October 22 1963
Dear Family;
    Last week I walked over to Dulago for our monthly visiting, and again this exchange of visits, news, problems and information proved its value in raised spirits and stimulation. In spite of our *two* cultures which are proving to be *one*, we have no regrets that we are "next door" to each other. The trip over was quite opposite to the last one two months ago.
    The day before I left we had five inches of rain and Kaliam, two young teenagers and I found that wading across the river was impossible with the flood. So we used the overhead single cane-vine "rope" and pulled ourselves across—half submerged—hand over hand to the opposite bank. It was not too difficult for me—I had only myself—but it fell to Kaliam to make three trips with my overnight bag, my knapsack, and the boys' bag tied to his head and just staying out of the water. Not only was our river flooded, but also all of the 10 other streams one must wade through on this road, and it made the going rather tricky and slow. We got to the 1st village, Silop (on top of the mountain), in an hour and 15 minutes and waited out a light drizzle before setting off for Yambon and Dulago. Shortly before Yambon the rain began again and we decided to take a shortcut "breaking bush" to by-pass Yambon. We came to a large garden and walked beside the 6 foot fence and the rain began to fall in buckets-full and continued to do so for the next hour plus that it took us to reach Dulago. We sloshed over old paths, across rotten log bridges and once we reached the "main" road again, we found it to be a temporary stream bed. But there are times when walking in the rain can be enjoyable and this happened to be one of them. With the promise of dry clothes, hot food and drink, I sloshed happily onwards, absolutely drenched and only wished that the NGS had thought to provide us with underwater cameras as well.
    Ann and I dined on partridge, pheasant, caviar and eels (the last local) and planned our Christmas trip to Rabaul [for a 10 day break] and listened to her radio (mine's still not here) and read each other's fieldnotes.
Love Jane

Dulago, Tues. Oct. 20?
Dear Jane;
    Paiyali has just suddenly conceived a desire to go to Umbi, so I'd better take advantage of the opportunity to get at least a little mail out. I hope you're doing better for resident population than we are. I'm going to start tracking them to their bush houses in a very short order.
    The betel nut-husks in the men's house are partly because it's tabu to throw the rinds out the door during the rainy season—or swamp *i stap long nus bilong haus* (a swamp will form in front of the house). The dry season is OK. They [the husks] are used for cooking on as advertised.
    Can't think of anything interesting that's happened. I just went down to check on my potential swimming hole and found it already totally dry. But it's worth it to have some sunshine. Are you getting rumors of the 'number two'

Kiap's incipient arrival (after the Aid Post is finished)? It seems to me rather more likely to be true this time. I hope to God he doesn't come when I plan to send my carriers. Oh, well, I should know better than to worry about rumors at this stage.

I also am feeling threatened with missionaries. Just got a remarkably silly letter from one who was at Pomalal and he says they want him to visit here. His instructions to the men here have been to keep the children in the village so they won't learn the *pasin bilong bigpela man* (way of the elders) and there seem to be great plans for schools and catechists. So I may not be so lucky after all. He tells me that he's a teetotaling Irishman.

Got at the same time (via the same messenger) a much more detailed account of the sorcery which killed Kanegit. If you haven't heard all this (the story is that several men are serving jail sentences now—Luluai of Sankiap, [among others]), let me know and I'll send it over pronto.I can hardly tear myself out of the sun.

Love, Ann

Umbi, October 23 (Thurs.?)

Dear Ann,

Had a chance to send you a *pas* (letter) via Lelus, who's finally decided to go home, but it was presented to me at breakfast, and I couldn't function fast enough. Anyway, I expect a messenger from you either today or tomorrow with outgoing mail. I'm still hoping Saturday's excursion will go as planned. Have sent word to Arihi to expect Kaliam and the cases on Sat. but I'm not sure how the cases are going to get there. The last Pomalal delegation (of aid-post builders) has not returned and no men have been in the village this week, only two of the delegates' wives and assorted children. But hope to persuade some of the *manki* (young lads) to take them (patrol boxes).

The recent good weather has brought a spurt of energy to Debli and Kaliam. I have a new "small" house [latrine] at least 10 feet by 10 feet with a new roof and a roofed entrance, but over the same small hole. Thus there is a new problem—find the hole! But if the roof doesn't leak progress has been made. [My previous privy was demolished by a falling tree seconds after I had vacated it.] They also burned some of the brush in my new "garden" area yesterday so I finally reactivated my camera for the event. Otherwise— nothing—as usual—has happened. I will have to have a late November trip for supplies as food is still short here. But I have been getting some from Arihi and Hulem.

Your messenger just arrived—Yes, I have heard rumor of Kiap's coming and the Umbi-ites seem to be taking it seriously too. However, Umbi is almost totally deserted except for Debli and me and the one couple I can't stand! No I haven't heard details of Kanegit's poisoning so please do send them over. Re missionaries—The Umbi-ites say the *Popi* [Catholics] missionaries are "hard." They insist the children stay in the village all day, whereas the *Englan* (Church of England) missionaries only want them in the early a.m. and late p.m. Good luck. Love, Jane

PS. I've run out of tobacco and practically out of money but gave [your] messenger 2/ to carry this back to you.

Umbi, Sunday night, Oct. 27
Dear Ann,

I can't begin to relate the ins and outs of "cargo" but some Arihi and some Umbi carriers took off yesterday with me *dinau*-ing (credit arranging) on some of the payment and believe it or not Ningbi returned today carrying 1 bag of mail (up to Sat. a week ago) plus 3 lbs of tobacco! I don't yet know what I will do about the house boy situation but I'm saying nothing one way or another at the moment. (Ningbi has come home sick—throwing up blood in Arihi! So I gave him some Sulfa and we'll see what happens in more ways than one!) Kaliam has gone with the Cargo.

I read TAA's [Trans Australian Airline's] letter, regarding our flights for December's holiday in Rabaul, but didn't see one from the Cosmo [Hotel]. I expect more mail with the cargo—optimist me.

Umbi has been deserted except for this weekend, when at least half of the population turned up to patch the roof of the *haus kiap* (rest house). I shot 3 and a 1/2 rolls of 36 exposure film to celebrate. Had a dream last night that the NGS sent Terry over to investigate what the hell we were doing or rather—not doing. When he got here it was pouring but he insisted on taking *you* off somewhere to photograph you doing something—then I woke up feeling totally guilty about everything—so was glad to have something to "shoot" today. I'm including these [films] to go down with any you have with your trip whenever that takes place. Do let me know *if at all possible* when you expect to get anyone off for Kandrian.

Dave writes that my radio was returned (from the shop in Rabaul) and he played it for two hours when it conked out again. So he's sent it back. I plan to have words with B. Wong [where I bought the radio] at Xmas.

My messengers seem to be getting younger and younger but these two volunteered and said they wouldn't get lost. I've given (or rather will give) them 1 stick @ and told them you would pay on delivery. Please keep the mail bag and send it on to Kandrian.

I have just now been getting more info. on Kanegit's poisoning, but would like to hear your version. I've also been questioning various about the suspected cause of the woman's death. Only today Kasli said they suspect poison and will eventually work a *toktok* [inquest]. I wonder who they will accuse this time with 3 notorious poisoners in jail already.

By the way, Kasli is (he says) getting rid of Ulengme (his second wife). Her "husband" came back from work and complained to the police at Pomalal. The police said for him to talk to Yiangme (the first wife) first—because if *she* was happy with the situation it was all right with the Kiap. Yiangme isn't happy at all and threatens to "*hangupim*" [hang herself]. So Kasli is going to send Ulengme back to her *kandere* (mother's brother)—not her husband. He also says sororal (*tupela meri won susu*) [two women with one mother] polygyny isn't the custom here. It is for the Miu. If two women who are *barata* [siblings of the same sex] marry the same man, they are likely to fight as in this case.

Love, Jane

Umbi, Oct. 30 1963

Dear Ann,

I'm fed up! After increasing my pay for cargo by 33.3% I've just been through the worse hassle ever with the Arihi contingent threatening to murder or court (take to court) Kahame, and demanding £1.0.0 @ to carry (help carry) a case as far as Arihi and refusing to carry it further. Kahame gave them the money and now with pitiful countenance wants some payment for his efforts. He carried cargo for nothing having given all the money out. On top of all this I asked Eddie Yun for £30.0.0 in shillings and didn't count it before handing it out and now counting it I only have £21.10.0 left. I can account for all but £2.10.0 but am sure in the heat of the argument I overpaid to that amount and this makes me even more furious! One case of cargo is still in Arihi locked up in the Church of England "brother's" house and all the "brothers" have gone away and won't be back until Sunday. I am enclosing £8. Keep your £2 and when you get more send £6 back. When you come over we can straighten the mail situation out. (I'm paying 15/ per large bag of mail Kandrian—Umbi.)

[If we seemed to be as overly concerned with money as with food and mail, it was because we had to order shillings from Eddie Yun in the same fashion as the other two items. The local population saw that we could merely write a letter to the store and get money and food, and led to the constant demands for increased pay. There was just no way to convince them that our money was limited.]

What's the cure for blood poisoning? Debli has an extremely sore leg due to infected tattooing and is now complaining of swelling in the groin. At this point he can hardly walk. Of course he didn't come to me until it was really bad because he didn't want to lose his tattoo. Now if it had been but a minor scratch—it would have been different.

One, or rather two, bright events to report. I got my first *kapul* (possum) yesterday, and a very large tender leg and ham of a wild pig today. I've decided to buy fresh meat at quite high rates and hope more will come. It's so good. The 2 dogs [puppies which I had adopted] got the bones and they were ecstatic.

Love, Jane

PS. There is a wild pussy cat howling near by and Ningbi is out to kill it—Oh dear!

PSS. If you write to the NGS tell them I haven't really forgotten them but just didn't have the time to get a letter off (Gilka's Sept. 3 letter to me just arrived).

Washington DC September 3

Dear Miss Goodale;

Greetings, I've just looked at your first shipment of film from New Britain. I didn't see any great pictures, but I think that with improvement you forest dwellers may come up with enough photographs to illustrate a magazine article. Both of you are having trouble with underexposure. A couple of rolls in this shipment showed color shifts which indicate the rolls were left in the camera too long after exposure. Miss Goodale's four rolls arrived wet, although they were in a tin can. The most interesting pictures show people doing something. We are shipping more film by air today to each of you.

Sincerely, R. Gilka (Director of Photography NGS)

Dulago, October 31

Dear Jane,

Word has been relayed through the bush telegraph—yodeling, that is — that there's a letter from you at Dulago, but I'm well and truly in the gardens. The man I'm with is the one who took my letter to you the time you were in the gardens and talks grimly of "backing" (paying back) that episode. He's totally disinclined to leave his work to take me back, and I certainly wouldn't trust myself to find my own way, so I hope your messenger can hold out for a while. I've just run out of film and am cursing myself for not bringing more. It's hard to realize how much you use up when the weather is moderately good, though a lot of these were just shots of plants for teaching.

The word is that the priest who's visited Pomalal has told them to follow the *kivung* [cargo cult] so they will. That figures; he's from the area where the Catholic Church is deeply involved with these cargo cults.

I've had one *kapul* [possum] and no other fresh meat since the eels, but just got a fresh pineapple today. The only thing I know of for blood poisoning is antibiotics taken by mouth (Aureomycin, etc.). I don't have anything appropriate myself. It's just the kind of problem I was unsuccessful in buying antibiotics for, in Rabaul. Love, Ann

Umbi, Nov. 2—9 p.m.

Dear Ann,

Kahame has just announced he is going to Dulago at 6 A.M. tomorrow and asked me if I had any *pas* [note] to send. Here is the September weather report which I neglected to send last month. October's is not yet ready.

[The weather service in Lae wanted me to send them monthly reports, covering daily temperature/humidity ranges and rainfall, for comparison with the daily reports radioed in from Kandrian on the coast.]

We're having a feast of meat tonight. I was offered a choice of 1/2 a very large *sikau* [wallaby] or a python. The boys voted for *sikau*. It's lovely but wish they would spread things out. Kahame's coming over to you to find out the

ETA of a rumored patrol of a doctor. I hope he (the Dr.) doesn't hold up the cargo. Excuse scribble in haste. Love, Jane

Dulago, Nov. 2

Dear Jane,

They had a singsing all night last night which, what with both *dokta boi* (Doctors) in my house as well, interfered more than somewhat with my struggles (to complete) a book review. I still expect carriers to leave tomorrow. Maybe, I can survive today with the help of No-Doz. The python [which I had sent to her via Kahame] is most gratefully received. I was brought a small rat last night, but was planning to feed it to the kitten and eat something that was too small for both of us myself. Must get back to picture-taking. See you in a couple of weeks, I trust. Love, Ann

Dulago, Nov. ?

Dear Jane,

I'm feeling cheery because: 1) it's a beautiful day; 2) I've just had a pleasant trip to a distant garden with no strain on the knees, even though the trip is extremely hilly and I fell flat on my face at one point; 3) I arrived back to find a waiting possum, on a night when I thought Paiyali and I would be reduced to (canned) casserole steak. By the way, you were well advised not to take the python; it was literally skin and bones. A sad waste of money.

Paiyali and I had a knock-down drag-out fight the other night—oh, dear. (Don't mention it in Umbi, though he tells everyone here about it.) Things are back on an even keel at the moment, but I suppose there may be other rifts in the future. Oh well, it's the eternal servant problem. And how is your complex household going?

[The eternal servant problem was largely in the dual role we asked our assistants to play. It was expected by the community that we would hire one or more of the local residents to work for us for money, which would then circulate our wealth throughout the community. But the only *services* we wanted were for them to cook any locally obtained food (bats, possums, eels, taro, etc.), to wash our clothes in the stream, and sometimes to sweep the house. But most importantly we wanted someone who would be available some part of every day to answer questions, teach us the language, and offer explanations; i.e., to be helpful and friendly informants. This was particularly necessary when the rest of the population was so small and scattered throughout the vicinity.]

My carriers got off so early on Monday that I have hopes that they'll be back tomorrow. So many went that I'll be lucky to escape arguments for paying by the case, but we'll see. I didn't get off a letter to the NGS, but I'm getting low enough on film to start feeling nervous. Are you still planning to send down sometime this month?

They're all trying to persuade me to go to Pomalal when they have to go see the doctor, so I won't be eaten by *tamberans* [ghosts] if I stay here alone, but I'm determined not to make that trip for nothing. The obvious thing is to join one of the old men who's too feeble to go, but my Sengseng really isn't up to it.

Friday—Just had a visiting Catholic priest (the one who wrote me the silly letter). I'll tell you all about it when I see you. He reports that, as far as he knows, no one is replacing Dave [on leave], and the Grants have gone *finis* (departed for good), so maybe with any cooperation we'll have a [empty] place to stay at Kandrian [en route to Rabaul for our Christmas trip]. All the better if he's correct in thinking that the station (Kandrian) singsing is on New Year's. In any case, he reports that the Catholic Mission is planning to have a big singsing in February—inviting people all along the coast—to celebrate their Jubilee. We're invited, and photographically I think it might be very well worthwhile.

Carriers arrived back today, and thank God no problems (in spite of the fact that John Yun didn't pay them there; apparently I'd cleaned him out of cash). I got up at 5:30 this morning to see the Mass at Yambon. Unfortunately it was held out in the woods. Too bad; it would have made great pictures for *The* magazine. I thought I'd better know what he (the priest) was telling them so I could spot the distortions.

Fresh meat situation has improved, thank God, and should be even better with the cargo line back from Kandrian. See you soon. Love, Ann

Umbi, Nov. 9
Dear Ann,
    You caught me this time basking in the sun by the river (alternately swimming) and I'm just too lazy to go up to the house to collect the *pas* I started to you. The *pas* [letter] I wrote to you is a full description of my latest cargo affair. I'll tell you all or rather get the *pas* to you sometime. I may be able to get mail out sometime, such things are touch and go at the moment, but people are going to Kandrian. I haven't written the NGS, but shall do so— about film (I'm practically out of 36 exposure film but have a full package of 20's).

    I've been housebound by various extraneous events, but hope soon to get out to the gardens, but mainly I'm waiting until the food situation gets a little better so we won't be "imposing" quite so much. Yesterday, I bought my first "local" taro and tapiok, so I hope it won't be too long.

    We'll expect you the 17th. I do hope you will be able to go swimming as it's glorious down here and very relaxing mentally and physically. Must send your messengers back. Love, Jane
    PS. My household has been most solicitous particularly after my outburst! [See below.]

Umbi, November 1963
Dear Family,
The last cargo trip caused so much trouble and fuss that I gave up arguing and cried instead with the most amazing results. Previously I always had to fight the exorbitant demands alone, but when my tears appeared one man offered me money to pay extra to the two carriers (I refused the offer). Ningbi did pay £1.0.0 to one of them and backed me up for the first time. And one carrier gave me 10 shillings to "shake hands"—which I accepted. Since then demands have slackened, debts paid relatively promptly, and I have more offers to carry cargo this time than I can use and everyone has told me to do nothing for the one carrier who didn't apologize—not to buy food from him, or to treat his sores and cuts, and not to let him carry cargo for me. One man said, "We can't get cross at you; you are like our Grandmother and boss of this place." I am sure he meant it as a compliment! The real result is that they now know there is a limit to my money (and patience) and I'm sure part of the problem is that shillings are so relatively new to them, they have no value and they can't imagine they have any value to me. Ningbi expressed this idea in his speeches "backing" me up and I hadn't realized this fully before.

[I was to learn in the months to come that my behavior was also typical of, and appropriate to, *bigman* and *bigmeri*, men and women of importance. When pushed to the extreme by a friend or equal, influential people cry (rather than argue), exchange valuables, shake hands (*sekhan*), and continue the relationship. Any other response on my part would have terminated all relationships with these individuals involved. Learning through participant-observation can sometimes be extremely painful.]

Your candy has just arrived and is a big hit. Debli who can't [without lower jaw] chew betel nut, calls them his betel nut and savors each one. I've given them out to the kids who accompany me on "expeditions," and with few exceptions they are delighted with their "pay." Love, Jane.

[Ann visits me November 17-19 and we plan our trip "outside," to Kandrian and Rabaul over Christmas and New Year's. It will be our first and only trip out of the bush country, in which we had lived for over five months.]

Umbi November 22
Dear Ken (Weaver, NGS)
It's been a long time since I sent a "report" in to you and the NGS. I am quite surprised at how time flies up here when really in many ways life is quite dull! Off hand I could easily say *nothing* has happened of newsworthy importance. The rainy season is tapering off slowly. We usually have some sun every day as well as some rain. The daily temperatures are delightful—it's cool in the shade, 75 to 80 degrees, and hot in the sun and many days I've taken off to the river to swim and bathe and relax.

We are planning to go to Rabaul over Xmas to get a break and eat fresh meat and salad and drink beer! and see a movie. We are also going to inquire about chartering a small Aztec (plane) in the hopes we can fly back in here and take aerial photos of our area. There are many "ifs": if the plane is free, if the weather is clear, we shall do this and take up the NGS's offer of extra money for something special. We hope to be able to coincide with the Kandrian *singsing* on our return, when a large number from the area gather with feathers and other finery and, I guess, sing and dance. So far we haven't heard of when exactly this will take place—just "at Christmas." We will let you know how this works out. At the moment it is pouring rain. As ever, Jane.

Umbi, November Wed. Night
Dear Ann,
This (incoming) mail will probably take you by surprise as much as it did me, but although you may not have anything ready to come back, I figured you'd want it as soon as possible and Sakhun has volunteered to take it to you—I told Sakhun you'd pay him. (As far as I know he doesn't speak a word of Pidgin.) I hope to get people off for Kandrian a week from Saturday so if you get outgoing mail over next week it will get off—all things being equal.
I got a "horrifying" letter from Rainey [Director of the University Museum, University of Pennsylvania, our institutional affiliation for the purposes of our NSF Grant] enclosing a perfectly terrible news-clip concerning us and the singsing (for Kanegit) at Angus and a picture of me, and about two dozen glaring sensational-type errors of information! Evidently Rainey reported, to the Member's Night crowd, from my last "newsy" letter to the Staff (of Univ. Museum) and it was picked up by the Bulletin [Philadelphia's leading newspaper at that time]. Rainey also admits he gave it to the Museum publicity man. I think I'll write Rainey and ask him please to have all stories first cleared by Ward [our former professor Ward Goodenough]! But I don't know what will happen. I'll bring it to Pomalal-Rabaul or send it over later.
Glad you had a nice day to walk back in (at least we had one here). Went to gardens today and got more information on sorcery, so your visit was inspiring. Love, Jane

Dulago,
Dear Jane,
Your letter caught up with me en route to a funeral (which everyone fully expects me to attend). Don't want to hold up the procession—we're carrying a pig—so more later.
Love, Ann.

Dulago, Saturday
Dear Jane,
I'm sorry I didn't keep your letter, but as you doubtless gathered I was in something of a hurry. I didn't see the actual burial, which was done inside the

house with no women present, but there was a certain amount of interest. Do you suppose anyone in these parts has yet been buried where the Kiap tells them to? Not this one certainly, and her father is the Luluai of Hutkihyu. They had a singsing that night which shocked me a bit, and I'm about to sink a tooth into a leg of one of the pigs killed. The shell exchanges produced total confusion. However, on the whole I had a jolly two days with women and children from Hutkihyu and Seuk. I didn't spend either night, as I should have, but really—good old Rainey! And when you think of all our efforts to evade publicity, too. Do send over the clipping when you can.

Tuesday—I've finally been to Seagit, which wasn't nearly as far as I expected, though it is an exceptionally hilly track. Took 1 hr. 40 min. each way. I've got quite a backache, I guess as a result of juggling walking stick and umbrella simultaneously while slithering down the clay banks. Today I'm more or less taking time off to wash my hair, write letters and maybe even tidy up the study. There are rumors of an impending visit from the priest, but I can't believe that he'd return so soon. I've had so much fresh meat lately (past three days) that I've turned down a snake, a frog, and a small hand [foreleg] of pork. However, I fear the feast is over, but the pork and shrimp have been awfully nice. I wish some people would come buy bananas, though; we're really overloaded.

Lovely attempted abduction in Yambon the other day. The man came to be treated for knife cuts the girl gave him. He saw her bathing, removed his laplap and walked about *nating* [naked] to approach her, and tried to drag her off, but (how unlike the Lakalai and I imagine, the Tiwi) all the time intending marriage. No dice, though.

I've acquired four nice new flints since I saw you last (one picked up by Kasup on the way back). One of the boys just brought me the most beautifully chipped one I've seen yet. As soon as I get more film, I'm going to take some good (hopefully) pictures of them.

I'm feeling very lazy all of a sudden, but maybe a burst of energy will develop. What I really need at the moment is to pin down Paiyali or someone to go over all the newly dictated words (of about two months, now) which haven't been translated. Unfortunately it's a task we all hate. Better go rescue my drying clothes; it's awfully threatening out. Love, Ann

Postscript

With the good weather beginning we began to move out of our immediate villages and confirmed what we both suspected, that the people live most of the time in or near their gardens and rarely in the village. Gardens were scattered so a visit to one for a day meant contact with very few people, perhaps only a couple and their small children. New information came at a slower rate. Boredom was frequent.

We both felt the need to refresh our spirits, and mental and physical well-being. After five months we looked forward greatly to a week in Rabaul over

Christmas and the opportunity of selecting for ourselves canned food and other supplies that were getting low. This concern was particularly intense as our patience was being sorely tried by our supply problems—worse now as the rains had lessened and the local people had far more important things to do in their gardens than go to Kandrian for our mail.

What really ticked me off with my big cargo hassle was that the person who shouted injustices at me in the loudest voice was one of my best friends (I thought) and in my culture friends should not act like this. Nor should they in Kaulong. It was sometime before I realized that my response, tears and all, was also the appropriate response in Kaulong and is followed by the exchange of shell valuables. However, what was very different was that in Kaulong, arguments between two people are allowed to be carried on for what *seemed to me* to be an extreme length of time, before interference from others, *if any*, takes place. It's a subtle point, but it is out of just such painful moments that experiential learning comes best.

Our interest in human bones and in chipped flints came from our training in both physical and archeological techniques. Indeed both of us had significant experience in archeological fieldwork, and had taken at least two or more courses in these anthropological fields, although we ended up concentrating on cultural and social anthropology.

The Australian Government had forced the reburial of human skulls, which until recently had been housed in the men's house. The observation that the unearthed skulls had been painted with red ochre led us to inquire about discontinued and outlawed rituals of postburial disinternment, ritual treatment and display, and accompanying singing, which included pork exchange (Goodale 1995).

The chipped flints (all surface finds) were, as far as we knew, the first to be reported for New Britain, and therefore of considerable interest to us.

Chapter 5

Because of the Sick

Umbi, Tues. Dec. 3

Dear Ann,

First—if Tuesday isn't Dec. 3rd, please correct! I feel I've lost track somewhere and without a radio, can only check with you! I expect the cargo tomorrow—only four locals and two neighbors turned up to carry and the two women I had thought were going to carry kerosene for me were conscripted by two of the carriers to carry rice for them—so goes it. However, I estimate I have enough kerosene to last me and as Debli was one of those who "stole" a girl to carry rice (for him) instead of kerosene (for me)—I don't feel so badly about leaving him in the dark without kerosene when we go on our holiday. We'll see what tomorrow brings—I shall be eternally grateful if no problems arise.

I've been lazing along all weekend. We had a grand "to do" Sunday—held at the Solomon's (Missionary Brother's) house—when practically the entire registered population turned up and everyone decided to collect *dinau* (debts). Ningbi's comment when I asked him for details was "*Ol i baim ol long dinau bilong ol mor yet*" [Everyone is paying/collecting debts of each other in a big way]. I gather it was a chain reaction—do wish I understood the language better!

I'm enclosing some "lovely" shaggy-dog stories which I got from Gospo on Monday after I fed him some taro as he said he couldn't tell stories on an empty stomach. The *imlo* (flint) one, I think, is particularly interesting and I rechecked again as to the unique richness (in chipped flint) of the Silop area, and all said it was true. Silop certainly deserves a closer look. Could it be a quarry? Gospo says he has plenty more stories, but can't be hurried up and I assured him to take his time, but tell away. He only appears about twice a month, so I plan to pump him when I can.

[The story tells of Imlohe, who chased some girls from his garden by throwing *imlos* (chipped flint) at them, which he pulled from his anus. The girl's uncle (the cassowary) goes to their rescue and kills Imlohe at the place called Silop (between Umbi and Dulago), which explains why we continually picked up *imlos* on the trail there more than anywhere else (see Goodale 1966).]

Belo [my male puppy] nearly got killed today by the Tultul's son [Porkpudli] who was chasing a cat with a bush knife. Belo, also chasing the cat, was mistaken for the cat, and received a deep gash in his forehead. Porkpudli [aged 8] took off for the bush and his little sister said he went to Kandrian where their mother is. (He appeared after 3 hours.) Belo, after sleeping all afternoon, is now chasing pigs and eating old rats he's stashed away, plus all his dinner so I guess he'll live. I plastered (taped) his forehead, but don't know how long the plaster will stay on. So what's new with you?

Wed. night

We had our (first?) spearing today (better keep quiet about it at Dulago until word reaches you through normal channels). Soksili (Ningbi's Brother) and Utsili, his wife, had a real fight down on the line [in the village clearing] at 7:30 A.M. Utsili received 2 spear wounds in the back of her left knee, and a number of bleeding cuts on her back from a beating with a stick. No one I've asked seems to know why they were fighting, but their poor children were mixed up in it and it was a "merry" time! Soksili departed for parts unknown and Utsili went into the house down in the hollow behind mine. About 3 hours later, one girl came up and described Utsili's wounds and I said, if she wished, I'd treat them. The girl went back and soon Utsili appeared and I started cleaning the spear wounds when suddenly Utsili toppled off the patrol box in a dead faint. No older women were about. The kids were frightened. Ningbi and one other man did nothing. I finally got her back to her house where she fell on her bed and I insisted one girl take the 1 year old out of her hands so she could sleep. When Kasli came in with the cargo and heard the story, he said I wasn't to treat Utsili anymore because it was a court case and Soksili must take her to Pomalal (aid post). Of course, Soksili isn't here, but they don't seem to think about Utsili in this at all.

The next thing that happened was the dribbling in of the cargo. The second contingent with Debli reported that Sutli had cut his big toe on a rock all the way to the bone and he couldn't walk and was at Angus. Ningbi said he would go back with a bandage and tell him he should come in for proper treatment and to help carry him, if necessary. Ningbi left at 3 and at 4:30 Gospo staggered up to the house with 6-foot Sutli on his shoulders and with the others, gasping behind. Truly, it's a *very nasty* cut—for once they were not exaggerating. If he were an easier burden to carry, I'd send him to Kandrian, but as it is I don't have the heart.

On the bright side of events today was no complaints on cargo and the fact that they talked one Arihi man into going along to carry kerosene for me. Debli just came in and said that John (the shop keeper), who collected the mail from the office, collected yours too, but there were only magazine and papers and my case was too full to put yours in too. Debli insists there were no letters for you—if there had been, he would have brought them, he says. (The case was filled with 7 packages from my mother—Xmas trifles, she calls them. I haven't opened them yet!)

Incidental information: John charged me £2.10.0 for a bag of rice, and for the exact same bag he charged Sutli and Slabli £2.14.0 per bag! Naturally they are furious and John is a fool if he doesn't realize prices are one of the chief topics of conversation up here. Love, Jane

December 4, 1963
Dear Family;
Six packages from you arrived with this mail. They are resting at my feet and I feel it's Christmas already. I've put off opening them in spite of entreaties from my two assistants who have shaken and weighed each one. I think I will open them one by one, day by day.

With my cargo came a note from the Chinese storekeeper saying they have changed the schedule for planes to and from Kandrian-Rabaul. Of course no one thought to let us know before, but he thought we might "be interested." This effectively puts all our previous [vacation] plans, for which reservations had been made, out of action and I don't know if there is time to make new reservations for going to Rabaul on the 21st and returning the following Saturday. I am sending this happy (!!) news to Ann and poor gal, she'll have to decide what we do and then do something. I've suggested it might be easier to postpone our outing until after the holiday reservation crush. At this point I don't know where we will be on Christmas day...We will certainly get somewhere OUT in the near future if not Christmas. This is the first time I've regretted the lack of direct voice communication with Kandrian and Ann...

Wednesday, Dec. 4
Dear Ann
No mail for you was picked up. Probable reason a) Algy (the PO) didn't read pass, b) John (shop-keeper) took letters up to office and collected mail (Instructions re mail were in my letter to Algy.) Very sorry indeed, but brace yourself for worse— I received *no word* from Algy regarding anything. I wrote him saying we had confirmed reservations for the 22nd and would like to know about housing and when was the (Kandrian) singsing? Had he replied we might be in a better position to decide what to do now. I'm willing to go to Rabaul via Lae IF we can get reservations all along, i.e. plane and hotel. I'm (also) willing to postpone our visit until the beginning of January—perhaps hitting the elusive [Kandrian] singsing on our way out, if this makes reservations possible—but I'd hate to descend on Kandrian on Xmas Day. But see John's invitation enclosed [to a party].

Can you get someone to go down to Kandrian and if so I'll leave the decisions to you (poor gal, I hate to do it, but I'm quite sure I can't get someone to go again from here)—Your mail is there, the boys say. This is a frightful mess and I very much doubt whether anyone in Kandrian will take the initiative and make changes in reservations without word from us. Perhaps TAA has already written you, but without your mail—who knows!

It might be easier all around to postpone our outing until after the holidays and here's a thought, why don't we go to Mt. Hagen instead! and come back via Rabaul to shop. The new schedule gives us a week. I'm just tossing ideas out—wish we had telephones between us and Kandrian.

If you decide to postpone and would like to discuss with me person to person, let me know and I'll hike over for our monthly visit. But if you wish to go ahead with plans for Xmas (via Lae) time is of the essence.

In compensation for no mail I'm sending you some of my new magazines. I'm also sending a few 20 exp. films—I'm running low too and so far haven't found the one film John says he sent. Love Jane

[The following letter from Ann was written both before and after she received the above from me.]

Dulago, Sunday

Dear Jane,

I want a vacation! How about you? I suspect I've now hit a stretch where trips to the gardens won't yield anything but exercise and a change of scene, and that this will last till I can understand the conversations a lot more fully. I do feel moderately happy about the language at this point; a lot of breakdowns in communication result from my suddenly forgetting a word I should know. Still, when I compare it with my progress in Lakalai it's awfully discouraging.

Do you seem to be having an epidemic of dysentery or something similar among children? I'm getting cases almost daily, and it's very worrisome, especially in view of four known deaths in our immediate areas in the past two weeks.

My hiking shoes [which we both obtained from the U.S. Army Quartermaster Research Unit for testing under "extreme hot/wet conditions"] have both developed holes in the uppers, which really seems excessive, considering how little I've used them I think I'll save them for the Kandrian trip and try to break in something else for the short trips to the bush. I can't say I'm looking forward to the experience, though.

My clock has now conked out, what next?

People, one informant I should say, here absolutely deny that all women lived in one house. However, pre-Kiap all *haus marits* [married people's houses] were of the sloping roof type, essentially open across the front, which explains various features such as houses built facing the bush and the tabu on unmarried men coming near them, which were baffling when I thought they were fully enclosed. Also got a whole series of tabus, connected with the general ones on women being above men [thus polluting the men], which govern behavior of young men in the houses (i.e., they can't eat food cooked on the fire between the beds [with the assumption that women have stepped over the fire]). If your people have none of these tabus, it would be a really interesting difference.

Sorcerers were heard here the other night, and Paiyali sat up all night with a spear guarding my house against them. Isn't that touching? I think they were primarily worried about their own things which are stored here, but still— I've finally had an encounter with a poisonous plant, and have a terribly itchy rash down the side of my face and neck. I don't dare use any of my stronger remedies on it, so it will probably be troublesome for quite a while.

My initial data on kinship and *ulal* [courtship fighting initiated by women] turns out to be correct. The women with whom you can fight are especially the daughters of women you call *taso* (father's sister). Daughters of men you call *veheng* (mother's brother) are all right too, but the focus is on the patrilateral cross-cousin. It's a clear case of a difference in behavior toward cross and parallel cousins without, so far at least, differences in terminology.

[In both Kaulong and Sengseng parallel and cross cousins are referred to using the same terminology as for a true sibling; i.e., they are called brother and sister.]

Still to be straightened out are all the distinctions between the women you can fight with, the ones you can *tok plei* (sexually joke) with, the ones you can *plei* (court) with (not sure whether this is a different category), and the ones you can marry.

I'm enclosing the kinship system as far as I know it. The terms on the extreme right are used in such phrases as: "they are siblings" and "they call each other *kandere* (mother's brother's children). Some of them need checking, and I'm sure there are more.

Tuesday

I've just struggled all morning with a genealogy only to discover that I was given two entirely divergent accounts of a crucial group of siblings (Yanli's grandparents, given by a man whose grandparents they were too). Hell! I'll have to wait till I get my hands on him. But it's the first genealogy I've been given as a descent group starting from a semi-legendary Miu woman and going on for about eight generations, though very thin at the top. It's primarily for the Seagit people, but I have the name of another Miu woman who is supposed to give rise to the Yambon people. It's certainly not a matrilineal group, however. I did turn up a marriage (in this village) between a man and his mmzdd [mother's mother's sister's [z] daughter's daughter, or second cousin.]

The whole corner of my front porch collapsed today as a main cross-beam broke. Fortunately Paiyali (not I) was on it at the time; he managed to jump unharmed to the ground, bringing down the radio aerial with him, whereas if it had been me, I'd have been lucky to escape with a broken leg. Considering that it's less than 6 months since those timbers were cut, I don't feel too cheery about the future.

A Typical Open-faced Garden-hut

Thursday—The *Philadelphia Bulletin* article (about us) wasn't as bad as I expected. I might say that I wouldn't be surprised if Ward did have a hand in it despite those mysterious cannibals and head-hunters. You'd hardly know that New Britain contains the most progressive natives in the whole Territory, would you? And I love the picture of us so starved for company (and so energetic) that we spend virtually half our time visiting each other or en route to do so. Don't you wish that wild pigs were so common that they could just rush out and catch them like that?

They are working on the site for the damned *haus lotu* [Church]. Hell!

The Luluai crossed [scolded] Paiyali yesterday for taking my ax which the former had pretty well appropriated. Now I'll have to intervene, which promises to be nasty. The Luluai's wife is really my favorite woman in the village, but very short-tempered.

Ethnography has been very thin lately, and the fresh meat supply has been nil. I hope life is more fruitful up your way.

After your letter—Jesus! I don't have a clue as to whether I can get anyone to go down, but I'll try. We just got a rumor that the Kiap has sung out for people to come down and cut grass [part of keeping the vehicle roads near Kandrian clear]. If so, I might be able to send things with one of them, or possibly persuade someone else to go. In any case, I only have enough food supplies to last me til Christmas. Actually, I should be OK except for tinned fruit. I can't imagine that we could get reservations at this late date. If we delay it, I'll certainly want to see you. I'll think about what to do when I have a chance to talk to people. Thanks for the reading matter; here's a bit in return.

The weather looks very threatening, and I don't want to delay your carriers. I'm enclosing a guess at what I owe you for the coffee (from the label on the tin) and the chocolate, not knowing how much it is.

It's possible of course that TAA changed our reservations themselves, but I doubt it. I can't believe they wouldn't have written however. Until later, Love Ann

PS. Chances of getting someone off to Kandrian look pretty good, but I don't know yet what I'll say to Algy. However, I think it's unlikely that we'll go before Christmas, so do plan to spend that here.

Kandrian, 2-12-63

Dear Jane,

Plane schedules have been changed starting last week with result that the plane to Rabaul is now on Thursday while the return trip is on Saturday still. If this schedule remains unchanged, I doubt if your Rabaul trip will be worthwhile.

Accommodation is a bit tight with full staffing again, but there is a new unused AR2 house vacant at present but no furniture has been received. McLeans still willing [to accommodate you]. Singsing is due on the 1st January, 1964. No wireless as yet. Cheers, Algy. [Bessasparis-PO]

Umbi, Sat Night (Dec. 5?)

Dear Ann,

I don't know what sending on to you Algy's reply (received today) is going to accomplish—but here it is: (see above). I don't mind sleeping in a house without furniture, no different from *haus kiaps*! Debli says he asked John [Yun, of Chin Cheus] if the Kiap had written a pass to me and John said, no, and shooed them out so he could go and eat.

I was totally deserted by both Ningbi and Debli today, quite inadvertently. Ningbi went to Silop last night to see if they had been able to catch a pig he owns half of. Debli went to Parangin this morning saying he'd be back at noon. Both turned up at 5 and were very surprised to find the other had left me alone. Meanwhile, I made out fine and got some typing and other work done, and both have been very conscientious doing all the things I usually have to remind them of. Ningbi had quite a tale of pig chasing. And three men, who are all good pig hunters, got bitten by this pig with teeth going right through legs and arms (none have turned up for treatment). The pig is still loose and they have built a fence and if the pig goes inside, they will *pasim dua* [close the door/gate]. What then? No one seems to know.

Word of the "sick" that's hitting children your way reached here today— but no cases here as far as I know. Sulfaguanidine is supposed to be good for dysentery. Do you have some? I do, if you don't.

Sutli, the one who nearly cut his toe off, insisted on hobbling down to his garden yesterday (fortunately only a 10 minute walk) to cook rice for all the gals who were cleaning his taro using coconut shell-scrapers. As I watched the work, I noticed a spot they missed and fortunately I was sitting practically on it when the gals all rushed it, cleaned it, then "killed" all the taro (bending the leaves), and then jumped and ran away shouting. Later they "planted" their scrapers in the center. Naturally my 20 exp. (film) ran out in the middle of this! But Sutli says *kawawar* [ginger] is planted there and this "activity" will make the taro big. If you haven't seen this—be prepared. It's the last thing the gals do.

I haven't had a chance to check your information on male and female house tabus—but I just got a matrilateral 1st cross-cousin marriage. I'm having a hard time getting genealogies in depth and nothing like your semi-mythological foundresses. Probably a good deal of my trouble is I'm still operating mostly in Pidgin and the Pidgin speakers are too young.

How's your itch? I've developed a mysterious itch on my arm which started as a mosquito bite then an incipient ulcer, which was all healed when ugly red bumps appeared all over the ulcer spot. One person who saw it said "grili" [ringworm], but I don't think so. I hope it's not an allergy to my neosporin antibiotic—if it is, I'm reduced to sulfa drugs [due to a penicillin allergy].

I am resigned to staying here over Xmas and would love to visit you at that time. I'm OK on all supplies except fruit too, and I think my mother has sent some goodies, although I haven't opened them all yet. But I'll bring some things with me to make a semblance of a feast. Let me know when anything's decided. Love, Jane

Dulago, Saturday
Dear Jane,
   I'm starting this just because I have a stomach ache and don't feel like working, not because I have much of anything to say. I sent a letter off to Algy Friday, and a group led by Paiyali to get additional cargo and presumably bring back the reply today, so something may develop. At the moment I don't trust anyone at Kandrian to lift a little finger for us, least of all the Kiap, but they're not supposed to come back without a reply. (Sunday—Ho, ho, see below.)
   The Luluai has refused to answer the latest summons from Kandrian. I'll be interested to see if he gets calaboosed. My two best informants have gone and the rumor is that they'll be there till Christmas. It's the final touch to a dismal week, only cheered by an excellent snake last night, with a couple of baby birds for tonight (and one of those fearful lizards for tomorrow).
   I'll spare you the ins and outs of why they're collecting cargo for me. Sort of a now or never proposition. It may well mean that Paiyali won't be coming when and if we do go, which will be fine with me, except for the clothes washing problem. But we could always get them washed in Rabaul, which might be a good idea at that. Clothes are on my mind because I haven't been able to get any washed all week. Paiyali was truly repentant last night, but still left immediately after breakfast. Ah, well, fastidiousness was never my strong point, anyway.
   Sunday afternoon—Just got back from a pretty unsuccessful *ton* (lichee? nut) collecting expedition to find your letter. The expedition shook me because I found it such tough going—knees weak, head swimming—and it's just a week since I'd last been out. I'd been resting my plant poisoning, since heat and exertion bring out the blisters. It's all right now, and here's some potassium permanganate, my favorite remedy, in case that's what you have. Please decant some crystals and return; I may have another attack any minute. I use a very strong solution, but you'd better start with a weaker one. I do have Sulfaguanidine; the problem is knowing what kind of dysentery. Actually I assume my trouble today may be the result of anything from the fact that I was a little sick yesterday to the fact that the trek was made on a virtually empty stomach.
   All this avoiding the complexities of our present problems. Anyway, there I was all carefree and happy yesterday at 5 P.M. when into view hove both my cargo line and the men who'd gone to build the bridge at Kandrian, with the news that the Kiap had forbidden anyone from the bush to go near Kandrian for 3 weeks, because of a major sickness, nature totally unknown and locale unclear, and that he had said we were all to abandon the villages and live in the bush for that time. I suppose you've heard this by now. I expect it will be a couple of days before we get the full details; at present the question seems to be whether there are two or three weeks still to go. It means at the best, I wouldn't

be able to send anyone down before the 21st or so, and at the worst it might be the end of the month (in which case I imagine they'll delay the singsing a bit).

So please do plan to spend Christmas with me. If I get enough fresh meat between now and then, we may be able to avoid [canned] casserole steak, but I'm making no promises. I think our actual plans will have to depend on when the quarantine is lifted. But since I'd have to be sending down for supplies at the end of the month anyway, it seems obvious to at least go along and see the singsing. (It would also stave off starvation by a couple of days not to have to wait for the carriers to return. For that matter if the quarantine is lifted before Christmas, the carriers would probably run into store closed for holidays.)

What I'm leading up to is to say that if the quarantine is lifted before Christmas, why don't you come over say on Christmas Eve and then we could leave together for Kandrian on the 27th. You could leave your camping gear in Ningbi's charge to join you at Pomalal. If the quarantine is to run till after Christmas and the singsing is delayed, by all means come earlier than Christmas Eve.

My inclination would be to put off our trip into the outside world except for one major consideration. That is that in the period right after the New Year, with people at Kandrian for the bridge-building, especially the hatmen [village officials, the Luluais and Tultuls], we could be pretty sure that no major events would be going on while we were away. My suggestion is that we send down a letter to Algy with the policeman who lifts the quarantine and ask him to do what he can about getting us reservations. If he can get them within a week or so of the New Year, we could well spend the time visiting coastal villages, collecting linguistic data, etc. (The unfurnished house sounds like a satisfactory base.) How does all this strike you? I must say that after weeks of sleeping in the bush, no mail, and no cargo, I'll be as ready for a break as will ever be possible. For the same reason, any magazines will be welcomed with open arms. I only had a passing glance at the two *Times* that came with your mail before last, so if you've finished them, I'd love to see them (book supply is good, however).

The reason I'm sending Paiyali is to ask if I could borrow a bathing suit for the stay in the bush. We'll be camping beside the stream, and there'll be no one in the village to fetch water, so my only chance of bathing or washing the hair is to go in my clothes or...?

Kasup asks if I would remind you about the tobacco tin.

I'll undoubtedly be returning to the village during the day, to look after the cat *inter alia*, but my plan is to store our conch shell trumpet on the porch. If you send runners over during this period, tell them to blow it and someone will certainly turn up.

I envy you your stories, but I'm somewhat startled at the content. I bet they're not normally told in mixed company and that Gospo is enjoying telling them to you for more than one reason. Your story of Pondawildawil sounds as if they must have some of the same tabus (about women being above men).

Thanks for the garden tip—it's fascinating. Is Ningbi's pig the one of Naoli's that they've been singing over and trying to catch? Love Ann.
PS. Sunday night. Just listened to news for any clue as to what's going on at Kandrian, and [heard that] Kennedy is dead! Not a clue as to when or how, just a mention of President Johnson (God!) and "the late President Kennedy." I really do feel cut off now.

Umbi December 9
Dear Ann;

The first I heard of the quarantine was your letter, but it was verified by others who came with it. So we will go bush too, although I don't know where. Do you think we will hear the details of the sickness? There is one woman here who has just come down with something plus a very swollen breast. I have slight case of diarrhea, but am not worried. I have some Potassium Perm., so am sending yours back—I'd forgotten what it was for! (Writing this pass is difficult as everyone is in my house evidently expecting me to make some explanation concerning the quarantine.)

Since so much depends on the quarantine lifting—I can say your plans sound fine, but let's defer definite plans for my visit to Dulago to see if we get any further information on the sickness and when we'll go to Kandrian. As I don't know where I'll be, I can only say wait for further word as to what to do with messages to me, or else have anyone leave it on the table in my front room and I'll pick it up and "back" [answer] it when possible. Here are some new *Times* which I've finished. What a shock about Kennedy! I've just been reading these *Times*, which are full of the '64 election speculations.

I'm now waiting for a decision to be made as to where I will evacuate to, so Paiyali will know and can tell anyone who comes, where I am. (We also have a conch shell, I've just been told, but it's in the bush.) We won't be far as Sutli will be with us with his mutilated toe. This [tobacco] tin really belongs to a man in Arihi, but as Kasup's is the next tin I'll be smoking, I'll send this to Kasup and give his to the Arihi lad, when I see him.

Do let me know if you hear anything pertinent on your radio. I wish I had mine now. Hastily, Jane
    [By this time I had a long waiting list for my empty Log Cabin brand
    tobacco tins from people in all surrounding communities to use as
    lime containers.]

Umbi, Thurs. 12/12/63
Dear Ann;

I'll start this now as I don't know when we will exchange notes. I am at Sabilo living in a fortress, actually, my bed is built into the ficus tree and I'm using my tent as a roof. Sabilo is a very small Mountain top with very steep slopes on the East, North, and West and a more gentle approach to the South. It is a traditional refuge. On the other side of the ficus, as in a time of war, is the *mok* [women's shelter] and at present it's inhabited by some of the school-aged girls, the Luluai's wife and children, and her sister, and Utkunuk (the Miu woman) and children. Next to me is Debli and Ningbi's house and beyond, facing the approach, is the *haus boi* [single men's house], inhabited at present by Sutli (with cut foot) and some of the school boys. It's a pleasant group and is not as "artificial" as it sounds as it is a kin group of sorts! We are but 10-15 min. from Umbi and the (missionary) Brothers are maintaining residence there and holding morning school for an hour. Kilok and Belo (my puppies) are here with us and have settled into their new home well. We have a stream five minutes away and yesterday three boys took me up stream a short distance to a waterfall (10 feet high) with a nice pool underneath. But the water isn't flowing very fast and I hesitate slightly about bathing above drinking. (Later)—I've discovered drinking water comes from another source.

I got mad at both Debli and Ningbi today for separate reasons—Debli most contrite has apologized—Ningbi has disappeared. Thank God they finally killed that pig and he should be able to stick around and do his share of the work, but he doesn't and so I got cross!

Everyone has been *ton* (fruit) collecting for the past week, Debli and Ningbi included, and they keep saying it's not ripe when they come back empty-handed. But small children have been bringing one or two to me which are ripe! Ligiok, who disappeared with Ningbi, *just* brought me a bunch (of *ton*). *"I no mau gutpela"* [it's not really ripe], he says! Time out for eating them. They weren't ripe.

I spent the morning collecting a very involved genealogy from Gaho and Sutli and the most interesting thing which turned up was a woman married to her MB [Mother's Brother] (straight). This should knock out any matrilineal kin group idea. It's an old and well established marriage.

My allergy? has me baffled. I haven't tried your remedy yet as I have suspicions of ringworm and am trying Mitgal ointment whose label says "good for all skin problems." It has a raised rim which itches like mad, it's circular and gets bigger daily. I'll try PP (potassium permanganate) after giving Mitgal a chance. (Excuse small print but my notebook has become my diary as well and I have to conserve paper.)

Saturday—12/15—Gospo says he'll take this to you Monday. I don't want to send any small boys with passes as you're in the bush. So I had to wait til someone turned up. Since my blowup on Thursday at D and N, concerning the perennial problem of their feeding others MY taro and me not getting anything in return, all the children have been bringing me gifts of ripe *ton* (fruit) and *kindams* [shrimp] and other misc. small "game" and explicitly saying I can't pay for them. I went *ton* collecting myself yesterday, but don't want to get overheated until my arm clears up. I've also decided to stay out of the water. However, the Mitgal treatment seems to be working slowly.

I feel this bush experience is very valuable just for a concentrated dose of "daily activities" and close observation on children and unmarrieds. But lacking completely are observations on daily activity of married couples. So I'll have to go out again later if I can just persuade some couple to "invite" me along.

The story (rumor) which "arrived" yesterday was that the [Catholic] Father had arrived at Hulem and was holding school there for all the children of Hulem, Yambon and Dulago and, at least at Hulem, no one was "allowed" to hide in the bush. What's your story?

Sunday, 12/16—We all got our "medicine" last night—sung-over (bespelled) ginger—and the dogs were given some spit down their throats! Then Ningbi took some to spit *long lain* [in the village] and on the path. On the way back, in the dark, he was attacked by *three tamberans* [ghosts], who clawed (chewed ?) him and fought him hand to hand. He arrived back in a state of shock and later full of interesting data and stories.

I spent five hours this p.m. in bare feet and bathing suit. I took off with Ningbi and Noalong and four kids to bathe, wash clothes and hair, and eat *don*. We *daun* (cut) a total of seven large (*don*) trees and sandwiched in between, I did wash hair, underwear and myself. It was really pleasant and I saw some lovely waterfalls and quiet pools while I was walking down the stream to *Egi Ason* (the river Ason). My arm seems to have healed. I'm now writing this by the truly flickering light of my half-collapsed (non pressured) kerosene lamp (little), but I don't know when Gospo will turn up tomorrow to take this to you.

Now for the complexities of the current plans. At this point (and I've given it some concentrated thought) I can't see planning our trip to Kandrian with any certainty until we know we are allowed in! Also I cannot plan to leave for Kandrian VIA Dulago. In the present situation, I can't plan much of anything except my visit to you. (But see later).

I would like to stay here in the bush until the 24th and then come over Xmas eve for Xmas. I can bring some goodies like partridge and pheasant and Xmas Cake with me—also my mother has sent some cheese and nuts. (Do you *not* like nuts in general or only in chocolate! Let me know and if you *don't* like them, I'll eat them now). Then, I say, let's leave future planning for then and hope the *sik* is over and we'll be able to make definite plans. It's going to be tricky just to get people to come to Dulago with me and cargo.

What is your set-up? Do you have room for me in the bush? If you don't and/or it will be too complex to have me don't hesitate to say so—and I will (we can) pretend Xmas doesn't exist until we can celebrate it properly in the Outside World.

Gospo should wait for a reply, but should you wish to communicate further with me, tell your postman to go to the Brother's house. One boy is staying there with them at Umbi and knows where we are. We are within shouting distance, but there's no guarantee anyone will respond to a shout as they are afraid to answer such calls now. The spirit causing the sickness can hear shouts and even normal talking and be able to find us, requiring us to speak in whispered tones throughout our stay there. But the Brothers are "in residence" even if they're "out," they will return and will see I get any message from you (*they* can also *read*). I'm curious, did my letters get through to Kandrian or did they come back too?

Monday, 12/17/1:30 p.m. —Gospo hasn't showed up. I asked Debli to take this to you tomorrow and all of a sudden both he and Ningbi say 1) Kiap told them not to move about except in their own areas, 2) Debli has work tomorrow in his garden, and 3) all are afraid to go to Dulago. But (after much persuasion on my part) he said he might go on Wednesday. But the upshot of all this is, I think, it is *extremely unlikely* I can get anyone to take me to Dulago on the 24th. Such complexities. The best I can say now is: *if* I can come, I will, but, if I can't get anyone to go with me, '*maski mi stap*' [forget it, I'll stay here] as Ningbi puts it. Of course, if this is too uncertain, and/or the visit will be materially (not mentally) a burden, just say so and as I said before, I'll forget Xmas exists and become a perfect bush heathen. This may also mean we won't be able to exchange notes except in extreme emergencies (i.e. we get desperately ill). I mentioned these events to Debli to prove to him the importance of his taking this *pas* to you so you would know how to get in touch with me! They evidently hadn't thought of *my* dying, or even being sick. Damn Algy anyway. It would have been *thoughtful* of him to send *us* a note of explanation via the policeman [who stopped Ann's carriers from reaching Kandrian].

Later—More developments: Word has reached the Brothers that they are all to go to one Mission close to Kandrian for Xmas and perhaps to wait out the sick. They have agreed to Debli's suggestion: that I give them a pass for Algy asking for 1) information about sick and duration and 2) to let us know immediately it's over and we would be down in Kandrian shortly thereafter.

The other development is that all my companions (the children) will desert me and go to their parents. At first it was suggested that we go deeper into the bush too, but at the moment, I'm sitting tight. But it appears almost 99/100% sure that it will be *impossible* for me to get to Dulago for Xmas. Also with the Brothers gone, it will be rather difficult to contact me. However, someone goes back to the house once a day (usually early in the morning) and if a letter is left on the yellow table weighted down with a boot (also in the front room) it will be collected.

Noalong has said he will take this *pas* to you tomorrow. The tin belongs to Mongin. Merry Christmas! Love, Jane

Dulago, Monday, December 16
Dear Jane,

It's not that I expect a chance to send this out for weeks, but who knows? Who knows about anything in fact. The worst news first. I dislocated my knee again Saturday night—doing nothing, just climbing a hill (6 months to the day since the last time; isn't that cute)? It was a pretty ghastly few minutes, but Kasup straightened out the leg and I shoved the kneecap back with no real effort. However, it's gone out twice since then, in spite of Ace bandages. I've got on the sticky bandage now, and hope it will hold. I've now got a folded

Kotex holding it in place. Do you think the NGS would appreciate that? Obviously I'll just have to see how it is when the quarantine is lifted. Paiyali is hell-bent on our moving to the bush, several hills away, which I had infinitely rather not do under the circumstances, but the news of a case (of dysentery) in Seagit has them very frightened.

Paiyali fortunately suggested that I hold his wages and that he cut the firewood for the duration, so I will be able to buy food. As it happens, I'm being deluged with fresh meat; just when I can least afford it, but it helps my morale as well as the supply of tins.

I sent someone down to intercept the policeman, with a letter asking Algy to find out about planes for us when he knows when the quarantine will be lifted (sent your letters too). If the leg is holding up at all, I plan to make the trek if we can get down in time for the *singsing* and get a plane no more than a week after that. I asked him if possible to send word with whoever comes to end the quarantine. I must say I'm not cheered by this method of handling an epidemic by cutting all the sufferers off from medical aid. We've had one case of dysentery here, but the Sulfaguanidine apparently did the trick, though the effort of getting the pills down children leaves us all exhausted.

Tuesday—Your messenger just arrived, much to my surprise. We were told on Tuesday about the ban on movement between areas, so I hadn't expected to hear from you at all (though there's been a great deal of ignoring it, notably to attend a singsing the next night). I'm awfully sorry I didn't go, especially now that I'm buggered up.

We were just about to leave for the bush when your note arrived. I'll be camping out with Paiyali's family in an old *ples matmat* [hamlet/burial place], which is said to be very close. The official word was that no one but parents of small children had to go to the bush, which is why we hadn't left before this.

Could you pay your messenger? My tobacco has already gone to the bush, and I am desperately short of money, so I really can't afford to.

If by any chance the quarantine is lifted in time, please do come for Christmas. Conch shell is on porch, as advertised, and we are a very short distance away (and will of course be back if we hear in time). I do like nuts when not in chocolate. I'm not in the least optimistic though. Because of the leg I don't plan to leave the bush camp at all, so it will be easy to locate me. Paiyali will go daily to the house to feed Roo, too.

Mitgal certainly cleared up my ringworm. I can't recommend anything better.

I'd been virtually living out of the village til the knee (and finally saw a bit of garden ritual).

If you can persuade people to come over on Christmas even if the sick isn't over, I'll simply move back to the house for the occasion. At the worst I think I'll come back and at least listen to the radio. I won't possibly be able to send any messengers from here. I'd love to have you, and come alone without gear (or food) if you like. I will have enough.

Haven't heard a word about a Father at Hulem. Love, Ann.

Umbi, Sunday December 22

Dear Algy, John or "to whom it may concern;"

As Kasli has received word to bring some *kaikai* [food] to his wife in Kandrian, I am taking the opportunity, 1) to get a letter out to those (my folks) who will worry if they don't hear from us, and 2) to ask for some information concerning the present local situation. All our information is received here at Umbi third or fourth hand, and it appears to be quite contradictory.

We received word first, that *all* were to go bush and restrict local travel and visiting to an absolute minimum until word reached us that the yet mysterious sick was finished, and that we could expect that the sick would last for 3-6 weeks.

Yesterday, we received word from visitors from Hulem that 1) the Doctor, *Didiman* (agriculture officer), and Kiap were all at Pomalal last week, 2) all children of this region (except those who didn't get the news) received their second "shots" (of what?) last Thursday and Friday, 3) those who didn't go to Pomalal for the "shoot" must go to Kandrian NOW to get their shots or risk jail, 4) the Kiap was on his way up here and the Doctor had gone back to Kandrian, and finally, 5) that nothing was said that would indicate that traveling restrictions were lifted.

I am writing this letter primarily for my own sake, as I can neither send a message to Ann, send down to Kandrian for supplies (much needed) or make plans for traveling myself, until I know what the instructions on travel really are. Incidentally, one complication on our own travel arrangements is that I received word that Ann had dislocated her knee again a week ago. I would also like to know the nature of the sick, what it is, and where it is, if possible.

I'm not addressing this letter to any specific person as due to the *tok* (gossip), I don't know who is in Kandrian at the moment, but I've asked Kasli to give it to the Doctor, Kiap or someone else who can answer these questions. Many thanks, Jane.

PS. If Kasli can bring back any *first class letters* for Ann and Myself, it would be appreciated.

PSS. One young lad in our camp had two attacks of malaria this week. I've treated him with my own *limited* supply of Camoquin.

[Kasli met his wife an hour down the road to Arihi. His infant daughter had died in Kandrian and his wife was sent home—Kasli returned and my letter never reached Kandrian.]

Sunday 12/22 notebook entry

An off day. Mostly rainy. Went to Umbi for money, tobacco and weather report and arrived back at 9 a.m. Rain, visitors and resulting confusion until noon when all left. Debli and Ningbi slept. Woke at 3 p.m. and ate pig. Iamopli arrived back from *lain* [village] with news that *Doktaboi* (medical assistant) and wife were there and had a message for me. Went there in pouring rain. Got word from John S. (the European Medical Assistant in Kandrian who had banned all internal travel) that it was all right for *us* (by implication no one else) to come to Kandrian for Xmas! and word from Ann to come to Dulago for Xmas. Plan to do the latter. Sick is dysentery. Boys elect to stay bush.

Dulago, Sunday 12/22
Dear Jane,

Hope this (word from the *doktaboi* carried on to me at Umbi) means you'll feel free to come over for Christmas. My plan is to send off a couple of people tomorrow to collect mail and money and find out about the plane. If we can possibly get seats, I'm all for going down for the singsing and maybe even if we can't. But in any case I'll hope to see you Tuesday. If it's too difficult for you *maski, samting bilong yu* [forget it, it's your decision]. Thanks to the recent rain, we're back in the village, and I certainly hope that we'll stay here (the bush was a real hell-hole, and I was sick to boot). Love, Ann

Rabaul, January 3, 1964
Dear Family;

What a month this has been! [I told them of events up to Dec. 22—and then continued.]. . . Kasli departed with my letter [to the Kiap] back to his bush camp and we sat down to eat pig when a message came in that the *dokta boi* [indigenous medical assistant] was at Umbi and had a message for me. So, swallowing pig hastily, I set off (in the pouring rain) and received our first communication from "outside"—a note from the Kandrian Medical Assistant saying, the quarantine did not apply to Ann and me, and we were expected in Kandrian for Christmas (an impossibility due to the late arrival of the note). Since the messenger had been to Dulago first, there was also a note from Ann saying she hoped I would be able to get over for Xmas, since we *could* now move around. I did, of course, go—arriving Xmas Eve.

Ann had moved back to the village, as her tent leaked impossibly, so we spent Xmas together in comparative comfort—listening to carols on her radio on Xmas Eve, while munching on "Assorted Nuts From Around the World," lunching on "Assorted Cheeses" and rye bread, and dining on Scotch pheasant and rum cakes while reclining in true Roman fashion on the floor. Added to the immeasurable joy which your contributions made was the arrival of Ann's messenger back from Kandrian (she had sent him down immediately on receipt of the note from the Med. Asst.) with our Xmas mail, Xmas cards and, most important, news of what *really did happen to Kennedy*! The latter (was) not exactly cheery Xmas news, but you can't imagine what it was like to know only that he was dead and *nothing more.*

We also got a good laugh from *Security is a Warm Blanket* [a Peanuts cartoon book], particularly in view of our [very insecure] situation. Thank you one and all for all the presents. The cigarettes kept me going on the trip down, the rubber bands and safety-pins retired my solitary pin and rubber band to a well earned rest!

We also, at this time, got confirmation of our suspicions, that the *sik* was indeed dysentery. Ann had several cases from other villages (to treat), Umbi only one, which we were able to treat with Sulfaguanidine.

Since Ann felt her knee was in satisfactory enough condition for the hike out, we made plans to leave on Sat the 28th and I left Dulago for Umbi on the 26th—a very wet day. Slept that night at Sabilo and moved back to Umbi on Friday, happy because four men had volunteered to escort me to Kandrian and carry my two patrol boxes (on the down trip filled with books [to return], camping gear [for the trip] and clothes and what little food I had remaining—a fairly light load), but unhappy and dirty, because it was raining and no washing of clothes was possible. That night one of my carriers arrived, no word from the others.

Saturday morning still only one carrier. At 9 a.m the carrier and I left with Debli who said he would help carry one case to the next village (Hulem) where we would (hopefully) find a replacement and he would return to stay in Umbi to look after house, garden and dogs. Ningbi would wait (in Umbi) for the other two carriers and then join us and continue with me to Kandrian.

Got to the next village at 11:15—deserted—blew a conch shell and eventually the Luluai appeared and a messenger sent out to the bush to find one to three volunteers for cargo. Ningbi caught up with us and reported that *no one* had showed up at Umbi! I then realized that the case left in Umbi contained all my clothes, bedding, tobacco and papers, and money!

Finally at 3 p.m. the Hulem messenger appeared with one volunteer to relieve Debli and I sent him back to see what he could do about the remaining case, and left for Pomalal, where I was to meet Ann.

Arrived at Pomalal at 6:30 just before complete darkness fell. We were both overjoyed to see each other—I, because I could share her bedding and clothes if necessary, she, because she was sure I wasn't coming as she couldn't conceive it taking me so long to get there. I was at this time in a furious temper and it was a relief to be able to explode! We agreed we could wait until noon the next day, but no longer, to see if my case could/would catch up and after a rather uncomfortable night on the limbum [split palm] floor without padding we relaxed and bathed in the stream the next morning.

At 10 a.m. in staggered two men with my case. One of them was Sutli, who had cut his foot so badly 3 weeks ago that I had previously refused his offer to carry (for me). The other was his brother, Kaliam—my ex-temporary houseboy, who had given up an important work project to come. My gratitude to these two for coming is great.

So off we went—Ann, I, Ningbi and four Sengseng and four Kaulong carriers. From here we were told to follow an old road as the usual route was *tabu* [forbidden] because of the epidemic. We passed through Emoia—an inhabited village and then hit the road to Migili—an abandoned village, which, however, was said to have a *haus kiap*—or rest house. The carriers went ahead and it was only because we could see their track in the grass, that we knew we were following a road. The bush had grown up, the log bridges decayed and broken (but as the streams were dry, this was not much of a hardship). We three walked on and on, slowly because of Ann's knee and began to wonder if Migili really existed.

We did come up to it at 5 to find the men roasting some breadfruit by the *haus kiap*. It was true desolation. We are not sure when the village was abandoned, but the houses, although standing, had broken ladders, missing floorboards and great bare holes in the *kanda* roofs. The *haus kiap* was nailed shut, so Ann and I went up to the main row of houses, through the tall grass and picked out one house that had a ladder, half of a roof and two *plank* [board] beds and laid claim. The men took over the other houses. The men then said there was no water, and they were hungry (there was no one there to buy food from). We made a deal which worked—we offered them biscuits and four packages of dry soup (about all we had) if they could/would make the effort to find water and they ran off and shortly returned with two buckets full and we were all happy and soon well fed and in bed.

The next morning the men left (after another round of soup and crackers) going ahead to see about the "bridge" over the Ason (Ann's Xmas mail carriers had come this way and finding no bridge had cut two small trees and laid them across, but we were all doubtful whether 1) they would still be there and 2) whether Ann and I could negotiate them). After an hour's walk and an extremely precipitous descent down to the river, we found two of the eight carriers waiting for us. They had added a few more logs and a hand-vine and fortunately the logs were at water level (which gave a feeling of security although the water was quite deep and swift in its narrow gorge). With a helping hand we crossed (in the pouring rain with the water lapping our heels) with little difficulty and breathed a sigh of relief.

For two more hours we followed the abandoned road and then reached Ngala—another abandoned village, but found a man, wife and child there who accompanied us on to Akak, their new village. Just before Akak, we met David, the policeman who had accompanied us in July. He had been sent by the Kiap to bring us out from wherever we were—it was the first evidence of concern about us from the administration (as far as we then knew).

We stopped for lunch at Akak and decided to move on as far as we could although this was the last *haus kiap* on the route to Kandrian. We reached Audi, the next village, at 3:30 and although we could reach Kandrian before night, we decided to stop there for the night, get food for the carriers, and not arrive dirty and exhausted just at dinner time. One old man offered Ann and me his house and taro to the carriers and we were quite comfortable. We sent David back to Kandrian with a note of our expected arrival the next morning and arrive we did at 10 a.m.—absolutely filthy and hot, as the last part of the road is a tractor road—wide and with all trees cut back 100 yards on either side and the sun blazes down—plus we had an added layer of charcoal acquired from hitching a ride on a wood collecting tractor wagon for the last mile, sitting on top of the already charred logs.

Our first stop was the store, where John Yun took one look, led us to the back room, sat us down and poured ice-cold Cokes for us. Properly refreshed we staggered up to the office to find Algy Bessasparis [the Officer-in-charge while the Stevens are on leave] and then on to his house for ice-cold beers. We had an invitation to stay with the Mcleans (malaria control) so we went there for lunch (after a shower) and gratefully accepted their invitation to eat all meals, except breakfast, with them and explained that we were turning down their offer of beds, only because of our need for room for cargo packing and organizing.

This was New Year's Eve and the Yuns were having "drinks at their house" to which we were invited. Fully expecting to fall asleep at our usual hour of 9, we went and had a wonderful evening. Drinks, intelligent (comparatively speaking) conversation in a yard decorated with Chinese lanterns and balloons, exquisite hors-d'oeuvres, and a delicious supper at midnight with champagne and a 2 minute barrage of Chinese firecrackers. We left at 2 a.m. (the party continued until daybreak).

The next evening was the native *singsing* with invitations extended to all the tribes [*sic*] in the district (except for quarantined ones), and we spent the afternoon photographing some of the coastal dance groups in their varied masks, headdresses and costumes. The bush people (ours) with their *planks* (shields) and spear dance were rumored to be waiting in the bush for midnight, when they would arrive, and we felt an unexpected tenseness in Kandrian because of fear of these bush people.

We were quite exhausted and decided to sleep in our clothes before their arrival and our carriers said they would wake us when the *planks* (shield-people) arrived. This was at 11 p.m. and we went down to the field and in the full moonlight saw dancers from the Gimi, Miu and a few from Kaulong, massed with their shields and spears. I met a Luluai from one of the Gimi villages, who took me up [to his group] and "introduced" me and then later talked to me for an hour or more (mainly, why didn't I come to live in his village). Ann had a similar conversation with a man from Miu. We watched the dancing (which is the same as we've seen in our villages but without *planks*) for an hour. The Police were hovering very close by us, but we felt no alarm. These were "our people." However trite that may sound there was no doubt that we were regarded, even by these strangers, as belonging to the bush country, as a different breed from the other Europeans, and as "exhibits" by our own villagers who showed us off with pride, bringing people up to us to introduce to us or vice versa. We were constantly being surrounded and forced to exhibit our as yet limited knowledge of the language.

We returned to bed at midnight, promising to return at dawn to try to photograph. Up we got at 5 a.m. and staggered down again—we were the only Europeans. As we started to photograph, the crowd of bush people obligingly lined up and started to charge us with spears rattling—(presenting) perfect picture subjects, but immediately the police rushed in and forced them to line up 20 yards from us in static poses. But we did take pictures by dawn's rosy

Visitors from the Interior at Kandrian Singsing

A Lunchtime Conversation under Jane's House

light, of people and faces, and returned home to find Ningbi had disobeyed our instructions "to go to the *singsing* and forget about making our breakfast" and had in fact made hot coffee for us. We needed it for we had to get our carriers loaded for return to Umbi and Dulago (with fresh supplies) and us packed for Rabaul and we departed at 12:30, arriving here (Rabaul) last night.

We are off again at 5 a.m. tomorrow for Mt. Hagen (New Guinea), returning to Rabaul next Thursday and to Kandrian on the following Saturday. We decided we needed a *real change of pace* and on the spur of the moment made these plans.

Many thanks for Christmas messages awaiting us here at the Cosmo (Hotel) and at R.W. Hancock (our agent)—we feel in a good holiday mood now! Happy New Year to all! Much Love Jane

PS. [from Ann] As you've probably gathered from Jane, the only reason we had any Christmas cheer at all was thanks to your packages. Thanks to two really spectacular failures of our always bad mail service, the only mail at all that I received in six weeks were the letters that arrived on Christmas day and it was only when we got to Kandrian that I found both my family's Christmas package and your delightful present. We are now celebrating the New Years on them, but you all really made our Christmas. Many thanks on behalf of both of us (things really were rather dismal for a while, but we've been recovering our spirits steadily since Christmas Eve). A belated Happy New Year! Ann

Postscript

Unexpected events and/or disasters can prove full of rich information of another culture—but we never anticipated the feeling of utter powerlessness that came when the "sickness" blocked us from all outside communication with our real world. We realized that should this outside world disappear, we would never know. We even feared that our communication with each other would become impossible as we found ourselves held prisoner by this mysterious sickness.

At first I could lessen my anxiety by considering the sickness to be due mainly to sorcery, a causal factor in which I did not personally believe. Later, I began to worry for my health along with that of my companions, particularly when I learned this sickness/sorcery was directed not just at other sorcerers, but at all Umbi residents and in addition sometimes involved mysterious substances (poisons?) acquired from the outside world. It's hard to remain objective when under personal attack. Umbi's sorcery war with Womilo continued at least until after I had permanently left the Umbi region seven months later in July.

Gender tabus began to reveal themselves to us—first to Ann as Dulago held to a strict form where no man may go under a place or structure where a mature woman has gone on top. In addition to isolating women who are actually menstruating or giving birth (two intensely polluting times), they believe that all sexually mature women can pollute and cause illness and death to men at any time should these tabus be broken. In both Dulago and Umbi men and women used the covered space underneath our raised houses to cook food on an open fire, and as a place to gather and talk. Men may not eat food which has been cooked on firewood on which a woman has sat.

Ann's raised house was tabu for sexually mature women in contrast to my house in Umbi where Kaulong women were frequent visitors inside. Ann herself was classed with the grandmothers or postmenopausal women, while I was classed with the sexually mature mothers, but I was not considered to be capable of polluting men as Kaulong women were.

Although there was a difference between Dulago and Umbi, my second community, Angelek, showed the Dulago pattern. After I had been a year in Angelek (where my house was built close to the ground and only small children could fit underneath), a man asked me directly, and for the first time, if I menstruated, but before I could count to 200 (my usual delay for difficult questions), he said, "I guess only our (kind of) women do that." I felt at the time that he didn't want a yes answer at that late date to make his and other men's lives more difficult. The women were as always unconcerned. I believe that the inhabitants of Umbi (as in Angelek) decided not to make their life more complicated by my presence and declared me and my house outside of these tabus. Ann found that the Sengseng, like the Kaulong, did not believe that European women menstruated.

Kaulong and Sengseng courtship is (to a European) a rather violent affair and provided me with amusement as well as data as my two young male assistants were targets for many young women. At times I would curse them loudly as they carried on into the small hours of the night around my fire underneath, while I tried to sleep above, but it was refreshing to me to see women having the upper hand. Kaulong and Sengseng men are not permitted to actively initiate a courtship, but they may allow a young woman to beat them with sticks (sometimes knives) in *ulal,* or they may choose to run away. Men may not lay a hand on the young woman or they will be liable to a charge of rape. They may, however, use bright colors, pungent fragrances, shiny healthy bodies, and sweet panpipe compositions to entice women to choose them for *ulal.* To stop the attack men give gifts (tobacco, money, etc.) to the courting female.

Courtship (*ulal*) and marriage (*nangin*) are two very different and unconnected concepts and activities. *Young* men may choose to engage in *ulal,* but will swear they will never get married, or will do so only when they are old and ready to die, in order to have a child to replace them. Sexual intercourse inevitably results in marriage (*nangin*) and also in death, they believe. Sexual intercourse is intensely polluting to men and results in men expressing real fear of getting married and of early death. Some adult hamlet leaders (we found through genealogies and from informants) never married and yet were able to achieve fame and wealth.

Chapter 6

They Held an Election

Umbi, January 19, 1964

Dear Family,

Arrived back on the 17th feeling much refreshed by the "outing." We had a marvelous time in Mt. Hagen. Ann had never been there and it is such a nice spot I had no reservations about going back. [I had previously visited Mt. Hagen in 1962 en route to Kaulong, to visit a friend.] Cool Mt. air (alt. 5,000+ feet) was so refreshing and yet so stupefying that we slept like logs. We took afternoon naps, strolled about the town enjoying the colorful locals (because we didn't have to ask them any questions) and eating delicious food and drinking with the local expatriates. We even saw a movie (an ancient western) at the local "club." We arrived back in Rabaul Thursday after a stop over in Lae and did all our necessary shopping and saw another movie and caught Saturday's plane to Kandrian. Again the McLeans undertook to feed us while we slept in the empty and light-less house and straightened (sorted and packed) cargo for the trip back. And we enjoyed our stay with them very much.

On Tuesday at 7:00 a.m. we left. As Bruce McLean was also going on patrol and had the use of the tractor and cart, he kindly delayed his departure to give us and the cargo a lift over the blazing hot, miserable tractor road as far as our turn off—approximately 5-7 miles. As this is really the worst part of the trip (except where there is no sun) we were eternally grateful.

We had a fairly easy four-hour walk to Mihak where the Luluai offered us his house for the night. Mihak was about to kill a pig in celebration of an important marriage and all the big men from the vicinity were there, dressed in their finery. Unfortunately for them, our arrival with its accompanying demands for carriers the next morning, forced the postponement of the all-night singsing.

[I remember that we offered to postpone our departure for 24 hours
so they could hold the singsing—and so we could see it. This offer
they refused.]

We were accompanied by two policemen for the express purpose of
negotiating for carriers and to return with the six patrol boxes which we had
borrowed to bring up a two month supply of food and soap. It was fortunate, for
we ran into carrier problems the next day. After the four hour walk (including
the crossing of a cane suspension bridge 80 feet above the Ason, which was
rotten) we arrived at Sahi and the Mihak carriers immediately departed to go
back and kill their pig and we could gather only enough men and women to
carry one case apiece with food and bedding to Pomalal three hours further on.
One of the Policemen stayed behind with the remaining cargo. One half hour
before Pomalal we got caught in a torrential cloud burst and arrived drenched
only to discover our cargo contained only (dry) shirts—no shorts! However our
expensive [Abercrombie] "safari" shorts proved their worth by drying in record
time as we stood over the fire.

We spent the next day at Pomalal (a very nice village) waiting for the
cargo to catch up and taking the opportunity to swim and wash hair and relax!
The cargo arrived at noon, but no relief carriers. However, by 8 a.m. the next
morning enough arrived to carry my cargo to Umbi and as my police escort was
in a great hurry to get back to Kandrian, we left trusting that Ann's carriers
would arrive in time for her departure to Dulago. In six hours we arrived in
Umbi and within fifteen minutes the borrowed patrol boxes were emptied and
the policeman was off with them to Kandrian. This last part of the trip
definitely proved that my walking condition has improved. The mountains
didn't seem half as big (as before) and I even did our own "little" hill-climb up
from the river to the village without stopping (it usually is a "killer" after a
long walk).

Thank you for the lollies [hard candy], toys etc. They are a great hit and
the lollies buy a bucket of drinking water any time. We made exit plans (back
to the USA) while in Rabaul. Tentatively we plan to arrive home around
September 15, via Bangkok, Manila, Hong Kong and Hawaii....Love Jane

[I paid the younger set (four to twelve years old) a lolly for each
container, of any size, filled with fresh spring drinking water. The
smallest four-year-old lad carried my canteen, and the largest a
plastic bucket. I never lacked for water carriers. They filled the large
yellow plastic trash (now water) container every morning, providing
drinking water for any villager who wished it, and the adults made
sure this drinking water was pure enough and uncontaminated for
their children to drink.]

Umbi, Jan 19, 1964
Dear Ann,

Bruce's [Malaria control] cargo has just arrived here, so I expect Bruce to
follow momentarily. We heard the conch shell blast this morning so I've been

struggling to write letters. (Continued 10 p.m.) He arrived just at 3 and we've had a pleasant visit, but I've only got a few of the necessary letters finished.

Arrived back here [from Pomalal] by 2 p.m. due to the policeman hurrying us up as he wanted to go on to Arihi to sleep! (He didn't make it, his carriers reported, but slept in a *matmat* on the way.) I didn't get a chance to write Algy—so if you think we have anything to say to him—do so.

A real household crisis developed when we (Ningbi and I) discovered the entire bag of rice had been consumed in the week between the time it got back up here [while we were off on holiday] and last Monday when Debli left for the Arihi singsing. Debli was still in Arihi and arrived back at noon today.

One thing about these people, they may steal from their mothers and lie through their teeth, but they are also the greatest tattletales I've ever known. Everyone was only too willing to tell me *all* of Debli's misdeeds—feeding rice to lasses and pigs, giving tobacco to lasses, smoking my tin tobacco and not doing any of the housecleaning (quite evident), none of the major washing or garden weeding and not looking after the house at all. He did look after Kilok and Belo [my puppies] very well and got the new mission Brothers to feed them while he was away. There is more but I'm sleepy—anyway I got properly mad when he did arrive and tried to lie his way out. If it was anyone but Debli, I would have fired him on the spot—as Kasli [the Tultul] suggested. However, he said he would work without pay until he made up the deficit and I added the severe penalty of going to Kandrian to carry up another bag of rice (but I guess I'll have to buy it as he has no money). He's been working like a beaver all afternoon, washing clothes, weeding the garden and cooking. (Ningbi has retreated into the background.) He (Debli) has been clamoring for his "presents," but I think I'll withhold them for some time. He needs a good lesson. Oh, but I'm mad! So with a plunge, we're back to normal, but if this had happened before the vacation, I'd be off the deep end tonight. Now, I'm rather enjoying the fight.

Anyway, Debli will be going to Kandrian sometime soon—when I don't exactly know—but if within the next few days, you have more outgoing mail shoot it over. (I'll also instruct Debli to pick up our first class mail—he alone won't be able to carry more and *I won't* pay anyone to help him.) With Bruce's arrival we really didn't have time to finish the fight, so things are still a bit up in the air. Must to bed. Love, Jane

PS. Your water bottle was discovered by Ningbi in the bottom of my rucksack, under the onions, when we unpacked. (Quiet! I can hear your curses over here—and I don't blame you a bit!)

[We both suffered greatly from thirst while trekking and although there were usually many streams, they were often undrinkable because they were considered polluted by the locals, and also begin to dry up or go underground at this time of year.]

Dulago, Tuesday Jan 21
Dear Jane;

Bruce just left and Mangdali just announced that he was going to Umbi, so I don't have time to do more than write this. I'll try to get someone over on Friday with letters and especially with the reports [to National Science Foundation and National Geographic Society]. I hope that won't be too late for you. I just did not have the strength to get the reports done before Bruce's arrival. The trip up, however, wasn't nearly as bad as expected. We left Pomalal shortly after you, when the Hutkihyu line turned up, and arrived at Valngin to find the *entire* able-bodied male population of Dulago plus females, waiting and fed to the teeth, as you might expect. However, though there was plenty of carrying on, the only real statements (about how tired they were of being summoned to Pomalal) were directed to the policeman, and relations seem to be OK at the moment.

Trip took only two hours to Valngin (vs. over three on the way down) and a little over two to Hutkihyu. I think we got in a bit after 3 (and I paid a fortune, but we'll ignore that for the moment).

What a horror story about Debli. I'm glad you're in fighting trim. Especially because the trip back was so much less grueling than expected, I don't regret a moment of the vacation. Finding it a trifle hard to settle down to work, but the village is back in residence. Four reputed cases of dysentery waiting for me (and three bad burn cases), but the former seem all right now. No news of any consequence that I know of. I've been pretty thoroughly occupied with unpacking. Left my toothbrush at Pomalal, by the way. What a mind! Road to Kandrian strewn with my gear. Love Ann

Umbi, Jan 21
Dear Ann,

I feel in the middle of a 3-ring circus: When Bruce left, a large contingent from Miu arrived with spears and skirt materials [fibers and leaves] to trade, and Kahame killed a huge fat wild pig—then today in the middle of the transactions, we worked a talk [local court procedure] about my stolen goods and it looks like the talk will go on for sometime and perhaps end with a handwashing trial [with "poison water"]. But I am *not* involving the Kiap in this. This is for public announcement, as we have so many visitors here, the whole region will and should know the facts. I am asking that money be backed (returned) and in the meanwhile I'm deducting from Debli's wages. What was stolen were 2 tins of fruit, 2 tins meat, 1 nylon clothesline, 20 sticks tobacco, 3 spoons and some taro (the latter not mine). All very small fare, but "it's the principle of the thing."

Debli, today, admitted (faced with the crowd) that rice was not stolen and he's responsible for its disappearance. He will be going to Kandrian sometime in the next week—I think, and one lad from Arihi has volunteered to go and collect our mail. So if you get things over here Friday, they will be sure to go. I can't make it more definite at the moment, as I feel he (Debli) should be here during the *toktok* (discussion).

Not only all of this—but I discovered the rain gauge empty when I arrived and my informers (*sic*) say, Sutli drank it! [He later told me that he *skelim* [measured it] before drinking, as he had seen me do, and then told me how many measures it totaled, so I could write it down.] I just haven't got around to resuming weather observations and tonight Ningbi broke through the steps to the *haus kiap* [where I kept the thermometers] which totally collapsed—so now I'm less anxious to take temp. readings. In fact, it wouldn't surprise me at all to find the thermometers broken! And to top it off, we have three new (missionary) Brothers, one of whom considers I welcome him in the house and arrives day and night for a chat. As he is the one who fed the dogs, I find it difficult to be uncivil to him, but soon I will have had it.

Four houses have been torn down "to be rebuilt for the Kiap" [in anticipation for annual census patrol]. The Luluai of Hulem killed a pig of Kahame's which had gone wild [killed with permission, that is] and parts of it are *mumuing* [baking] in the village tonight. With this and parts of the Arihi pig, killed and distributed after the singsing, and Kahame's wild pig kill, we've not lacked for fresh meat (one contributing reason to my tranquilized state in all of this). The village is humming with people I haven't seen for months, including the lad who I mentioned to you as one I hadn't seen for three months. (He was working on the road.)

Wed.— It appears the kids are responsible for the missing tins and shillings are gradually being brought in. The Luluai of Seagit is adding his authority to seeing the money is backed [repaid]. Soksili has backed 1/ for a stick of tobacco which he admits taking.

Tried to take a shower yesterday after Bruce kindly unfastened the previously clogged spray for cleaning but the force of the water, pouring into the bucket, broke through the canvas in the bottom! It's very rotten—so I guess it's sponge baths and swims for the next 7 months. What next? I haven't done any "work" since I've come back unless you count the stolen goods business as participant observation. Love Jane

[At this period, and after the holiday, I felt more confident in my knowledge of the culture and of my linguistic ability (being what Ann called "in fighting trim"). Expressing complaints and arguing points, and thus bringing it to their "court" of public opinion, were really tests of my understanding of the legitimacy of the issue in the minds of the locals. Once the legitimacy was acknowledged, the solution which resolved the dispute was quick to follow.]

Dulago, Monday, January 27
Dear Jane,

I was hoping to send down mail this week with the Luluai of Hutkihyu, who's presumably going down to meet his brother from Talasea, but now that he's just been beaten up by the Kiap [CPO], I don't really feel I can ask him to go to the office (later—just heard he's in jail).

R. [the involved Kiap], by the way, was on his best behavior here, full of charm, interest in anthropology, and so on—in singular contrast to the way he has acted on the road. Since he brought my mail, umbrella, and airletters, I was very kindly disposed, and fed him supper before he left again for Pomalal (at 9 p.m.), dragging the reluctant inhabitants of this village behind him, through flooded rivers. All very mysterious behavior, but we'll discuss it when I see you.

[In preparation for the first elections of Papua New Guinean members of the National House of Assembly, all Luluais, Tultuls, and senior men in the region were ordered by the Kiap to assemble at Pomalal for instructions and education. It was unfortunate that the representative of the Government conducting these sessions (a CPO) lost his temper and (quite against the code of behavior for administrative officials) slapped the Luluai of Hutkihyu. Aside from the personal insult, this incident erased from everyone's mind any positive aspect of the education for the coming elections. The involved CPO was shortly transferred. [For further information on the elections see Goodale and Chowning, 1965.]

I've had no fresh meat at all, though I've been well supplied otherwise. Several pigs in Hutkihyu are threatened with death (for eating taro), but this has been going on for months, so I don't dare count on anything.

I hope you've recovered your stolen goods. Nothing missing here, thanks to my nasty suspicious nature, it was all locked up tight. And, after hearing about you, Paiyali assured me again that he "wouldn't dream of stealing from me" because he's "too afraid of the Kiap!" As usual, no mention of any other reason. Love Ann

Umbi Jan 26 1964
Dear Family,
On Friday at 10:30 a.m. rumor was received that all men, women, and children were to go to Pomalal where the Kiap was and if they didn't arrive by 4 p.m. (it's a four to five hour walk) they would all go to jail. At that moment practically everyone was in the bush. Suspecting the whole rumor was false, Ningbi blew the conch shell to call people in (no one heard it, they say). Ningbi (left) and arrived back with a native policeman at 4 p.m. in a drenching rain (3 and 1/2 inches in 2 hours). The correct version was that everyone was to go to Pomalal on Saturday to hear election education speech by the Cadet Patrol Officer on Sunday. All but one elderly and one very pregnant woman and 2-3 kids aged 2-10 years left. I cooked for myself which was a pleasant change and conversed almost totally in Kaulong for 24 hours.

They all arrived back late this evening and I've only had time to question a few as to what the CPO told them. One lad about 13-14 years old said they had fenced New Britain dividing it in half and one fence belonged to the whites and another to the blacks (in reference to the electoral divisions I expect). Debli said the CPO showed them a book with pictures of men in it but he didn't point out any of them for election and that they were to go back to Pomalal, but he hadn't a clue as to why, except it was something about a house for whites and another for blacks!

Umbi, Monday, Jan 27
Dear Ann,

Many thanks for your 2 notes (and return of my bra). Debli hasn't gone yet due to "one thing or another," which includes my no real urging of him to go in order to get as much correspondence out of the way—including three months of weather reports. I'm returning the financial data (pertaining to our NSF Grant) to you with a copy of the report I will have sent to the Museum. I can't imagine how we managed to spend $600 on camp supplies in the States, but am only curious, not worried. I accept fully your recommended "revisions" and have warned the Museum about travel expenses increasing and have requested them to hold on to our remaining $3000 until further notice.

Big news today, and big dilemma. At four, Debli and Ningbi came running up to my house shouting for me to go stop Maulme from killing one of her newborn *twin* boys, who were born about 200 yards from the village! They, D and N, had already sent some women to talk to Maulme, saying it was against the law and if she didn't kill one, the Kiap would give her lots of money. But they (the women) returned saying Maulme was going to kill one. What would you have done? I said I couldn't *tok ples* [speak adequately in Kaulong language] to the women and even if I could, I wouldn't, as it wasn't any of my business—and D and N should get the Luluai or Tultul to talk as this was *their* business (as Village officials). Kahame [the Luluai] appeared at that moment, so I repeated it to him. However, I believe, he did nothing about this affair as, immediately D and N accused Kahame of calaboosing [jailing] Idaso for not having built a village house and the discussion regarding Idaso went on for at least an hour. So I greatly suspect one twin was strangled. Maulme was the one who I was sure would have "produced" while we were away as she was enormous a month ago. During the past week, small boys were laughing at her walk and imitating her. She has some bad leg TUs (tropical ulcers), so I hope they will be an excuse to visit her soon. For heaven's sake—keep this whole thing quiet—(see later).

The affair d'Idaso is very interesting. He was the one calaboosed before for not having a house at all, and now, since his return, is the only one who 1) has a new strong house and 2) whose house was completely missed by the Policeman, as it's hidden between me and the Mission! Both D and N say Kasli deliberately calaboosed him. Kasli denies this and so does Kahame. Idaso is the only one in jail. "We" are full of indignation at the Kiap's behavior and *completely confused* as to the elections. But four houses have been torn down and two are being built above the ground—"we" are also *scared* [of the Kiap's annual census patrol].

Just before all were summoned to Pomalal, a troop of Mius (Miu people) came visiting, including Dengli—the Tultul of Iemduh—a good Pidgin speaker and one of the most "sophisticated" young men from these hills I've met. Full of questions about what we were doing, our financial position, our life in America and work opportunities there. They were good questions. Also an invitation to come over there. He *says* they are moving out of the mountains to a place one days walk over straight roads from Kandrian and near the Alimbit river and in good coffee-growing country. His inducements—fast cargo service, good water and no Mts. to climb. If it's true, there go the "wild men of Iemduh" [to quote one patrol report]! In return for all this talk, I got about one and a half hours of Miu vocabulary from him and although I skipped some of the harder concepts in the basic Swadesh list, I have a good sample of the major phonemic shifts: (P to H, i.e. *Homasang* (people), and prefix *Bi-* to *Hi-*, for place indicator. [B and P are the same phoneme, as we found later.] This latter is not completely confirmed in all instances, but I now have a good basis for tackling our Miu widow. I would have gotten more if Pomalal hadn't interrupted their visit as he was only quite willing as an informant. But when all went to Pomalal [regarding the coming elections], they [the Miu] all went home [in the opposite direction] ahead of time.

We have eaten 5 wild pigs since my return and one *sikau* [wallaby]. Due to intense questioning as to what you (and the Kiap) wrote in your notes, Kahame says he will kill a pig and sell enough to me to be able to send some to you.

Wednesday—Went to visit Maulme today and both twins are still alive and adorable! Yesterday a woman said, in Kaulong, they were both alive because Kahame talked to them, but I had to see for myself. Also yesterday, Kasli asked me whether I heard that Maulme carried *one pikanini*? I caught the stress on the word one, and said I'd been told she had two. He said *"bai wan em i dai"* [later one will die] and, *"mipela blakskin no savi karim tupela wantaim"* [we blackskinned people don't give birth to two children at one time]. I repeated my "it's none of my business," but today other men too have asked me, "is one very small?" and expressed the feeling that one would eventually die. The women, on the other hand and Maulme included, don't appear so pessimistic. One baby is smaller than the other, but both appear healthy and both are nursing and Maulme has her hands full, literally. While I was there, she bound both of their heads for the first time (approximately 40 hours after birth). You will probably hear of this through normal channels, but I think it wiser to say nothing about my reporting it to you. At the moment all *pas* [notes/letters] received here are followed by worried and detailed questioning.

[Ann notes that a local PO had outlawed head binding on the grounds that the local people needed to enter the twentieth century and that Luluai hats looked ridiculous on a pointed head. However, nearly all infants born while we were there had their heads bound. The binding is of soft barkcloth over which a very thin vine rope is wound around firmly but not tightly. The binding is loosened at least once a day and merely molds the skull with gentle pressure into a desired high crown shape. Unbound heads of those who are born close to the coast are considered by Umbi and Dulago people to be "ugly." The binding may be terminated anywhere between one to six months.]

How is your house standing up to the wind? My roof is torn to pieces on the NW corner and I pray no rain will come until something can be done. And this afternoon all the men forced me out of the house, convinced it was going to fall down. Debli cut three large posts and braced the house against the wind and it seems to stop the major shakes, when people "heavy-foot" [stamp] about. My room is half inch deep in *kanda* (thatch) shreds—most discouraging. Love, Jane

PS. Kahame says the Luluai of Hutkihyu is at Pomalal in *haus sik* (aid post), not in jail, but that all his *lain* (village) have been calaboosed.

Umbi, Wednesday, Feb. 5
Dear Ann,

Mail arrived 7 p.m. last night. So far (7 a.m.) no volunteers to carry your mail to Dulago. Will put pressure on if anyone shows up. Saturday's plane "shot through" [could not land in Kandrian] due to rain, but Algy held my carriers over for a diverted Monday Lae-Rabaul flight which did have our mail. As you can see it contains: no film, and three misdirected letters. On the vague chance you may send someone down before I do, I'm sending them on to you (to return). Included a note from me to Algy as he has requested information from me on the true state of Idaso's house. He's released Idaso and says there is no hurry about informing him.

No real news here—twins moved back to village yesterday. The Luluai keeps asking me, what should they do about them? i.e. take them to Kandrian or stay? I still feel hesitant about suggesting *anything*. Question—does nature usually/normally provide enough milk for two?

Terry's (NGS) note to me, in effect, said my pictures showed a "monotony of activity, only a few pictures of food preparation, and that in the sun my technique was rusty!" My house is still up, but I lost a number of nights of sleep, too! Love, Jane

Dulago January 30
Dear Jane,

Lelus just arrived with your [previous 1/27] letter and with the news that the person to whom I gave the bra yesterday "threw it away on the road" and he picked it up and took it to Umbi. The person involved is Pehedli, one of Yangli's sons, and he had announced while here yesterday that he was en route to Umbi. Admittedly I rather forced it on him, but I'm still pretty annoyed. Second time recently I've had refusals to do something very minor from

Yambon men. I'm plotting my revenge; I think the only thing is to refuse to buy food from him. He has so many relatives that it's rather tricky.

Ngolu appeared just before Lelus with the news that he'd talked the Kiap out of jailing the Hutkihyu men (the Luluai went straight on to Kandrian to meet his brother's plane) and tried to do the same with Hidaso [Idaso], but the Kiap insisted on seeing Kasli about it. Ngolu's story is that Kasli wanted to get Hidaso in trouble because he was angry about not receiving a share of payment for the latter's marriage. (All this before I got your letter.) What's the story there? How fascinating about the twins, I haven't said anything. I think I would have done what you did; poorly developed moral sense on our part, I'm afraid.

The $300 apiece for gear in the States seemed to mount up, what with duffel bags, shower buckets, boots (a fortune in themselves), and pretty well all clothes taken into account. I threw in vitamins, knives, ammo cases and anything else I could think of. What went here and should have gone elsewhere was photographs, physicals, et al. I think we really did spend that much. What really appalls me is the amount spent in Rabaul. Really! But I fear our budget estimate last year (in the application for a grant) was ridiculously low. Incidentally, I seem to spend about £60.0.0 a month here. In all cases where our expenses were uneven, I've doubled the larger number.

Sunday—Word of the twins has reached here. I was naturally asked why I hadn't told them, and told the truth. Haven't gone into it any farther yet. Have you heard the story yet about one of the Fathers interfering with the CPO's progress through Kaulong? God knows how much of it is true, but it will certainly win plenty of adherents for the *Popis* (Roman Catholics).

We've got three new houses being built to date, with presumably two more to come. Unfortunately, I feel I know all there is to know about house-building, but at least it keeps a few people in the village. I feel I'm accomplishing very little ethnographically, but have finally gotten back to typing notes, and it really is useful. So, in fact, is the several month's delay in doing so. I can fit things together and spot some at least of the discrepancies. But I must buckle down again to questioning.

I don't think my house has been damaged as much as yours by the *lambur* [NW winds] (it's a couple of months younger of course), but enough thatch is off one end to make raining into the study a serious problem (plus several new leaks). So far I haven't been able to get anything done about it. What was really doing me in was lack of sleep, what with the heat and shaking of the house. I do hope the worst was over, though I gather that sometimes it (the *lambur*) continues for weeks.

They've just had a tooth-blackening [male initiation ritual] at Valngin, but no one from here went, though they did from Yambon, and I don't expect to get much in the way of useful details. Is it all right for us to meet at Silop on the 15th?

[We planned to hunt deliberately for the chipped flint tools *(imlos)*, which we had been picking up casually in this location on every exchange visitation trip.]

We're having, by comparison with the past, a real plague of flies and mosquitoes (latter certainly bred in my privy while I was away). Also the drinking water seems to contain frog spawn, and tastes foul. And still no fresh meat. Otherwise all is well. Tabus on saying one's own name here apply only to children, who won't grow up if they say them.

Congratulations on your Miu material. I still feel guilty for neglecting my one opportunity to get data on the [Karore] language across the Andru (river). Ps. In Lakalai (on the north coast), there was a tendency to let one twin starve because they were considered too much trouble, but both Lakalai and Molima (in the Massim region) had plenty of living twins. That's all I know on the milk question. Love, Ann

Umbi, Feb. 16 1964
Dear Family,
Ann is here to visit and goes back to Dulago tomorrow. On Saturday I hiked over the mountain to the village of Silop to meet Ann and do some concentrated collecting of chipped flint artifacts, of which we have always found one or two on our monthly visiting hikes. Iamopli and Ligiok, two lads of 10 and 14 years, accompanied me, and as we ambled over the trail with our eyes glued to the road, we found a number of rather poor specimens. Then we settled down by the Silop stream to wait for Ann. There we discovered the stream bed literally lined with very crude, but unmistakable large flint (core) tools. Ann arrived shortly with her two carrier-companions and we spent the next hour accepting or rejecting specimens brought to us by our eager hunters. We found at least 30. We were limited really only by the constant problem of weight limited by what we could carry back to Umbi. Just after leaving the stream, Iamopli (the youngest boy) found a perfectly beautiful specimen. Since these are the only chipped flint tools ever to be reported from New Britain we feel these are quite exciting. We've decided to deposit them with the Australian National University in Canberra because we've received a specific request, and so they will be in a central location for any future archeological investigations out here. We are, however, quite mystified for the range of types indicates extensive woodworking of which there is no evidence in the present culture.
Love, Jane

Umbi, Feb. 21, 1964
Dear Ann,
Ningbi says he's going your way tomorrow—so what's new with you?
We have had quite a day. The culmination of several events. A lot of people were in residence and this (as is becoming customary) resulted in airing of grievances and settling *dinau* [debts]. First there was pig business—you see—the pig of Nauli's which was killed at Angus was one of two of his which were accused of taro stealing. The second was killed the day after, and the day after that they discovered the 2nd pig (already eaten) was innocent, and it was a

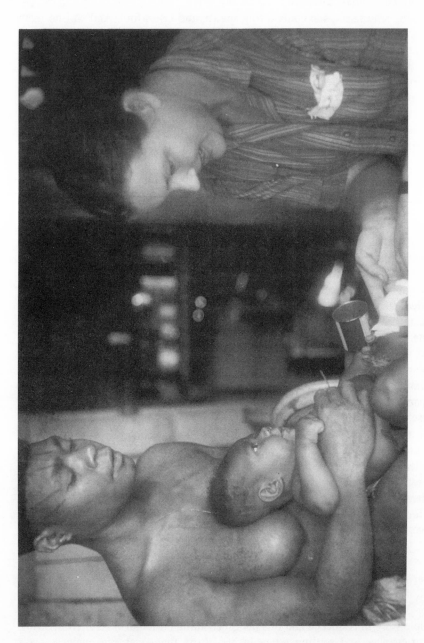

Tending a Burn Victim

pig which belonged to two other men which was guilty, so *that* pig was killed yesterday. As you can imagine the paying (of resulting debts) was complex, but the pigs delicious. (I also got a large *sikau* [wallaby] in between.)

The next business of today was Liem getting *"kros"* [angry] with Utkunut, with the result that Utkunut has taken her two youngest children to Miu. This episode I was just trying to straighten out when Kasli (Tultul) returned from Pomalal (a story in itself—see later), and tried to get everyone together to hear what he had to say and as usual some women remained by their house and Kasli shouted in Pidgin *"Yu no kan sindaun long plati as bilong yu bai yu kan harim mi"* [You must not sit down on your (contested word) ass if you want to hear me]. The words *"plati as"* produced an explosion from Kahame (Luluai) and other big men (none of whom except Kahame can speak Pidgin) as they interpreted this as *tok nogut* [swearing].

A discussion resulted in which I was included, of what in *Tok Pisin* is *tok plei* (permitted sexual joking) and what is *tok nogut* [obscene swearing]. I bowed out at this point. Ningbi says *plati* (bloody, in the British/Australian slang sense) *as* (ass) is all right in *Tok Pisin* and so is *bulsit* [bullshit] which Kasli also used, but *bastid* [bastard], if used to another, is a jailable offense. Anyway, I expected spears and they were mentioned, but Kasli decided to go to the Kiap (in Kandrian) to prove that he hadn't used *tok nogut*. He ran to my house and grabbed his official (Tultul's) hat and set off followed in half a minute by Kahame with *his* Luluai's hat, and one of the other men who had been offended. They got as far as the Silop turnoff, when Kahame suggested they all return and *stretim tok* [settle it] at Umbi. Kasli returned, but only to wait for the Kiap to come here. Kahame and family have gone *long hap* [off somewhere]. Kasli is fed up (I don't really blame him).

He (Kasli) and wife and Sutli were the only ones to reach Pomalal [for election voting]. Kahame was sick. I really did think he was sick as he was sleeping in the *haus boi* [men's house] all day yesterday, but today I wonder if he wasn't faking an excuse not to go. About six other men left to go to Pomalal, but at Hulem were told two reasons they should not go further. First: Only men who had previously fought and killed with spears and *plank* [shields] were to go to the election. Second: All women must discard their *purpur* [skirts] before coming to Pomalal. Kasli heard the second reason, but went ahead with his wife who did put on a *laplap* [calico], but the other men (hearing only the first reason) came back. Kasli is mostly furious because of people returning and not following *him*.

[The men who returned told me that only fighters were to go to Pomalal. "Weren't they fighters?" I asked them. "Yes," they replied, "but the Kiap had told them to stop fighting." Faced with an incomprehensible and unresolvable conflict in Kiap orders, they chose to be prudent and do nothing. It was many months later when it suddenly dawned on me that all the while the Kiaps had been saying *"election,"* the Kaulong had heard the word *leksun*, which, in their language, means to fight one another. Little wonder that they were confused.]

I wrote a note to the election official who turned out to be Bruce Cowgill [Agricultural officer], asking for any information on the Kiap's [census] patrol and also informing, whoever, about the mix-up over the [rumor regarding] injections. Bruce wrote back that he felt it was important for the Kiap to make a patrol up here "as soon as possible" because of the *kivung* (cargo-cult talk) and also evidently about the "medical problems at the Aid Post." He thanked me for the injection information and said he would include it. As a PS. he said "incidents regarding the CPO are in the hands of the ADO," whatever that means.

From Kasli's report of what Bruce told him—I'm impressed. He [Bruce] first told Iangme (Kasli's wife) to go get her *purpur* [grass and fiber skirt] and put it on and second, that if strange rumors come, don't all react, but send someone to Kandrian, or to the source, to find out whether the *tok* is straight or not.

We have found your little *imlo* [flint] projectile point. Am holding it here for you. I don't want it to get chipped. Nothing else of note except I seem to have a lower digestive upset. Perhaps it's all the fresh meat! Love, Jane

Dulago, Thursday (Feb. 20?)
Dear Jane,

First, Easter is March 29. Second, I did send your letter (but not the film) down to Algy. The main reason was that I got back to find that the whole village had left in response to one rumor that the Kiap was coming at once, started back on a second (rumor) that he wouldn't come for three weeks, turned back on the road with a third (rumor), that he was coming on schedule, and meanwhile a whole group had set off on the basis of a fourth (rumor), that all those who didn't make it to Pomalal for shots were to go to Kandrian at once for the same! Jesus. In the midst of this Milingli claims actually to have seen the Kiap in person (I'm dubious because I don't see how he could have made it back here when he did). In any case, he's done so much walking that I'm afraid that he either won't go to Kandrian at all or will go straight on from Pomalal (and unfortunately without instructions to pick up my mail).

The word Milingli brought back was that absolutely everyone was to go to Pomalal. However, Paiyali tricked me by giving instructions to his mother and one little girl that they were to stay with me. I didn't find out about this till so late yesterday afternoon that nothing could really be done. (I did think they'd become awfully docile about the idea of leaving me at the mercy of the *tamberans* [ghosts]. Maybe they do have some slight personal affection for me after all.)

I'm feasting on masses of *pitpit* [*Saccharum Edule*]—first so far. Have you had any yet? My last watermelon vine is dying, though. One tomato is developing.

We did quite well on *imlos* on the way back—rather hard on the tobacco supply, but a couple of really nice specimens. With four of us looking, we could hardly fail, but I was a bit embarrassed when Nehebi picked up two good ones on the Yambon-Dulago road.

Paper-eating insects struck last night. I'd hoped this place was free of them. It'll be an awful bother to have to put all papers away every night.

Saturday—I was thinking of adding this when Ningbi arrived. Glad to hear about the little *imlo*. I've suddenly been so overwhelmed that I've had to cut prices to half-a-stick. Four (flints) were brought me from Valngin yesterday (by a boy who accompanied us from Silop, and then went to the elections), and then at night four excellent specimens were brought me from our drinking stream! So we (me and 2 little boys) spent the morning wading through it, and did fairly well. It's nothing like Silop, but it's still pretty good and indicates that there'll be something to do on those dull trips to the stream.

I wrote Bruce about the *purpurs* and various other rumors and was also impressed with his reply—and the cookies!—though I swear I'll never say any more about your spelling, after reading his!

Paiyali has gone to the beach (coast) along with half the population to collect *dinau* [debts]. Another third has not returned from Pomalal, including Milingli, who did go on to Kandrian. (I fear others have too—annoying because I'm likely to run out of supplies before I dig up enough people to go again.) Also I find I don't seem to have any mailers (for films)—but do have a spare biscuit tin. I think I'd better send the film back to you, in view of immediate prospects. I am desperately anxious to get more film before the [long-awaited Dulago] singsing. Plans are still to have it *very* soon, but there's one more trading expedition necessary [to acquire shell valuables] after this one returns, so it'll certainly be a couple of weeks.

Life here has been very dull compared with yours. Obviously you just got your rumors a little later—but no worse than ours.

Love, Ann

Dulago, Monday (2/24?)

Dear Jane,

Nehebi says he's going over, so I'll take the opportunity. I'm really irritated with Chin Cheu, though not awfully surprised. I really feel threatened by missionaries. Ngolu and Milingli report that the Father (White) has ordered them to build the church between here and Yambon, and that he'll be back up here after the bishop's departure. Well, maybe the conflict of cultures will bring out things I'm not finding out otherwise.

Nothing of interest has happened. Paiyali's not back yet, and I'm knee-deep in dirty clothes and dishes. Finally was brought a few shrimp yesterday and today—first fresh meat since Umbi. The report is that you'll be sending someone down this week, so please do try to arrange for us to get some more film. I feel awfully frustrated not daring to take pictures. Sorry not to have limes for you, but the Luluai and his wife are away, and who knows when they'll be back. So what fascinating things are happening in Umbi? Love, Ann

Umbi, Feb. 25

Dear Ann,

So what's new, you ask? We are in the middle of a crisis—Don't breathe a word of this, as at the moment I'm the *only* one, aside from the principals, who knows. This morning Debli "lost" his laplap and trousers [exposing himself] in front of two young girls and instead of spearing them on the spot out of shame (the old law), he is leaving tomorrow for Kandrian and Talasea (he hopes), for [an] indefinite period of time as he is full of shame. A number of people have asked me why he's leaving, but I've been sworn to secrecy.

The other event was that Gospo and Naingli snuck off to Kandrian yesterday without telling me or asking if I had any cargo for them to carry down or back—the bastards!, particularly so, as Gospo borrowed 5/- last week and said when his foot was better he'd go to Kandrian for me. So I don't know who, or when I'll be able to get anything back up here. Debli will take our films down to mail. I'm toying with the idea of giving him a "*pas*" [note] for Gospo should he meet up with him in Kandrian. I'm holding fast to the films that I have and will save them for your pig-feast—unless we sacrifice a virgin here first!

Can't think of anything more, except I have new *kanda* [thatch] on the john and on the end of the house and I hope Ningbi and Debli will finish the rest of it today before D leaves. I'm also hoping I can talk Ningbi into working alone for me, as I think I will be far happier. Love, Jane

Umbi, 2/28/64

Dear Ann,

Dalian says he will be happy to carry a *pas* to you when he finishes helping Ningbi patch my roof. Debli did *not* go to Talasea. His shame was bought off for the price of one shell! Damn! But he did go to Kandrian yesterday on a cargo trip junior style with three young lads, Ligiok, Iamopli and Lesum and two young ladies. And they will collect our mail (perhaps minus newspapers if the load is too much), but with either NGS or Chin Cheu film, and all first class mail (this is, of course, assuming John [store-keeper] follows instructions), and some tins. Today Kaliam and Dangit took off for Kandrian to buy rice for themselves and I persuaded them to bring up some tobacco. So if you get desperately short of supplies let me know. I feel I'm living from day to day, but will be in fairly good shape when they come back with some items.

Spent a delightful day yesterday doing absolutely nothing and alone in the village except for Litem [5 or 6 years old] who evidently was told to keep me company.

By the way a whole slew of Yambon females are now sitting inside my house with a cooking fire underneath! Nothing more of news. Sent my (never working) radio back and demanded money refunded. We shall see. Love, Jane

Dulago, Saturday

Dear Jane,

I'm really delighted to hear you've managed to get someone off. My present plans are to send a line a week from tomorrow (March 8?) so send over any mail you have.

Paiyali, who swore (*mi no giamon*) [I'm not lying] that he'd return from the beach last Monday, is still not back. I held the fort alone for quite a time, but now Leklam is cooking my *pubak* [a native green] and washing my clothes. I'm doing all the primus cooking, which gives me an excuse not to give him tinned meat, on which we're awfully low (thanks to getting almost no fresh meat since my return).

The big news is that I've finally started getting story texts. The main informant is Nehebi (I finally deduced from the eyes that he must be Lelus's older brother, which he is—otherwise known as Sulubo). As you will see when you compare his versions of stories with yours, they are both condensed (dictation speed is awfully wearing) and expurgated (I don't think they were at first, but Leklam's reaction to one tidbit inhibited him), and I suspect full of Kaulong-isms (mother is from Hulem). They also leave a lot to be desired both as regards recording and translation. But they are nevertheless full of useful linguistic and ethnographic data. I'm typing them up in order of ethnographic interest.

I conducted a tour of the wettest portions of the house during yesterday's rain, and got the usual expressions of concern, but still nothing has been done. Unfortunately the study receives the worst of it. Monday, they finally put 6/ worth of new *gorgors* [thatch] on it.

A family from Valngin has just announced that it's moving here because it's closer to their *ples matmat* [graveyard/hamlet] in which they live. I hope they will, mainly because the wife (from Seuk—one of Paiyali's numerous first cousins) speaks Pidgin.

Monday—The people who visited the beach finally started trickling back yesterday (including Paiyali). They've brought loads of mussels which are giving me a couple of day's relief from the tins (but not Paiyali, who says he was sorry over the delay because he missed his tinned meat so much).

Tuhung's baby was born dead (circumstances are slightly suspicious, but it's long been thrown into a hole in the ground), so there go my chances of observing infant care. I suspect that Ilme (wife of the old man with the goiter) is pregnant, but I'm not sure she'd have the baby before I leave. Much discussion is going on because men here have heard that the Yambon men have called them "women." Maybe something interesting will develop.

It seems awfully late in the day to have learned that boys cannot say the names of girls who are in the "potential spouse" category, but so it goes. Ramifications must be explored, but it seems definite that a boy cannot say the name of a daughter of a remote relative he calls *taso,* [father's sister], girls who also engage in *ulal,* courtship fights, with him, whereas he can say the name of the true father's sister's daughter. And at your end?

We're raising a ruckus because my one really large ripening tomato bears the deep imprints of someone's extremely dirty fingernails. The idea is to keep the other five intact, if possible. My watermelons have all died by slow stages.

Tuesday—I'm feeling very guilty for not going to a three pig singsing at Yambon last night (we had a one pig singsing here, and I now have a leg). The reason to go was on the chance that I'd see some *ulal* [courtship fighting]; the reason I didn't was that I was really afraid to tackle that path at night after hours of steady rain with the knee still stiff. If I don't see *ulal* at our dance [the long expected singsing over the large tusker pig], I'll make a real effort afterwards. Love Ann

Postscript

It was inevitable that problems would arise between our household help and ourselves. Stealing, telling tales, and at times disappearing were not unexpected behaviors, but always emotionally difficult to handle. Our household help came from the villages we worked in and Ningbi and Debli both told me that people were getting cross (jealous) of them, and they had to give most of their pay to these relatives. On the other hand, only we knew how limited our money and supplies were and we had no relatives to help us—as I tried to explain to them. Perhaps the most insightful comment came from Ningbi who said, following one argument I had with Debli, that of all those in Umbi only he understood me (my values) because only he had spent sufficient time living with Europeans to learn their ways. "When you, Jane, say something you mean it!" he told me, emphasizing that indeed I was correct in thinking that Kaulong never tell the truth deliberately. Once I understood this I found it much easier to live with my hosts. I came to understand that it was as if they were living in a continuous poker game, where one should always try to hide one's hand, lie, and bluff to win political position and power.

I also came to understand that this "ethos" was behind the constant and nearly universal sending of predominantly false rumors. The problem was that one never was sure if the next rumor was for real, or not. However, no matter how much power and authority a headman (Luluai) or hamlet leader *(midan)* might have over other hamlets and persons, none came close to the authority and power of the Kiap and his minions. Rumors said to come from the Kiap could not be safely ignored without considering the consequences.

In my later (1967 to 1968) work in Angelek, I asked the people to list for me the behavior characteristics of Kiaps they knew, who they thought were "good" and those who were "bad." Quite surprisingly, because it was directly opposite to my own evaluation, "good" Kiaps were those who gave out orders and "laws" and always jailed/punished when these were not carried out. "Bad" Kiaps gave out "laws" too, but they did not *always* punish someone for not carrying them out. Instead they talked, and talked and talked, to everyone, about it first. And they often did not require the same punishment. The former were "good" because "We know exactly what they will do if we don't follow the 'law'. Therefore, it's up to us to choose to follow or not follow." With "bad" Kiaps "we never know what to expect." Clearly and logically, unpredictability of another's behavior is psychologically unsettling to say the least to *all* concerned.

Waiting for the Kiap to come to take the annual census and inspect the village to see that all previous orders had been carried out regarding houses, latrines, and graveyards was a very stressful time for everyone. Would their village houses (in which they rarely slept) pass inspection? Would the village be clear of all grass? Does every house have a latrine? Are any deaths suspicious to the Kiap? Should they have taken the twins to Kandrian as ordered? Will he notice (outlawed) headbinding? Who is really going to bring a threatened argument to the Kiap to adjudicate? Does anyone have a tropical ulcer or illness he or she should have taken to the *haus sik* (aid post)? Since all of these are thought to be jailable offenses, the ultimate question is: Who will go to jail *this* time?

With the constant and conflicting rumors of imminent arrival of the Kiap, it is no wonder that all of us got fed up with this interference with more important activities. It's hard to appreciate that this is politics as usual when one is in the middle of it.

The flint tools which we collected at Silop (and which Ann continued collecting in her later trips to the region) eventually led to preliminary archeological excavations there beginning in the late 1960s (Specht et al. 1983). In the most recent excavations (in the 1990s) a date of 35,000 years before present has been calculated by radiocarbon for the earliest habitation in the region (Pavlides 1993). The collection that we made in 1964 is now located in the Museum of Papua New Guinea (in Port Moresby), with the exception of a small collection of thirty pieces housed in the Department of Anthropology at Bryn Mawr.

Chapter 7

This Marriage Is a Gold Mine

Umbi, March 6 1964

Dear Family,

Wonders will never cease. I sent down a small cargo trip last Friday to collect our six weeks-plus mail and today five others have *volunteered* to leave Monday for Kandrian for more cargo and there are rumors that more will be volunteering before Monday. I think the changing factor is that I've split large loads, which four men changing places used to carry in a patrol box, into four small loads which each person carries without relief and everyone's happy (and I even save money). This also means I can make small enough loads for the youngest lads aged 10—16 years to carry and *they* don't complain.

[I paid the young carriers in advance at a rate of a shilling per can of food. Some of the smallest kids were now able to earn money (to spend at the trade store), even with a load of only ten cans. For loads such as kerosene and rice I paid 15/ to a single carrier, usually a woman, who could balance such loads on her head better than a man. For the young lads and women this was, for most, their first opportunity to earn money to spend in the trade store and thus the sudden volunteering—for more trips than I could afford or need. Ann was unable to follow my lead, for her carriers had to pass through Kaulong territory in which, they believed, lived many sorcerers. Sengseng men would not permit their young people or women to journey to Kandrian alone.]

The Tultul (who has been the most helpful of the two headmen) almost left for good yesterday because his wife wouldn't talk to him, nor feed him and he was "shamed." I was upset at the thought of his leaving, but when four other men "struck in sympathy" and said they too would go, leaving Umbi gardens in poor shape for two years, the wife and Tultul shook hands and exchanged money [resolving the conflict]. One of my best informants, Gospo, however, really left for two years plantation work because the widow of his mother's brother has claimed her deceased husband's taro which—because they used to strangle widows and bury them with their husbands—rightfully (under Kaulong law) belongs to the deceased's sister's son, in this case, Gospo.

[Leaving the scene of a conflict is a frequently used strategy to delay resolution until both parties are over the heat of the argument and ready to resolve the problem—when the departed person returns— often many months or years later.]

I have had a fairly good supply of fresh meat once or twice (and rarely three times) a week. Mainly pork (both wild and domestic), fish, flying-foxes, and possums. Ann, on the other hand, reports almost none. But we are both awaiting for The Big Dulago Pig killing and singsing, which is scheduled sometime this month. Dulago has been planning this for nearly a year—since before Ann's return last July (1963). They have one giant sized pig to kill and a number of small ones will be killed at the same time. Pork has been promised to at least one Umbi-ite, and so there will be a contingent from here going. I, on Ann's invitation, plan to go with my tape-recorder (assuming it works). I haven't tried it recently and Ann's doesn't work. By the way, Dad—since you ask—in case of emergency, an urgent message from you to me should be cabled c/o ADO Kandrian and a police runner would be sent with a message for me and vice versa. I can get one down to Kandrian by runner. On this cheery note...Love Jane

[My father, after nearly a year, suddenly became worried about my safety. I am not quite sure what set him worrying at this late date.]

Umbi, Sunday March 6 1964
Dear Ann,

I'm feeling in a very mellow mood at the moment for tomorrow an entirely volunteer line is off again to Kandrian. In fact I've had more volunteers than cases or cargo to carry!

Yesterday both Debli and Ningbi wanted to go bush—fine, I thought, I'll write letters in peace, but they insisted that I go to Olias (hamlet) with Ningbi. I only went for the exercise and except for some useful unexpected items, it was the usual boring day. I was left in Olias with two old men and five children (none Pidgin speakers) from 8-12 a.m. while everyone else went to carry planks [hand hewn boards] for the new [hamlet] house. The interesting items were: we were all given ginger [bespelled with anti-sorcery medicine] to eat, which I later found out was because the night before the men had chased (with spears) five poisoners (suspected from Sankiap and Womilo) from the village and that this wasn't the first time. It all ties in with Kanegit's death and the Womilo (dysentery) deaths and our two females (deaths). A good revenge feud situation.

The other interesting event was that the pigs at Olias have been rooting in the old house-grave site and the 2 older boys finished excavating 2 tibia which they gleefully threw at me and we were all set to dig further when the parents arrived and put an end to our "fun." But I later asked Soksili (one of the parents) about two large stones on the grave and he picked up the smaller one and scraped around a little with his knife and unearthed a skull unfortunately not enough to identify, he said, but enough to prove to me that this is where Sutli buried all the Parangin skulls when the Kiap came. They are going to build two plank (new board style) houses here. One on the old site where Yiaragit [the old man without a face] will live until he dies, and one replacing the *banis*-type (fence/log construction) house where the recent and future burials will take place. They are hoping that their efforts will be appreciated by the Kiap (when he does come) and that he doesn't enforce his original demands for a new graveyard for Umbi.

By the way, I've got from Ningbi some clarification on shell exchange at pig killing. In case you haven't also—briefly it's this: The owner (of a pig) usually contracts with a receiver (for head, *het* or rib portion, *banis,* before killing), and the receiver "R" gives owner "O" a shell as evidence of a *contract.* At the killing, "O" must 1) return R's *contract* shell, and 2) repay (*bak)* any *dinau* [debts] owing to "R." I'm not completely sure this is obligatory [it is]. Then "O" must give one of his own shells *'wantaim pik'* (together with the pig-portion) to "R." "R" does not have to pay "O" [with shells] for the pig at this time and I suspect, usually doesn't. But later "R" must pay "O" what he ("R") thinks the pig was worth. "O" is able, at that time, to demand more if necessary. "R" must *also* [at that later time] *bak* [exchange] a shell of his own for the shell he got earlier from "O" *wantaim pik* [with the pork].

All this came out because, evidently Sutli has agreed to be an "R" at your forthcoming pig killing and I wanted to know why? "Because I was asked," he said. And he added, "because I am a man to whom pigs are given" (i.e. because he is known to have shells). Anyway I won't have any problems getting carriers to come with me and the word [of the Dulago pig-kill] should reach us through normal channels. But written notification is, of course, better! Love Jane

Dulago, Friday
Dear Jane,

Having put in a solid spate of letter writing so's to have time to write a "Comment" on a *Current Anthropology* article, I've just decided not to do it. (The deadline is already past, and what I have to say is certainly not important enough to be treated separately), so I'm now bracing myself to settle back to work after two glorious days of reading mail and writing letters. (Everyone was sacked out yesterday after another all night singsing). I've also just been infuriated by Mubudli's making a conscientious attempt to get Paiyali into trouble with me.

Did you get a letter from the new (NGS) man (Moldvay) on the photographic scene? He certainly must not have looked at our earlier pictures (I take it these comments are on the Highlands trip) since he tells me they'd like to have pictures of people building houses! Much kinder than the other two, though, and I needed a kind word on the subject of my pictures. Have you seen the uproar because an anthropologist referred to patrol officers (at an ANZAAS meeting) as "boy scouts"? I can truthfully say that's an epithet that never occurred to me. We'll be darn lucky to escape the repercussions of that. I'm getting increasingly dubious about when or even if the carriers will leave. Things looked bright a week ago, but they don't today. We'll see.

Monday—Carriers just left—considerably fewer than I wanted or needed, but at least I can stop thinking about it for a while. It'll be sort of a relief to get back to regular work. They may get to you first (on the way back), if the river is flooded. Do you get the horrid impression that they think the rainy season has started? I can hardly face it. The house is watertight at the moment except that the afternoon rains blow in through the study window.

Life has just been cheered by the best leg of pig I've had yet, plus fresh pineapple. The pig was dead (in an accident) 24 hours before they cooked it, so I was a trifle nervous, but no ill effects so far.

It's not significant that Yambon (Sengseng) women were sitting in your house—*they* (the women) don't mind violating the tabu. The question is, were any Yambon men sitting underneath it or eating food cooked on the fire? On the way back, Dudame was teasing Milingli about his reaction when he found there were women above him in your house.

Had a really exciting morning yesterday watching a solid hour of garden ritual (preceding the first planting in a new garden). Now if I can just find out what it was all about.

All talk about the pig killing seems to have died down and no one is game to ask since a quarrel on the subject a few days ago damn near led to bloodshed. After all, they were talking about holding it in (last) September, too. So why don't you come on over whenever you like—immediately would be fine, as far as I'm concerned. Thanks for stuff on pigs and shells. That makes sense of a lot that I've seen.

Later—Cargo just arrived fastest time yet, despite some justifiable complaints (because John sent almost everything I'd crossed off my list, when I saw how few carriers there were). No real trouble, though, and it's a great relief to have the stuff. Like an idiot, I ordered coffee instead of Nescafe. Do you know how to make coffee in a saucepan? Love, Ann

Umbi, March 12, Thursday
Dear Ann,

The returning cargo took me by surprise today and Lelus and Lesum say they are going your way tomorrow. John put my small amount of mail in with my cargo, so don't worry when you see there's none with yours. But Algy's letter is for both of us so it's my excuse to send a note. How will the (transferred) CPO do at Hoskins (on the north coast)?! But Umbi greeted the news with sighs of relief. Any news of the Dulago Pig Killing from your end? It would be just our luck to have it on your birthday.

Umbi had been virtually dead with the cargo line gone. But in spite of the lack of anything going on, I still haven't got down to typing for I was never let alone enough. I did, however, get the opportunity for some interviewing as people dropped in to check up on me, and one day I traipsed off with Hingme and Tihime [two young women] to Elwai (hamlet) to stretch my muscles and establish "rapport" with Hingme. The day was almost totally useless as far as information went, but quite satisfying as all conversation was in Kaulong (language) with the two girls and with Sakhun's family whom we visited. It was a pleasant day. I did check with Ningbi on the *dinau* (debt) aspect of pork selling and if the Owner owes *dinau* to the receiver, he *must* 'back' [repay] it. But pig is (also) sold to people to whom no *dinau* is owing and in that case, of course, none given!

All the returned carriers are "dying" of hunger and pressuring me to sell them some of my rice and I'm being hard hearted! But this trip too went without complaints—two in a row—I can't believe it! Love, Jane

Dulago, Sunday (March 15)
Dear Jane,

Either Friday or Saturday (for your visit?) will be fine. I can't imagine that the singsing will be held this week; if it will be, preparations have been mighty secret. As far as I know the last trading expedition [to Kaulong— essential for getting shells to pay debts of potential pork receivers] hasn't even left yet; certainly it hasn't returned. Someone from here left for Kandrian on Saturday and has instructions to pick up our mail. I'll send it over or let it wait for you, depending on when he gets back and whether anything looks urgent. I assume that, like me, your thirst for mail is somewhat dulled at the moment, but I don't believe in passing up any chances, and it also gave me an opportunity to get some Nescafe. Life has been very dull for the last couple of days, and I've returned to typing. My sleep is now being interrupted by a marauding dog who comes in at night to explore tins and pots and devour the cat's food. Kasup is also building me a new privy, which at the moment looks no better than the old one, but should at least be mosquito-free.

Can't think of a thing of interest. The *Times* are extremely welcome. I should also have some *New Yorkers* (for November!) for you by the time you come over. Love, Ann.

Umbi, March 23
Dear Family,

I've just got back from Dulago and feel refreshed mentally, but we both have a feeling that time is running out. Only a little more than four months more and all along time has been rushing in spite of the monotony—we can't quite understand why.

My companions this time were two 12-13 year old boys and we had "adventures." We met a "poison-man" (known sorcerer) who hid in the bushes hoping to be unobserved. But we did see him so he emerged. [Umbi was still in the middle of the sorcery war with Womilo.]

We broke bush (left the path) on a short cut and saw some lovely country around a large stream and visited with a family at their garden. On the way back we spent three hours at this garden because the boys found they could be fed there, and so we sat eating *tapiok* (manioc), sugar-cane, yams (wild and domestic) shrimp and (large fat white) grubs. This route may be a short cut in distance, but it certainly wasn't in time! We also took time hunting for *imlos* [chipped flint tools]. It was a different trip and the boys were pleasant (if at times exasperating) companions.

Ann was fine, her knee almost totally recovered and we arrived just in time to share pieces of three wild pigs. I had planned to take my functioning tape recorder over to her for she has had many village singsings (and hers doesn't work) and the night that I tested mine I suggested—as a test—that one man tell a story. The story he told was when he killed his mother because she had "crossed" (became angry with) him. Then another man related how he killed his sister, because his brother killed their mother! And we were off! I got four hours of stories of murder and revenge that night and three hours of them the next night, and a wealth of information all told. They first told the story in Kaulong and then repeated it in Pidgin and everyone had a grand time listening. The house was filled with boys and story tellers and all chipped in with names and events.

The next day the Tultul, who was to come with us (to Dulago) and carry the tape recorder, bowed out because of boils and so the tape recorder remains here and I'm hoping to get more informative sessions. The last murder I've recorded was about 10 years ago. The high incidence of murder didn't "shock" me as much as the realization that in my house at that one time were sitting three murderers, all calmly "confessing." There are about 10 murderers in the village.

Your latest package of [plastic] "Real" lemons and limes in all forms and lollies arrived. The sour lemon lifesavers are wonderful for the bush hikes and the empty plastic lemons make perfect whistles and/or squirt-guns, and my tea is greatly enhanced. Love Jane

Dulago, Tuesday March?
Dear Jane,
Talk about not knowing your local *masalais* [spirits]! The one that Osio saw while you were here lives underground in this village, emerging from a hole which is practically within sight of the house. If it appears in the daytime, a man will die unless the people promptly "offer" it a shell and a pig, which it doesn't take. However, appearances at night, like the one that just occurred, are not bad omens, except for the pigs it's presumably after. In the time of the distant ancestors it tried to drag a tusker [pig with tusks] like ours down its hole, but the hole was too narrow.

The supply of pig legs continues unabated, with another promised for today. However, no indications of a singsing, and I suspect the reason is (I just found out) that the (Catholic) Father is said to have sent word that there are to be no singsings till after Easter. I don't know whether he actually meant it to apply to all these villages or if the word was just picked up down the way (presumably by Osio at Pomalal), but I find it exceedingly annoying. That's why Paiyali stopped the children from singing on Friday night. Love, Ann

Umbi, March 25

Dear Ann,

The Brothers (C of E) left yesterday to spend Easter at Apugi [the Church of England mission] near Kandrian and Lesum went with them. I gave Lesum some mail, including our films, to take down and he will stop in the office for mail on the way back, but he says this won't be back for three weeks. However, Nehibi and others started for Kandrian Monday and returned in 1 hour, because they had no money and said they were going down Saturday to work on the road.

All is well here. Within an hour of the Brothers' departure, Kasli brought some of their *kaukaus* [sweet potatoes] to me and in addition everyone went bush last night. Aside from we three, there were Kaliam and my 2 boys in the village. Today, just Ningbi and I—which I like, because I can pump him for information. However, he's been off washing clothes and collecting water all morning.

I've paid these boys (actually the older one whose name I've forgotten) 4/ as we agreed—I have not given them anything with this letter. Also yesterday Noalong and the boy he passed your note on to, appeared and although Noalong said when you gave him the 2 sticks (tobacco) you didn't say anything about his giving one stick to the person he got to carry the letter here- he paid me back 1/ without too much fuss.

Hope Payali is shaping up. At the moment D. and N. are in good humor. Love, Jane

Umbi, April 2

Dear Ann,

I am being slowly driven out of my mind by two small (6 and 8 yr. old) boys who were left to "take care of me" today. Every minute it's "*Dion, elemen?*" [Jane, what is this?] or, more usually, something totally incomprehensible. I've come to the conclusion that these two converse primarily in "married talk." An interesting observation, but very frustrating for me. These two boys have been left in the charge of Sutli and Kaliam and for the past three days, the four of them have made up the total population of Umbi together with Debli and me. The first day I went with them to the gardens— frightfully dull.

[Affinal names and similar sounding words are tabu for married people, so they must use a different (and largely individual)

vocabulary from that spoken by unmarried people. Children often learn to speak using the "married talk" vocabularies of their parents—as in this case—before switching to the standard vocabulary used by the unmarried.]

Yesterday, I stayed alone hoping to accomplish a lot, while all went off including my dogs. However, at 10, the Hulem kleptomaniac, Lelwali, arrived with 2 ham-less (lower) legs of pork demanding 10/ apiece. I paid 5/ each and then he offered to recook them for me and I gave him some tobacco, taro and biscuits in return. The climax came when he started to leave and from his laplap fell a large hunk of pork right on Belo's nose (my male puppy had returned from a pig hunt and was sound asleep). "*Dok bilong yu kisim pik*" [Your dog took some pork] says the quick witted thief, and as I grabbed it from Belo, Lelwali takes off!

I repeated this story to Sutli and Debli, who found it, as I did, both typical and amusing. All this effectively botched up the day. Debli arrived at dusk with more pig which he said Belo had killed (with Kasli's help) that morning and we six had a mammoth feast with more to eat this afternoon when the men return.

What I should be doing today is photographing the *imlos* [flint artifacts], but somehow the effort involved seems overwhelming. Also it's HOT out there in the noonday sun! Or, I should be typing—to excuse myself from these tasks, I write to you. (The two boys are now completely hysterical over something— but at least they've stopped singing!)

It's been an interesting week—On Sunday, Koran came over from Hulem and showed me what was quite unmistakably a *mokmok* [stone valuable]. I finally asked him if he wanted to sell it and he said, "yes for 10/." So I bought it. Sutli then looked at it and said "*niglak bilong masalai*" [Mokmok belonging to a spirit], because; (1) it's completely round rather than oval or disk-shaped, and (2) it's a very heavy black stone rather than multi-colored or light. Sutli says he knows of another one and will try to negotiate for it. Whether masalai's or *bigpela man's* (i.e. really considered a true mokmok), I feel it was well worth the 10/ as all of a sudden, Sutli started to open up on local masalais (spirits) with such rapidity, I was swamped. Few items: 1) invocation of one particular *masalai* in a taro singsing, of another (*masalai*) to catch eels, 2) the fact that the pig-singsing songs are songs which belong to *masalais* (particular ones), bananas, *elans* [bandicoots], *sikaus* [wallabies] etc. etc. As I struggled against the losing battle to record this flood of information, Sutli and Debli suggested I get the tape-recorder out and they would tell stories and sing songs with translations. Then the crowning touch—I found the tape-recorder, in spite of new batteries, is very weak! I've ordered new fresh batteries, and hope it's as simple as that, but I have my suspicions. Anyway—if it doesn't work, I've at least got most valuable leads into the Religion, and willing informants.

Monday was a mad-house. Simultaneous activity consisted of: 1) trying to get a continually expanding cargo line organized; 2) accepting the expected— that Ningbi was determined to go work at Manus (in spite of various bribes of future handouts in distribution of my worldly goods) and was off to Kandrian with the cargo line, but depending on when the Manus boat was due to arrive, may or not return to wait for it; 3) fixing sores, selling tobacco, and buying *imlos* [flint artifacts] from almost the total population of Umbi plus a large contingent of visiting Silop-ites, including Slebme and her week-old daughter; 4) the women "dancing" to celebrate Slebme's return as new mother, which was going on under my house, while I was detained above with all the foregoing.

I finally got down (out of the house) knowing nothing of what was taking place, but observing what in any civilized culture would be called a drunken orgy! I sat down on the "bed" to observe and as part of the "play" one woman sat on my lap and the bed collapsed! This so upset the women, they stopped the ritual completely and picked up bag and baggage and moved off. Then—I was told what had been going on! Damn!, Damn! and etc. Of course, no pictures [were taken] and, if I had known it was "something for real" and not just horsing around as it appeared to be, I would have been more circumspect about sitting amongst them. This didn't seem to bother them at all as was apparent from their including me in the play. It was just damn unfortunate that the bed collapsed and that I couldn't immediately assure them that "it was nothing," but there was no one to translate (my bad Kaulong) adequately.

Sulubo (Nehebi) went with my carriers to carry only your mail as he says that's what you told him. I of course, did not pay him, but I did give him 1 stick of tobacco (as all my carriers now get a present of such) and also included him in the rice/fish scale [ration in Kandrian which I now provided my young carriers in addition to pay]—as I felt if I didn't he would eat and smoke my carrier's rations. I said I would collect from you later.

(Later—April 4) Yesterday our C of E contingent (now 4) arrived back from Apugi carrying *our* mail. The Brothers left Lesum [who I thought would bring our mail when he returned with the Brothers] at Apugi to go to school. The Brothers, "feeling sorry for us," picked up the mail on Tuesday. I insisted on paying them 15/ as not only was your parcel in it, but also a large one for me from the Glicks [Len and Nancy, colleagues of ours], full of goodies and books—truly a "life-saving" package from people who know "what goes well with taro"—as their card read. The cargo-line is expected today.

Later—12:30—Nehebi and Ligu have just arrived as an advance guard. Nehibi did pick up some more mail for us which he said they waited for on Thursday's plane. I've *bunged* [put] it all together.

I spent the a.m. racing the approaching rain to get *imlos* photographed. I got two rolls of the Silop stream examples, but really rushed on the others, however, my conscience feels somewhat relieved. Including the Silop (stream) lot, I have just about 100 specimens here, not including the used flakes.

The boys say the [labor recruiting] Manus plane is not expected for a few weeks, so Ningbi (who had planned on going to Manus to work) is back for a while. How confused can a household get?

Dave writes he doesn't know when Manus recruiting will take place and that Algy is off on patrol and we may expect him in 3-4 weeks—hopefully just after the 18th [the date of Ann's expected trip to Umbi]. Love Jane

Dulago, Saturday, April 9

Dear Jane,

Life is very confusing at the moment, thanks to the Father's arrival in Hutkihyu yesterday. My cargo line was scheduled to leave today, but as a consequence has not. The plan now is for them to go Monday (barring word from the Kiap or the Manus recruiters). At the moment I seem to have plenty of volunteers. These things certainly move in mysterious cycles. Anyway, I want to get stocked up as far in advance as possible against the rainy season, the departure for Manus, and the general cussedness of the indigenes.

The delayed departure (of my carriers) makes our plans a little tricky, since it means the carriers will almost certainly arrive back when I'm away [visiting Umbi]. Paiyali's going with them, which makes for additional worries, such as the cat and a dearth of house boys—in case they're delayed on the road. However, I am still going to try to come over Friday [to visit April 17 to 18], since if I delay, I'll run into the day appointed for the Manus recruits to assemble (by a Kiuli man, who says the boat is supposed to arrive on the 26th—who knows) and quite possibly the Kiap. I'll do my best to make it.

Koriam [the leader of the cargo-cult] was elected to the House of Assembly for East New Britain. I'm flabbergasted (and horrified)—so much for the sophistication of the Tolai.

[East New Britain District encompassed the south coast (including Kandrian) as well as the eastern Gazelle Peninsula, with the major city of Rabaul, whose people, the Tolai, had been in contact with outsiders since before the turn of the century. The Tolai had participated in local government for a fair number of years prior to this present national election. Everyone expected one of the several candidates from the Tolai to win over people from the south coast. However, what evidently happened was that the Tolai split their votes and a south coastal candidate, Koriam, described in the newspapers as an illiterate farmer, won the seat. He was to hold this seat for eight years.]

West New Britain [including Cape Gloucester and the northern coast] is one of two electorates still not decided; Talasea airstrip (on the north coast) was closed down by rain and they couldn't collect absentee ballots. They're supposed to know today, but there's no local news [on the radio] on Saturday. See you Friday, I hope. Love Ann.

PS. The Hoskins airstrip [north coast] has been closed to DC3s! Curses! [As a first stop after leaving Kaulong/Sengseng, we planned to fly to Hoskins on the regular DC3 local flight, Lae to Rabaul, and visit with Ann's friends and former hosts, the Lakalai. This tabu on DC3

planes landing there meant we would have to charter a smaller plane
to make the hop over the mountains.]

Umbi, Tues.
Dear Ann,
Kasli, I guess, is after his *dinau* [debts], and has offered to take this to
you.
It's been one of "those" days, but with some unique events. Ningbi nearly
died with a massive hemorrhage this morning and is on the verge of being
married tonight! I don't think these two events are connected. (I wouldn't
mention the latter, it's not final yet.) It's been very interesting and I have just
now (8:30 p.m.) got the facts. Essentially, he doesn't want to get married (to
Ihime, the young adolescent who has been courting him for months) but forces
within the village are determined that he shall. In his very weak state after
hemorrhage, he's hardly able to stand up—literally and figuratively.
The hemorrhage was something and took place in the middle of the night.
He lost a lot of blood, evidenced with his showing me his soaked bedding,
laplaps and towels, but he insisted on walking down to the river to bathe this
morning. I insisted some lads go with him and to do the washing of bedding
etc. (and to be with him, if he collapsed, which I expected, but which he
didn't). The marriage talk has finally decided to be postponed until Ningbi gets
some sleep. Poor guy. I really feel for him and wish to hell everyone would go
home.
One group is off to Kandrian tomorrow to pick up rice—but no mail, as I
fully expect others to go the end of the week or early next week.
I must write up the marriage talk, so make this short. Love, Jane

Dulago, Tuesday
Dear Jane,
This is a just-in-case letter. Life here is insomnia producing at the
moment; yesterday all but one of the unmarried men (including Paiyali)
announced that they were going to Manus. If similar things happen in other
villages, and I've heard ominous lists from Yambon, I truly don't see how I'll
manage to get supplies not to mention informants (I'm not worried about
getting a cook).
Yesterday our regular Monday [government work day] quarrel was of
spectacular proportions. Three grown men in tears, one trying to burn down his
own house (and waving an ax menacingly), shells flying thick and fast and,
hordes of people stalking out of the village. The principal was Mubudli, whom
they're trying to persuade me to accept as my cook. Never!
The pig-hunting has finally ended, with the killing of a former village pig
that had gone wild. Incidentally, I was forbidden to photograph anything
connected with the wild pigs—lots of little ritual touches [and tabu for women
to see]. The distribution of the last pig was made the occasion for the removal
of the ritual pole, done absolutely without ceremony and preceded by a singsing

that wasn't even attended by any other villages. A completely nothing affair, and this seems to be it for the present.

I've been suffering from 4 A.M. diarrhea which does nothing to make me more alert (or cheerful) during the day. However, anthropologically speaking things are going well, and presumably will continue to till I see you. Now I'm sort of waiting to see what new shocks come (missionaries, no doubt; I expect them daily).

Sunday—We had an all night singsing last night, and I'm in my customary glassy-eyed state. Two projects are scheduled for today—a visit to Hutkihyu to see a newborn baby, and one to Yambon to watch a quarrel about adultery, but I suspect that neither will take place, thanks to a pig-killing in Seagit. But I'll sit around for a while before crawling back into bed; for one thing, I need to find someone to cook a snake for me (it's the kind Paiyali won't touch). We've had endless rumors and counter-rumors about when the ship for Manus is coming, but the only definite date quoted is the 26th. Kasup finally volunteered to cook for me (he's the only one who's not going), and that would certainly be the most satisfactory arrangement.

Monday—I laughed when I got your (earlier) letter, since I'd just gone through the identical experience of being driven mad by two little boys (our newly resident 3-year old, whom I can't understand) and a visiting 5-year old, given to interminable *elemei's* [what is it].

I'm delighted (and jealous) to hear your news about *masalais* and spells. I've recently been introduced to a third local one (*masalai*), who's inhabiting a deep pool at the base of a lovely waterfall which unfortunately makes it tabu for bathing. You must visit the spot next time you're here, anyway. With Belo, you should be able to find out about the ritual of wild-pig hunting. I'll tell you more about what little I know when I see you. I still plan to come over on the 17th.

Wednesday—I'm awfully glad to have a chance to get a letter to you. I didn't dare ask Debe to take it, there was quite a scene (not on his part) when I refused to buy the bananas he brought from Arihi—"because I pay so much better than you."

Kasli told all my companions that Ningbi was married, so it's hardly a secret at this end. I'll try to get a couple of letters written while Kasli is waiting for our Luluai to turn up. No one at all is in the village except the group of Yambonites I came with (I paid a sudden visit there, alone and in a fit of boredom with the locals).

I got a most peculiar letter from Gilka (NGS), devoted wholly to politics. All he said about film is that they're sending some more. What I'm getting low on now are flashbulbs. See you soon. Love Ann

Umbi April 13
Dear Family,
This has been a most hectic week. Beginning last Monday night when Ningbi was given a wife somewhat against his will. He had attempted to go off to work to escape (marriage), but the recruiting ship wasn't in Kandrian so he

returned to wait for it and was "caught." Tuesday, three men who were going to Kandrian for me postponed their trip, because one of them had to sleep with the bride and groom to see that one or both didn't escape! It's usually, I'm told, the groom who escapes, because the bride is asked beforehand whether she wants to marry this man, but the groom either stays or runs. Ningbi resigned himself to his fate and stayed.

His older brother came in from the bush, furious because he hadn't been consulted, and the couple are the wrong kind of cousin to each other. Everyone expected a fight, but shells were exchanged. This marriage is a gold mine for me as far as information goes. The young couple are under a multitude of tabus, on work, on food, on speech—they must only use the "married" vocabulary or die and Ningbi says his "mouth is so heavy" he talks in Pidgin or any other language he can think of because he's afraid of making a slip of the tongue.

On Friday I got incontestable evidence of Debli's pilfering of a dime [10c] which added to 2 other dimes which turned up in Dulago and were said to have come from Debli, who claimed they were sixpence [coins],was enough for me to fire him. I did this with the Tultul's backing and decided Ningbi and his wife would stay and work for me. It was an extremely hard thing to do because Debli has been so loyal in other ways. I knew he had taken tobacco and matches well before this and also a few sixpence coins, and I had recently locked all my American money, passport and a few other irreplaceable items away for the remaining three months. However, with the last incident of the dime, I had too many witnesses not to do something drastic. We had a fight, which is already being talked about as "big" and Debli so blatantly lied that even these habitual liars shook their heads in dismay. Debli stayed fired for 36 hours, and we finally both calmed down enough to talk and I decided to give him £3 (for past loyalties) and send him on his way. However, I also realized by this time that many things were involved.

He is a *kandere* of Ningbi (a very close relationship) and Ningbi had married a girl he (Debli) had been courting. Debli was cross at losing his girl, but Ningbi needed his financial support to buy the girl. I (with Ningbi's backing) got Debli to confess to *all* his pilfering (a major miracle) and Debli paid back what he had taken and Ningbi and I said "we would try him again," but the back of the house (my private quarters) is now tabu to him. He's been working very hard and volunteering all kinds of extraneous information (which he knows I'll be interested in, but couldn't be bothered to stop and explain before), and I think all has worked out for the best. It is really a case of trying to fire a member of the family in which you are a guest! It's not easily accomplished. Residual effects are being felt in that all sorts of people are paying off their 1-3 shilling debts to me. [I often gave out tobacco on credit to be repaid in food.]

On Sunday, in the middle of the first shell payments by Ningbi and his relations to his in-laws, Father White, the Catholic Missionary, literally dropped in. He had been over Ann's way arranging *Popi* affairs and decided to see how I lived. He stayed for lunch and then took off across the river to his "territory" again. On his way out of the village Ningbi, the only professed Catholic in the village, told him he was married and Fr. White insisted that Ningbi go to Hulem with him and talk, because his wife is "non-Catholic." Ningbi had already confessed to me that being married was hard work. Just as he arrived back from his "talking to" from Fr. White, he received a "message" (a knotted string) from a big man in Yambon saying that he, Ningbi, must buy Ihime with pigs and shells to be given to all relatives of hers, which is the old fashioned way and gives the husband's relatives the right to strangle the widow.

> [This was quite incorrect. I learned later that it's the widow's own close brothers (or, if more age appropriate, her father or her sons) who are expected to strangle her. The husband's kin must then give these shells back to the wife's brothers if they do not strangle her. In all deaths we were witness to shells were given back to the widow's brothers to make "right" her remaining alive and potentially sexually active after her husband's death.]

If Ningbi doesn't pay the full payment, this man will take his wife away and give her to someone else. This man is expected over here next Monday and in the meantime Ningbi has come back to sleep (alone) in my house. It's all fascinating anthropologically and I'm now rather glad Debli is back, for Ningbi is being kept so busy in his own affairs, he hasn't been much help in the housework. (However, his wife has worked doing the outside chores, so I've not lost anything.)

Continued next day—Yesterday, we had another death—an old man, who died at 11 a.m. and came back to life again at 2 p.m. and died again at 3 p.m. when he was buried. I did not go to the burial as my cargo arrived at the same time as well as the delegation from Yambon (of Ningbi's in-laws) for marriage transactions, but I wish now I had, as this "coming back to life" has started all sorts of talk of devils etc.

Today we are expecting the C of E Father and once he has come and gone, a group of kids are off again to Kandrian for "cargo" and on Friday, Ann comes over (it's her birthday). I have been saving "goodies" from your packages and one I got from my teaching substitute at Bryn Mawr and his wife and I'll do my best to make a proper celebration including a 2 oz. bottle of Scotch sent by another friend disguised as perfume. I may even have a watermelon! (We've eaten two already—very small as we've so much rain, but one more remains ripening in the garden.) Love to all Jane.

Dulago, Friday (April?)
Dear Jane,

This is a just-in-case note. Carriers finally off at noon on Wednesday and will wait for Saturday plane, mostly because returnees from Talasea will be on it. I have my own suspicions that they won't leave Kandrian till Monday, so the returnees can shop and they can all come back together, so I'm not really expecting them back before Wednesday. If it weren't for the (lack of) film, I really wouldn't care.

Some interesting recent data on childbirth and after, mostly from Ngolu, whose second baby has just been born. I was just bracing myself to ask *the* question (about how long they abstain from sex) when we were interrupted.

All my remaining firewood became tabu because a Kaulong girl who came with the Father sat on [and sexually polluted] a bench above it. They also "destroyed" a new bed in the HB [men's house] after she sat on it. I'll definitely be over on Saturday, in hopes of getting back before I get the curse. Whether I'll get carriers is another question.

Monday—Mubudli says he and his brother are going to Umbi tomorrow, so I'll finish this off. It would be nice if the mail came in time to go with them, since I'm going to have trouble finding carriers in this weather. What a blow, after these many days of sunshine.

I was feeling happy yesterday after a couple of days of interesting information when Mubudli informed me that Kasup [my cook] is dispensing tinned meat [mine] to friends and relations for miles around. *That* wiped the smile off my face, though I don't plan to take any action at the moment. Too much to lose, and as far as I know, it's only his own ration. This plus the fact that one of the women pulled up my only thriving morning glory today, has left me in a lousy mood. I think I need a touch of contact with the outside. Love, Ann

[Ann did visit Umbi over her birthday.]

Dulago, Tuesday (April 21?)
Dear Jane,

Bad news on the singsing front—they did have *ulal* [courtship fighting] *behain long mi* [after I left to visit you], but the good news on the religious front—the pseudo-catechist has gone home in a huff because two little girls made faces at him. Who knows for how long, of course.

The free hand [given to the Kandrian trade store] with the meat has produced some shockers (I forgot to forbid casserole steak) but a little variety. Didn't get well ahead on puddings, as hoped, but otherwise OK.

We just had a nice fight over Pamlik after the Yambon crew came for an all night singsing. I was there and with camera, but it took place on the path at dawn, and I was staying a healthy distance away (several were equipped with spears and shields) so I don't think it helped photographically.

Pehedli has just barred Selselio and his whole family from entering Yambon by "planting fire" (charcoal, I assume) on the path (reason being—a comment made by Selselio's daughter Mboime, about Pehedli's affair with Mudli). Anyway, a bit more about the sacredness or whatever of fire has emerged from this, and you might see what more you can get at your end. The standard statement is that fire is "something true."

Weather permitting, I'm off to Seagit tomorrow for a tour of caves (spirit places and otherwise).

The idiots at the Magazine Shop sent me your Sunday Paper. I know you don't care, but I do, so I'd appreciate a check to see if you have mine. I somehow feel that a week's mail is missing.

Friday—Letter from Hicks (District Officer in Rabaul) gives us complete permission to visit Lakalai, on the north coast, on our way out in August. He says there's Aztec (charter) service between Rabaul and Hoskins every Tuesday, so that will get us out (of Hoskins). I'll try to check on ways to get there. Might put the time up a bit, in one direction or another. My present thought is still to go on or after the planned date and just stay a bit later. I know this will disrupt our New Guinea schedules, but we'll see what offers.

I'm just back from a couple of grubby days in Seagit. Got to the river and to the cave where the spirits live, and I'm sure there's an element of deliberate fraud involved there. I'm distinctly footsore, and am looking forward to a couple of days of sitting around.

Umbi, April 21, Tuesday
Dear Ann,

It's something having *two* mail deliveries in one day! Even Philly can't do that.

Got a letter from Ann D. [Museum of the University of Pennsylvania] saying they are still depositing your salary checks (from NSF) as they can't think of anything else to do(!!!), and they can wire remaining money to American Express in Sydney and we can get Traveler's Checks there, and to let them know how much $$. What we now need to know is the price of our Airline tickets (which we will have to pay for in Rabaul). The latest *Time* says airfares have been *reduced* some as much as 20%! Got a note from C. S. Coon [for whom I had worked at the U.P. Museum] asking me to reserve a date in April 1965 to talk to the Harvard Traveler's Club! Leakey has found more bones in Oldoway and my mother sent me a clipping on them, so will save it for you when I've digested it.

We've had an interesting Monday with Kihungit coming to argue with Ningbi (settled for 3 shells), a crowd of Hulem visitors and the most interesting, a visit from a man whose existence I just heard about yesterday. He has always hidden in the bush from the Kiaps refusing to *lain* [be censused]. He is a middle aged married man with wife and several children and a huge pregnant dog. His brother works in Rabaul! They all came today to see me! Although the wife has still not showed herself to me. He's said to be Miu rather than Kaulong, but lives somewhere in between, well and truly in the bush with no roads or paths to his hideout.

Postscript

By March many events had ethnographic significance for us. Spirits (*masalai*) were all around us and people began talking about them to us. As pre-Christian religion was a subject we both were keenly interested in, it was rewarding to have our informants finally open up to us on this subject.

The shell exchanges, which we had seen in debt paying, we now saw in the context of pig exchange and marriage, two events with considerable complexity in the exchange of shells. I began to learn the "language of the shells," how they could be used to say many things without words. I began to learn the elements of Kaulong credit economy (*dinau*)—the management of which is the basis of political power.

The Kaulong taught me the significance of balance of internal and export trade between trading partnerships and between groups and the nature of the debt relationships within. Exchange is also the very process of *creating* individually a personal social (kin) network. The interlocking of these personal networks are the fabric of Kaulong/Sengseng society. In Umbi I began my education into Kaulong economy, but it wasn't until I was in Angelek in 1967 and 1968 that I completed my education.

People had told me that the reason they preferred to live scattered in small hamlets was to prevent conflict. "If two people live together, they will (naturally) fight." Many of the "murders" I collected on tape referred to a sanctioned killing because of a tabu being broken; for example, marrying someone ineligible (a sibling marriage), or a man's initiating courtship, which was considered rape, or adultery if he was already married and refused to marry the second woman. Other murders were committed when the man was "shamed" by exposing himself to women, by falling on the trail, or by being seen defecating. Conflicts over shells and pig exchange were expected to be resolved by nonlethal means, but of course some were not, and spearing was the result. This might lead to an interhamlet battle, with subsequent resolution with exchange of shells and sometimes pigs.

Domestic fights, over many problems, seemed quite frequent and were initiated by either wife or husband, who used similar weapons at hand to inflict wounds. Some of the wounds we patched up were those caused by courting girls who used knives as well as sticks (quite expectedly) to let the boys know they were interested in them or to repel the unexpected attentions of a young man.

By far the most significant event at this time was Ningbi and Ihimei's marriage, right under my nose so to speak. Kaulong women take the initiative in courtship as well as in capturing a husband. Tabus on newly married behavior, including those on food and speech, are marked. Whereas Ningbi could hardly talk to others because of name and speech tabus, he felt he could safely talk to me and let off some of his newlywed tension without violating any in-law tabus, and information poured in with major leaps in my understanding. Marriage is *the* most significant rite-of-passage for Kaulong, with the second being the rituals of death.

Prior to the first coming of the Kiap, people exhumed the skulls of deceased and kept them in the men's house, or so it seemed from our knowledge at this time. During my later work in Angelek, I was present at a major singsing at which the skull of a recently (1967) deceased man was presented to a former trading partner along with a portion of the sacrificed pig. The recipient then killed a pig and passed the skull along with pork to the next trading partner of the deceased man. Eventually the skull returned to the home hamlet where it was reburied with the rest of the skeleton. The old matmats (hamlets) were filled with buried skeletons of previous affiliates of the place.

This season, the last months before the rains began, was a period of greatly increased activity involving travel, trade, and singsings. The unpredictable and serendipitous nature of participant observation is obvious in the foregoing letters. Information was pouring in but in a completely random (it seemed) manner. It was hard to pause and probe more deeply into some of these matters before another fascinating tidbit of information interrupted and opened a new line of questioning.

Chapter 8

The Singsing at Dulago Was Terrific

Umbi, May 3 1964

Dear Ann,

Iamopli has a lot of *dinau* [debt] with me so he was only too willing to say yes when I asked him if he'd like to go to Dulago. I suspect your village is as confused with the Kiap [on annual census patrol] as we are—except we had "word" of his impending *immediate* arrival from two directions. 1st, he was in Arihi and going south to Asahi. 2nd (2 days later), he was on his way to Arihi and planning to "break bush" and come directly here (this from the Luluai of Arihi personally!), 3rd (1 day later), he had already been to Arihi and was now at Asahi and would be at Pomalal "tomorrow," 4th, he was at Aka when he got a pass to return to Kandrian.

We have been having [as a result of these rumors], several large harvestings of taro to be carried into Umbi (for all) to eat while the Kiap is here. What everyone will eat when he finally does come is anyone's guess! But yesterday, I accompanied all to a planting party of 23 men and women and uncountable children and I finally saw some more garden magic. Fortunately there was no rain and I got some pictures—ignoring the scolding looks from Kahame (the performer) and other men—but they didn't say anything, so I kept on. It was a thoroughly interesting day in the gardens for a change.

[Taro, once harvested, will only keep for a few days before rotting. The taro stalks must also be replanted within a few days before rotting, rendering them unable to regenerate new corms (edible roots). Normally a person will only harvest enough taro for one or two days for personal or family consumption. Taro, since it is continually replanted, does not have a "season" for harvesting, and large harvesting means large replanting and an interruption of the

daily routine of harvest—eat—replant, more or less assuring a
continual and adequate supply of this staple food.]

Just after our return from the garden, Debli announced he was leaving
Umbi for good, as Kasli and Langpapa are intent on marrying him off to
Tihime (a younger lass than Ningbi's wife who, when I last checked several
months ago, hadn't yet reached puberty). Tihime has been hiding in the bush
and yesterday, Bedli (a *kandere* of hers) [a mother's brother—matrilineal
kinsman] said he was taking Tihime to Yambon to stay. Hence Debli said he'd
leave and go to work so "*Tihime no lusim skul*" [Tihime wouldn't lose "school"
with the C of E Brothers]. I suspect Debli is also afraid of the marriage (Tihime
obviously is). Kasli went to Arihi "to meet the Kiap" and hasn't returned, but
Langpapa won't relent in his desire for the marriage to take place. Why? I can't
figure out (they don't get any shells out of it).

[I was wrong about this; only a bride's true brothers receive no shells
in a marriage transaction involving their sister.]

Debli has gone "*long hap*" [somewhere over there] to get *dinau* [debt] today
and plans to sleep here tonight (but a downpour at the moment may prevent his
return) and go to Kandrian tomorrow. *If* he actually does go (I've learned not to
count my blessings) I won't be sorry. Although having two married couples
attached to my household would be interesting, the actual situation would be
impossible.

I've come to the conclusion that the majority of the food tabus [for the
newly wed] are because of names of *tambus* [in-laws] being associated with the
food and are not general tabus. But these food tabus make great complications
in our diet. Ningbi has just announced that a pig, which is now being *mumued*
(baked) at Angus is tabued to both he and Ihime because some *tambus* (in-laws)
of theirs are buried there. Eventually he and she will throw shells on the graves
of their *tambus* (i.e. pay them) and the tabu is lifted. (I can't figure out who
picks up the shells as whoever does is also a *tambu* [in-law.])

[Food tabus turned out to be enormously *more* complex. The
matmats (hamlets) where the bride's or groom's in-laws are buried
are themselves also tabu until the bride or groom gives shells to their
dead in-laws. These tabus are related to other tabus about being
above (stepping over, raising one's hand above) an in-law. Affinal
kin who now live at the matmat will pick up the offered shells as
payment for their caretaking of the deceased in-law's grave.]

We had a fairly large and complex marriage transaction last week when
the Luluai of Arihi (a real mother's brother of the bride [Ihime]) arrived angry
(kros) about the marriage. After the *kros* was paid off, he gave Ihime a number
of shells to buy (pay) her *tambus* [in-laws], who then gave Ningbi shells to *buy*
[pay] his.

[All these transactions had to be made using different shells. There
was an attempt to make each transaction equal by giving each person
a shell of equal value to the one they gave.]

I have heard mumbles of lads wishing to make a trip to Kandrian (Debli and some others were planning on going next Sat.), but nothing definite yet, but if you have anything to send down, send it over. If Algy (the Kiap, expected daily) goes first I'll give it to him. I'm planning on giving Debli a few letters I've written, but am holding out on the film as I don't have too many. If you have any to send, send them over too. Also *if* your air-pillow is not in use, could you send me its *plug* (or the whole thing if you wish to get rid of it entirely). My plug is split across the top and I've grown used to sleeping on it. Love, Jane

Umbi May ?
Dear Ann,

I'm jealous, as word of your impending singsing *cum* fight has reached us and Debli is determined to go to the affair. I should put on my boots and go with them but I can think of all kinds of legitimate excuses, but the main one being laziness and a surfeit of Debli). Did Paiyali go to Manus? Only one of the five or six here, who said they were going, actually went.

Umbi seems awfully tame—no singsings, no arguments, no fist fights, only love and its problems. Nothing really new on Ningbi and Ihime except the trouble with Kihungit was settled with three shells. [My dog] Belo has just returned scarred and battle weary from his first love affair (lasting 4 days) and Kilok has reached puberty too (how long do bitches menstruate?).

Got more on *masalais* [spirits] here and the principal one (equated to your main one, name forgotten) is Wolio and secondary ones are definitely located in Humumu and "serve" this entire area. All taro belongs to Wolio and the garden magic [when replanting taro stalks after harvesting and eating the corm and leaves] is to get Wolio to bring the corms (at night) to the gardens and put it [them] on the taro sticks. If no singsing—no taro corms at all. Kahame says he will tell me his spells, but I wouldn't be surprised if he insisted on pay. He gets two shells for performing his spells for others. Nothing so far to indicate any changing character in the *masalais*. We have no "protector" against people or sickness in the form of *masalais*. I asked pointed questions.

Ningbi says his parents-in-law now call him *iok* (father) and their daughter (his wife) *inu* (mother) and all his *tambu* (in laws) do also! What is your information on this. (I've also got [the term] *wiok*, but Ningbi insists it's "papa" *iok*.) If so it will certainly confuse the issue.

Spent an almost worthless day off in Kahame's bailiwick [garden] only 45 minutes away, but up a big mountain. (I still claim they're mountains due to their steepness!) Thought I'd get lots of family life, but all mothers were away leaving only a few kids and Hingme and 3 piglets. Got caught in rain thoroughly on the way back and net/plus result was stretched muscles and honey-in-the-comb. I never seem to hit anything interesting in the gardens.

I will leave the homeward plans to you—glad we have permission (to visit Lakalai on the north coast)—shall we walk over? Love, Jane
Ps. The NGS seems to have forgotten me (I haven't written them either).

Dulago, Sunday

Dear Jane,

Sorry I didn't get a reply off with Debli, but he insisted on departing while I was still taking notes on the quarrel. He and Paiyali woke me at 1:30 A.M. to give me your letter! Naturally everyone's convinced it contained news of major importance. As you doubtless know, there was no fight [at the singsing], due to the Luluai's determination not to have another here just before the Kiap arrives. But at least I saw the business of breaking up opposing parties with fire.

[It was customary to expect a fight at intercommunity ceremonial singsings, and visitors always arrive carrying spears and shields, expecting a fight. Fire (a burning stick), it is believed, will cause harm to those who do not stop what they are doing when it is invoked.]

At the moment I'm dead for lack of sleep, but the place is full of Hutkihyu men looking at photographs. We received no news at all about Manus, so no one has gone. Different rumors daily about the Kiap, of course. I'm not sure about bitches in heat, but by now you doubtless know for yourself.

The business about kinship terms for Ningbi sounds fantastic, but I'll check. Many thanks for the additional data on Wolio. It's just what we need. Later: Paiyali says Wolio bosses taro here too.

How are you on films by the way? I'm down to 4 rolls. If you can spare any, I'd appreciate it.

Thursday—Paiyali *et al.* left yesterday, presumably for Manus, if the rumor that came through the usual untrustworthy channels is correct. I sent a note to Dave (ADO) asking him to send up our mail if any escorts or whatever were coming back, but Paiyali (who suggested the note in the first place) became so nervous that the Kiap would reject him for work if he gave him the note that I bet it never gets delivered. He also suggested, at one point, that the note was telling the Kiap to jail him. Guilty conscience about what, do you suppose? I'm now in the throes of teaching Kasup the mysteries of the stove and coffee. I've decided to stay home today; because (of a tabu) having eaten bat two days ago, I can only skulk around the edges of the garden fence which I did yesterday. Maybe I can get some typing done.

Ngolu was here briefly yesterday, and as usual, I got more from him in two hours than in two weeks with anyone else. Most fascinating data was on divining the cause of sickness. After making a singsing, they sleep and a baby-like spirit leads their "devil" (soul) to the sick person, cuts open his body, and shows them the cause of the sickness, which can be alleviated the next day with the proper singsing. The spirit is called *tisa* another mysterious ramification of the word, which here is used for "fire," "grandfather," and was applied to the anvil for beating barkcloth [*a polai*], which is a *masalai* [spirit].

What on earth has happened to Algy *et al.* [the Kiap patrol]?

Sunday—Sutli has just turned up, so I have a chance to get this out at last. I've been feasting on bat and eel, but the smell of an adult male bat I was brought nearly drove me out of the house. Don't know how I've escaped anything of the sort before.

I had two splendid ethnographic days followed by absolutely nothing, but that's the way it goes. I'm trying to force myself to settle down to typing again. Love, Ann

Dulago, May 4?

Dear Jane,

By now you've probably received the letter I sent via Sutli- Obviously nothing much has happened since yesterday. My (long ago) information on shells put on grave of *tambu* [in laws] by newly weds, is that anyone in the *haus boi* [men's house] in which they're buried can take the shell. I've got all sorts of fascinating tidbits on spirits etc. but will wait till I see you. We've also had numerous and conflicting rumors about the Kiap.

Under the circumstances, I think I'll take the time to type up my abstract [for a paper to be read at the November American Anthropological Association] and send it out. I certainly have no prospects of getting anyone down in the near future, what with house building here and the departure of hordes of Yambon men (including Kulbo) for Manus.

Your abstract [on shell transactions for the AAA] seems fine in the first paragraph, but the last one a little anticlimactic. I think you can strengthen the last sentence (or last two), and especially make a reference to shells in the last one: "To be successful, etc.—a man must demonstrate his ability to accumulate shells through hard work ("determination" if you prefer), knowledge/wealth magic and skill in interpersonal relations"—or something of the sort. If Algy comes through Umbi en route here and you have suggestions [for me], please send (my abstract) back. Otherwise better send it down as is; I'm getting nervous about the deadline. I can certainly get by another week or so without film so don't strain (of course if you don't have any to spare, don't worry). Love, Ann

Dulago, May ?

Dear Jane,

We're in the midst of a "Kiap is coming!" alarm, but the interest is rapidly dying down. It was just a matter of getting word two days ago that they had arrived at Pomalal, but absolutely nothing since then, and no direct word at all. I've at least got the front room straightened up [to allow the Kiap to sleep in the designated haus Kiap], but at the expense of having the other two rooms so deep in gear that I can't move. I've also just been infuriated by the Luluai, who ordered the grass at the foot of my steps removed contrary to what he knew were my explicit instructions; I've been trying to encourage it to combat the mudhole that develops there with every rain. So much for any influence I have in this community.

[Some Kiaps evidently believed that a grassless village was a clean one. Perhaps this is so on the coast where villages are built on sand.]

Kasup told me about the proposed Debli-Tihime marriage when we came back from Umbi, and also that Kahamei was opposing it because they hadn't consulted him first and the Kiap has said that they must do so. The hand of the Kiap appears in the damnedest places. I just learned that that's why Tibtibli is said to boss the men's house; some Kiap appointed him (and Kasup fully expects him to be jailed over its present condition, but of course no one is making a move to remedy it). They are, however, spending enough time tidying up the place that I'm getting no ethnography done at all, but have at least written a few essential letters—TAA, Hicks, etc.

Later—This [mail] just arrived. Algy writes that he'll be going to Umbi from here via Yambon on Tuesday and will stay there til Thursday when he'll leave for Hulem and points south.

No film came! If you have any to spare, please send back with Lelus. Love, Ann

Umbi, May 8
Dear Ann,

Many thanks for mail and word of Kiap. Yesterday we heard he was at Dulago, *laining* [taking census] Seagit and would be here today. How, and (why) do these rumors start? We shall expect him Tuesday. I too have had my house cleaned. Whether its clean state will last til Tuesday is anybody's guess.

I'm getting photograph shy—particularly after Ross's (NGS) note saying exposures are erratic. I've been bracketing (exposures) widely just because of mistrust in my meter. Now what do I do? Here are some films. I'm *fairly* well off.

No hopes of a cargo-mail trip till Kiap comes and goes. I'm getting very low on fruit and meat (*I* will be all right on the latter as I have various tins the boys won't eat). Algy is certainly taking his time. I've gotten *nothing* ethnographic for last 2 days.

I had heard too of Debli and Tihime marriage before, but not from Debli and with no indication that it was imminent. Debli has *not* left and he says he has straightened out the *tok* (argument) and it will be safe for him to stay. But I don't believe anything anymore.

This [empty tobacco] tin belongs to Poyme. I hesitate giving tins to anyone other than the actual recipient, so have decided to send it to you in the hopes that it may actually arrive at its destination.

If the Kiap keeps his schedule, I'll be over on the 17th and hopefully will have a cargo group off over the weekend. Love, Jane

Dulago, Saturday
Dear Jane,

Algy and Col [the Kiaps] mysteriously decided to arrive a day early. They're most amiable (and bless their hearts, they're not sharing my house), but I fear our conversational resources will hardly be equal to the occasion. I'm constantly badgered by the locals to intervene in court cases, but of course have refused. Nothing of interest so far.

Herewith tins (of food) to tide you over till you come. I can spare plenty more, but I don't want to overload you unnecessarily.

Many thanks for the film. I'm sending a nasty note to Ross (NGS) (whose only comment on his shipment was that he wished I'd take lots more pictures—with regard to a lot that contained only 3 rolls), though I know it's Gilka's (NGS) fault. I think one shipment of slides went astray since I received a later large batch (from someone else) marked: envelope 2 of 2, with no comment at all. They certainly vary weirdly in their treatment of us, don't they.

[Because of tie-ups with customs in Rabaul, and in getting mail from Kandrian, our communication with the NGS (films and letters) were constantly crossing theirs to us. The result was that the NGS continually asked us to take more pictures and we continually worried that we would not have enough film to photograph an important event such as the Dulago Singsing.]

I've also been going through the ethnographic doldrums, except for one good genealogical session, in which two major tangles were straightened out—one a simple matter of a man's two wives, but the ramifications are enormous; the other an omitted sister, who explains Yanli's ties to a lot of people such as Gaho et al. Yanli's mother's family was no use; all from across the river to the east.

I enclose my letters to TAA, theirs to me, and the form for you to fill out. Please add to mine and send on. As you see, they've given us the fares (but why no mention of Hong Kong?). The discounts in *Time* were on trans-Atlantic flights. Love, Ann

[Kiaps visited Umbi May 12 through May 14]

Umbi, May 15
Dear Family,

It's so quiet and peaceful right now that I can't believe it. Debli, who did not leave, is sleeping and two young boys are quietly looking at magazines and the rest of the village is out bush.

The Kiap has come and gone and life returns to normal. Algy (Patrol Officer) and Col (a new Cadet Patrol Officer) with Police escort and 20 followers, arrived here on Tuesday after spending two nights at Dulago and left yesterday (Thurs.) a.m. For the preceding five days the village was full with all the residents and about 15 other visitors coming to collect debts and with the threat of court action (from the Patrol). It was a mad house.

I expected Algy to be my "guest" but he requested that the (other) rest house be put in order for them, which meant quickly building an extra outhouse, cook house, and shower house all squeezed into the small space

Census Patrol, Umbi

available. To me it seemed a needless duplication of facilities, but as it turned out it was a nice comfortable arrangement. I entertained the two for dinner the first night and was entertained by them the second, playing "500" (a card game) until midnight and in between they were free to do Government business and I was free to try to do some interviewing (I got one large genealogy from a visitor). It was a quiet inspection. The twins were censused and the old graveyard, in which three of the recent burials have taken place, was approved (with its improvements), in spite of its being directly contrary to a previous Government order. All houses and out houses were approved and in spite of previous threats, no one brought their disagreements to the Kiap for court action. So no one went to jail and a big sigh of relief could be heard...

[Algy brought his large dog with him, which proceeded to terrify everyone and bit the Luluai's dog. Algy then tied him up. During the dreaded census, the dog lay under Kiap's table to which it was tied. Each resident, as his or her name was called, moved up to stand in front of the Kiap (and his equally fearful dog) while answering his questions. My female dog, Kilok, a quarter of the size of Algy's dog, made a sneak attack and bit Algy's dog on his nose, drawing blood, and then Kilok streaked for the safety of the bush. Algy's dog leaped about four feet straight up, collapsing the table and sending Algy's papers flying into the wind, eventually to fall into the mud. No one dared to laugh. But that night after the Kiaps, dreaded dog, and followers left, Kilok returned and many villagers turned up at my house with special tidbits of food given to her as the only village resident who dared to do what everyone wished to do—and then we all laughed.]

Today I am busy making arrangements for 21 carriers leaving tomorrow to bring up all the food for the remaining time (I only hope everyone turns up). Then on Sunday, I'm off to Dulago (with two young lads as escort) to have my birthday party. Love Jane

[Jane visited Dulago May 17 through May 19.]

Dulago, May 20
Dear Jane,

Sorry you were hurried off yesterday, especially in view of the good weather. We had a nice curing ceremony in mid-morning though unfortunately I was too slow off the mark to photograph it. The victim, a married man, was sick as the result of eating taro cooked on a fire alongside a bed on which a pregnant or menstruating woman had slept.

I was kept awake for hours by my (pet) sugar-glider's frantic efforts to escape and got up this morning to find that he had succeeded (despite a stone ax on top of the tin). Not a trace except that Roo looks awfully sleek and well fed. I hope you're having better luck.

[Ann had been given two of these tiny sugar-gliders (pocket-sized marsupial flying squirrels) called *sungek* in Kaulong. She gave one to me for my birthday present.]

I'd like to be working on the annual (NSF) report, but Haungin is here and maddening as ever. He and Kasup are conversing now, and I'm keeping an ear open for anything of interest, but so far it's Dullsville (though in the usual deceptively excited tones). But in re-reading the essential letter (herewith) [from the NSF], with its statement about a "short informal report," I've decided to drastically reduce my original outline, so we'll have plenty left for the comprehensive final report. Let me know if there's anything you think *must* go in at this point. Hope you can decipher this. I've spent a couple of hours trying to get two loudmouthed boys to shut up and let me think. *If* you can find a copy of our grant proposal, I'd be very grateful. I don't want this to be too repetitive.

Thursday—Bruce (malarial control) arrived simultaneously with your carriers, so things are a little confused. I've written Hancock [our agent] enclosing a cheque in hopes we can get the film through [customs] with duty. Curses! Love, Ann

Umbi May 20th Wed. P.M.
Dear Ann,

The cargo is dribbling in and all indications are that John has fouled things up by not dividing the cargo as I requested and thus putting heavy tins in the Patrol Box with the inevitable complaints. The case is still at Angus, plus other problems. But this is minor to the Hancock/Saunders letter. My only recollection is that Hancock has all the necessary papers. The new customs man must be a real horror as he "destroyed" a tin of cheese my parents sent me— *dim-min-he!* [an obscene Kaulong swear word].

[We had arranged with Rabaul Customs (with many essential documents) to receive our supplies of film from the NGS free of duty because it was for "scientific" purposes. But our clearance was "lost" during a change of personnel in the Rabaul Customs Office, and we had to pay enormous duty for film from this time on.]

The NGS says most of my pictures are now overexposed! but Brown (NGS) sounded encouraging, or at least not discouraging—who's Stewart (NGS)? I'm totally confused. I've just exerted myself and found the *one remaining* "grant document" from the NSF. Am sending it to you as I can't think of anything else to do (about the film) and the two carriers have just now (5:15) decided to go to Dulago today.

My parents are now quite sure I'll be murdered apropos of my telling them of my recording sessions on murderers and my rows with Debli!

Sungek (my pet sugar-glider) has diarrhea but aside from being terrified of new surroundings, I think is eating, but am not sure. He doesn't like the one sungek-sized pawpaw I have, but he doesn't mind sleeping on the wash cloth— in fact he prefers to curl up in it [in my shirt pocket] to riding on my shoulders.

Later 5:25—The two (letter) carriers have decided to wait until tomorrow. Having hurried up and condensed all the above—now what? We had a 3.5 inch rain here on Monday, but the Ason was not flooded—all the small streams were. Have just learned Kilok has gone (followed or was taken) to Miu (next language group) with Soksili! Presumably will come back sometime with him.

7 p.m.—Kongli (a carrier with my kerosene) just arrived and has accused Kasli of holding back 1/2 of everyone's rations to eat himself. (They couldn't complain to him at the time because they would be "shamed," and everyone who went to carry cargo *long ol* [on behalf of others], ate my carriers rations, including Kahame (who was given money to buy food for himself, as he said he wouldn't meet with everyone in Kandrian on Monday). But he did get to Kandrian and ate rations and kept the food money and *bought* [paid] a girl to carry my cargo for 5/- (keeping 10/ for himself). What a damnable crowd this is. (None of the culprits have come in yet). Ningbi is reported to be returning via Pomalal carrying rice *bilong ol* (for others) having loaded his wife with 28 lbs of sugar plus a mysterious tin of biscuits (large) when she should be carrying butter! I'm going nuts. Ningbi is reported to have arrived. Think I'll retreat into a mystery (book). Thanks for a lovely birthday. Love Jane

Umbi, Thurs. May 28

Dear Ann,

Debli arrived today with the enclosed mail and at the same time Sutli announced his taro was planted and he was off tomorrow for a bag of rice for me, and Iamopli offered to collect *this* week's mail! I thought he (Sutli) was planning to go next week, but this is the Passismanua, hence I've been madly trying to write letters this afternoon. I've written this new NGS correspondent and told him about our film problem and also asked him if he could let us know exactly where we were weak in content as we both? felt we had photographed the daily activities *ad nauseam* and if he could be specific about re-takes it would help (hope you agree). I also asked him not to send any more slides [with comments] back to me, but did not include you.

I think John Yun [store keeper] has been in association with the natives too long—after having substituted ordinary flour because he had no self-rising, he sent a double order of the latter with Debli—of course I had to pay for the carrying and at the moment I'm swimming in the stuff. Would you like some? I'll probably introduce "dampers" for lack of grease to make pancakes or anything else. [Damper is Australian unleavened bread baked in an earth oven].

Sungek (sugar-glider) is settling in—I've finally found a stump for his latrine. Before, he "performed" on my shoulders to the amused-embarrassment of all. He also runs for my shirt pocket to sleep in—after performing, and stays there quite happily for hours at a time. Bruce was quite "taken" with him and is going to see if Mary (Stevens) will look after him while they [McLeans] are on leave. He's donated nails and wire screening for me to make a more suitable house for him. The biscuit tin is really too small—he leaps for joy when I free him in the morning. He loves melon (all finished) and is eating bananas in small quantities and of course milk. Sorry to hear of your *sungek's* demise.

I have been finding it dreadfully hard to get back in the groove. Practically nothing accomplished. I have hopes of this phase being temporary—but the informants also seem to be fed up with the questions I'm fed up with the asking of!

Debli absconded with my playing cards and took them to Kandrian. And when he finally turned them over to me, they were in a dreadful state. I told him I paid 15/ for them and *olosem wonem* [so what now?], and he said he would buy them and I had absolutely no compunction of saying, "all right." Life is certainly smoother with just Ningbi around. Ningbi's wife fled to Yambon a few days ago. She (accidentally, I think) hit a young girl who is a *tambu* [in-law] of hers on the head with her knife while cutting *purpur* [skirt material]. She also ate food in front of the same *tambu*. Ningbi says she is shamed, certainly the young girl (one of her best friends) is not cross at her.

[Tabus concerning eating or drinking in front of any in-law are permanent tabus for all married people. I learned later that in-laws should not see your teeth—a sign of anger—one reason to have blackened teeth, and when in company of your in-laws, to cover your mouth while laughing, both undoubtedly related to the eating and drinking tabus.]

Ningbi's sister, who married a Miu, is here for her first visit since her marriage 10-12 years ago. Her husband is a red-clayed dreadlocks man, who is very shy of me. Udwali, the sister, is completely without shyness and bubbled into and through my house and acted as if we'd known each other for 10 months.

[Really important men, "big men," traditionally wore their hair long, in dreadlocks and covered with red ochre, perhaps related to the use of red ochre on the skulls we had seen.]

The annual report sounds excellent. If you'd like me to type it up send it back and I'll send it off with some other volunteers for rice collecting who are thinking about going soon. If they don't go soon I'll send it over to you again for your mail/cargo on the 8th. Love, Jane

Dulago, Saturday
Dear Jane,

Lainbo, who looks after *The* pig, came in today to tell me they're planning its killing (*vi-ngin*) —a nice linguistic example of a noun formative suffix again! A couple of excursions first and they'll also wait for Nieheli of Hutkihyu, just jailed for not finishing his house, to return. So I still don't trust them at all to hold it before we leave. But at least they're talking about it again.

Wednesday—I definitely plan to send carriers on the 8th, so send over your mail. Did you write Stewart? (He's head of the Photo Lab, according to the copy of The Magazine with the Gilliard article.) Still no limes—sorry. More and more talk about killing the pig, but—?

I thought you might like to send the (enclosed) slide to your family as proof that you're bearing up well.

Saturday (a week later) I take it something went wrong re Debli's trip to Kandrian? This is being written on the off-chance that you're sending someone over. Because all the men in the village are working full-time on the HB [men's house ordered rebuilt by the Kiap], I don't have a chance to send anyone to Umbi. The HB may also delay my cargo a bit, but presumably not much. (It's also brought ethnography to a virtual standstill.)

Judging from my recent experience, these *mulis* [limes] will ripen in time, so give them a try. The green ones seem to just be falling from the trees, which may mean that there will be a shortage. I've just reread my diary for (last) July to check on the weather (to expect on our way out). Horrors! Oh, for the wings of an angel.

Later—Your letter just arrived. Glad to hear your sungek is flourishing. Don't know what I could do with the flour, but no thanks. Love Ann.

Umbi, June 3rd (yet!) 8 p.m.
Dear Ann,

A ghost has just attacked Kahame down in the village which ensures me of peace and quiet up here. I have spent the afternoon trying to write letters with a new six-year old constantly bugging me. In this jumble of incoming-outgoing and stopping mail, you will find your copy of the NSF report (uncorrected), and a letter to the University Museum with the original (corrected), asking them to send it on to the NSF (and add the grant # which I no longer have). I also asked [the Museum] to wire all our remaining grant money to Amer. Express, Sydney by Aug. 1st. My only thought as I typed (the report) was: are these cultures really so "*extraordinary*"? But *maski* [what the heck]. Also in thinking it over I'd be hard put to defend *patrilateral* cross-cousin marriage on the basis of what data I have, but all this can wait and certainly our preliminary report isn't going to shatter the world.

It's been stop and go getting information this week. I saw Debli tabu his taro and learned that the black-nosed snake *yiabidwasun* [literally fire-stops-on-him] also controls taro (with Wolio) and there are singsings [spells] to him. (This snake is strictly tabu for eating here.) This information is directly contradictory to Debli and Kahame's previous statement that all singsings are to Wolio alone and getting this information from Debli was like extracting an impacted wisdom tooth. I practically had to knock him over the head to tell me anything that day—strictly from laziness on his part, I'm convinced, because after the initial shaking up, he did call me over to show me a dark brown caterpillar whose devil (spirit), when sung to (bespelled), watches over the taro after it's been tabued.

Then the other night (Sun.) all men present in the village took off to Sinit (a Hulem matmat) to dedicate a new house and Liem and Pahinbo and I were left in the village. The two women came up to talk and I decided it was now or never to broach the subject of sex. I started off asking about illegitimacy and pre-marital sex and got little response on the former and, on the latter, the statement with two case histories of couples who on their own decided to get married, slept in the bush 2-3 nights, and then returned and announced their marriage and as far as I could determine, there were no untoward repercussions, certainly they stayed married. One of these was the real MoBr-SiDa [Mother's brother-Sister's daughter] marriage of Ningbi's parents-in-law. I also got the information that when the couple first sleep together, the girl puts a shell inside the man's laplap—by demonstration, over his private parts, and in effect buys (pays) the man. I also got the term for copulate *sung*, i.e. *yulong sungsungwhal* [the two copulate together]. But when I asked for conception beliefs, Pahinbo said she couldn't talk as she was shamed too much. Even with prodding, i.e. "we're all girls here and there isn't a man within miles," and stories of storks and Tiwi (aboriginal) "dreamings" (of spirit children), I got nothing more, except a few age-grading terms for females, which I must follow up as I kept steering her away from them in order to get more intimate details.

[Concerning sexual intercourse and conception, both the Kaulong and Sengseng were extremely shy, and try as we might, we had had little luck in getting, at this time, much information about this aspect of their sexual lives.]

The only other interesting item was that *inaling*, a term of address for some *inu* (mothers), apparently at random, is/are also female *masalai* [spirits] of advanced years, who, if they nibble at food first and you eat it afterwards, will cause you to go *longlong* [crazy].

Outside of this, life has been dullsville. I'm sending your (exposed) roll of film back. I thought I had one to go with it, but I can't locate it. I just can't find anything interesting to photograph. I left my camera behind on the trip with Debli, because if it ever looked threatening, that was the day—it took all my conscientious efforts to persuade myself to venture out to see the ritual. Of course, it didn't rain. But the ritual was hardly worth the film anyway.

Soksili and Kahame may be going after the last two bags of rice this Saturday. I would love it if they suddenly decided to postpone the trip, but I can't afford to insist. But if they do go this Sat. I *won't* have them collect the mail (meaning an extra small lad going too) as I trust you will be sending off people soon. It's getting late and three small incipient TUs [tropical skin ulcers] are giving me hell, so I'm off to bed. Love Jane

Dulago, Thursday

Dear Jane,

I didn't get any criticism from the new man at the NGS, but he said he hadn't looked at my latest batch. Doubtless he'll have plenty then: I kept forgetting what film I had in the camera on the Seagit trip. Damned if I see what we can possibly do about weakness of content. Did he say anything else?

Boys just arrived. Thanks for your fascinating information. I got some stuff on illegitimacy, including an accusation on the part of the young men, that a girl here is pregnant. The wife of the Luluai of Seuk is said to have had and killed an illegitimate child (before her present marriage). Father known, but wouldn't marry her. However marriage is normal (follows sex, and of course pregnancy) if there's only one lover (see below).

I'm dying to pin the lads here down, but they've been thoroughly occupied with the new HB, and I've accomplished damned little. It's almost finished, thank God. The stuff on the snake may tie in with this business about snakes wound around taro and sickness resulting from eating it.

The boys seem to be sticking around for a while to cook a yam, so I'll go on. Your business about this sort of informal consummation of marriage agrees with mine, but this is not really premarital sex—sleeping together under these circumstances really gets them married. But in our discussion the boys told me of a woman in Moiya who has quite a large illegitimate child, and who couldn't get married because she said she didn't know which of her lovers was the father. Still to be checked is a general statement that a pregnant girl would be killed (from shame) by her family *if* she couldn't pinpoint a father. Add to all this, the statement that started it off: when Mekngin heard that the girl he is in love with is married, he said he won't get married but just have *pren* (lovers). So they are beginning to give, and I have hopes, though they still strike me as comparatively very prudish.

We had a major sorcerers or ghost scare the other night too. Two grown girls fled screaming (and reportedly naked) to where the boys were sleeping, for protection. Presumably they were carrying their laplaps; they were clothed when I saw them. But we had a rousing couple of hours.

The thieving dog died a natural death (starvation, probably), thank God. There seems to be a slight tendency to believe me responsible, since I once told them (truthfully) that I'd been taught a spell for killing dogs. It will be funny if I end up in a shell exchange.

I made the effort yesterday and photographed the rest of the flints. I hated to use the film, but I wanted to send them to Kandrian and had visions of no sun and no time later. I don't want a tin of flour, thanks.

Got a letter from CA (*Current Anthropology*) asking if I wanted to do an article on "The Ethnography of New Guinea." Just what I need for my spare time!

[In June Ann visits me]

Dulago, June Tuesday
Dear Jane,

Pleasant trip back and got to Yambon to find one man pounding barkcloth in the HB (men's house) and another painting it under a shelter outside. But with no flash equipment, I doubt if the pictures of either process will be satisfactory.

Got back to find a considerable ruckus. The reason Kasup tried to give me coffee at 5:15 on Saturday was that he was trying to flee the village before dawn. He'd just tried to give money to Pangsili, our local belle (Milingli's sister: her older sister is married to Kasup's older brother), in hopes of having an affair with her, and she had rejected him, with curses (references to his eating *pekpek* [feces], in front of all the dancers at a village singsing). He did leave, planning to go away to work, but turned back on the road. However, yesterday her father turned up and blasted him again, and he left again, and was brought back only by the tears of Pele, who is married to Kasup's 1st cousin. (All this second hand from Kasup.) He says he intends to stick it out till I leave, but is too shamed to face anyone, and won't take part in the (major) singsing (or, presumably fetch and paint his new shield). Meanwhile he's in danger of a real food shortage because he can't ask anyone to bring us vegetables, and he talks of leaving the village after dawn each day and returning at nightfall. Well, we'll see.

Wednesday—Spent an excruciating day trying to drag information out of Kasup who hung around the house but wouldn't give. He says he doesn't know any taro magic (confirming your statement, but suspicious because Paiyali [his younger brother] seemed to know more than he does), and that your *inaling* (here called *dinahi*, as predicted) only operate around Umbi. They are identified with the red parrot, *e-susu*, and you must also be careful not to drink from leaves they have drunk from and left lying in waterholes. No more information: you know how it goes.

Mail hasn't arrived yet, and both the brothers [who own the pig] are in Katektek collecting *dinau* [debts] so no further word as to when the singsing will be. They've built a platform to display the food on, and the women of Yambon are talking about clowning (*lis*) at it. My present feeling is that the only thing that will keep it from taking place fairly soon will be the weather. Even if it does take place, I fear we'll have a struggle photographically.
Later—Mail just got in, complete with another batch of film. Might as well keep it here for the moment, and you won't have to bring any over. However, since customs was presumably paid on this too, I think we should both send a doubly large check to Hancock. (The outside packet was just addressed to me so presumably the lot was charged to me.)

Mubudli and wife are reported to be en route back from Katektek, so I'll hold off on the mail in hopes of hearing about a time for the singsing in the next day or two. I feel very happy about the TAA letter [with our exit itinerary], except I rather think I'd like to spend only a couple of days in Rabaul, get to Lae on a non-Sunday (say Friday) and perhaps go to Moresby a little earlier. The relative civilization of the Papua (hotel) in Moresby appeals more than the Cosmo (hotel) in Rabaul. Otherwise, I wouldn't change anything. It seems to me that we have plenty of time in Australia for our side trips. I would still plan to come over on the 21st and (we can) leave on the 22nd (of July).

The person I paid to bring the mail spent the money and went off with the Kiap, and gave the mail to someone else. He's planning to sell me a shell, so maybe we can adjust the debt that way. It came back with three tins (cans) in the plastic (mail) bag and everything else (mail included) loose in the *non*-waterproof mail sack. Jesus!
Love, Ann

Umbi, Thurs., June 25?

Dear Ann,

Thanks for the mail. (I gather no official word yet on pig.) I think it's time for us both to get out of here what with Kasup and Debli. Had major fight with Debli last night, started by him because he turned up at 7 p.m. and I told him to get some *kaukau* [sweet potato] to eat as we hadn't *scaled* [portioned] rice for him (having already eaten). He told me to pack up and leave Umbi! Fortunately I had actual support from Sutli and Ningbi and it all ended up with Debli giving me £1 to "shake hands." But it was a tense moment and things are still tense as far as I'm concerned.

I will digest the TAA (letter) and bring it with me for the pig-killing. It's pretty definite someone will be going for mail around the 3rd or 4th. I have volunteers, but anything can happen. I got the curse yesterday, 10 days early! which coincides beautifully with our trip down—Hell.

I tried letting Sungek out last night and Kilok nearly consumed him, so I can't try that again. But Ningbi says he'll feed him while I'm at Dulago (and the 2 dogs). I told Slebme to bring her burned child (for treatment) to Dulago on Saturday, because if they killed the pig, I'd be there. Don't know what she will decide to do now.

Nothing more at the moment. Hope to see you soon. Love Jane.

Dulago, Monday

Dear Jane,

Sorry if you're living in suspense, but so am I. The decision as to the day for the singsing is to be made today, theoretically. Kasup warns that I'll get speared if I try to photograph the spear fight. Well, we'll see. If only the weather holds! That four days of rain was enough to bring back my foot affliction in full force. I went down yesterday to see the collection of taro for the singsing (complete with a couple of odd bits of ritual), and had one of those mysterious attacks of weak knees on the way back. Whatever it is, I hope it holds off for the trip home.

[Both of us periodically suffered from this sudden onset of severe physical weakness ("weak-knee syndrome" we called it) at unexpected and unexplained intervals. Eventually Ann correlated "weak knees" with taking our weekly antimalarial drug. Both occurred on Sundays.]

I was up at 5 (all night singsing) in hopes of seeing *ulal* [ritual courtship fighting] and I don't know why it didn't occur, considering the mixed bag of people, but no luck. I'll be glassy-eyed by the time you arrive: another singsing is scheduled for tonight, and I expect we'll get no sleep the night of the real thing. By the way, if you're still overloaded with butter, bring some along and we'll keep up our strength with buttered date roll.

Nothing fascinating ethnographically, except that I finally got that business of paying for compliments straightened out. High time, I must say.

[If a visiting big man compliments a local big man on some possession in which, under normal conditions, the visitor will not expect to share, the local big man must compensate the visitor. Both Ann and I were considered as our headman's "possessions" by a visiting big man. We refused our headman's request that we should compensate this visitor, thus leaving him to do his cultural duty.]

I've taken dozens of "nothing" pictures, in a what-the-hell mood. My temper is fraying dangerously, for no reason at all (except suspense, I suspect). I keep being afraid the rains will set in earnest and prevent the singsing. But it seems fantastic to me that we got to Kandrian a year ago.

Tuesday—Word is that they'll fasten [tie up] the pig tomorrow, so come ahead. I've been up all night, and am in something of a daze. Love, Ann

Dulago, June 30
Dear Family,

I am at present at Dulago. Arrived this afternoon and found Ann was planning to send mail out tomorrow—I am here for THE pig killing, a large tusker. Tuskers are pigs whose upper canines have been removed so that the lower canines can grow unimpeded into a full circle sometimes even reentering the lower jawbone. Pigs are tied up and are witness to the singing and dancing before being killed in the morning following the all night singsing. They are butchered and portions given to visiting pork-trade partners with elaborate shell exchanges. This tusker belongs to the Luluai of Dulago. Ever since we arrived a year ago talk has been going on about killing this pig and it now looks as though it is actually going to take place. Ann was to send me a note as to the actual date, but I came on anyway today (met the note at Yambon) as people have for the past three days passed through Umbi on their way to Dulago and the Umbi contingent decided we'd better be on our way.

Our river was quite flooded and we spent an hour crossing it mainly because my three young lads felt I would drown, and I thought they might. When we finally straightened this out we crossed with no more trouble than wet clothes. Arrived here with no further incident and in spite of being a day early Ann was glad to see me. She's had little sleep during the past 48 hours due to two solid nights of preliminary singing.

They plan to sing again tonight, catch and tie up the pig tomorrow, sing all night again and slaughter in the morning. The affair is drawing people from all villages for miles around and we expect to see the real thing, including the spear and shield dance *cum* fight.

At least at this affair we shall have a nice dry house to retire to as the dance ground is 50 feet away from Ann's front steps. The only hitch may be the weather but we have our fingers crossed...Love Jane

[The singsing was extremely interesting, quite the biggest one we had seen. For the first part of the evening the singers sang alternately from two positions, with the women and girls dancing and whistling in between the groups of singing men.

After many hours, the men began a challenging dance in which each group took turns in confronting the other group and at point blank range, turning and retreating. Older women led the charging men, and after the alternating challenges had gone on for some time, the retreating group unexpectedly turned around and met other group of charging men face to face in the middle of the clearing— and both groups were now poised with their spears inches away from each other's faces. The host's wife walked between the two groups holding a fire-stick and calling for peace. We were told not to take any more flash pictures, as they blinded the eyes of the men as they continued to dance challenging each other, and they were afraid of battle and bloodshed should they make accidental contact with their spears.

Early next morning the tusker and three other pigs were killed, butchered, and eventually portions given, with elaborate exchange of shells, to visiting trade partners. About noon, transactions were concluded. I spent the night at Dulago, leaving for Umbi early the next morning.]

Dulago, Wednesday
Dear Jane,

It's a good thing you didn't wait around on Friday [after the singsing]; they distributed the food at 3. I was finally given a hunk of pork (accompanied by a demand for payment—from the man from whom I'd bought the leg) just in time for supper, as I was muttering curses on the lot of them.

Mail got in at nightfall last night, and Sulubo will take it over to you when the weather permits. Not a word from anyone at Kandrian except the monthly account from Chin Cheu, but an exceedingly nice letter from the PO at Hoskins, who seems to be welcoming us with open arms (tired of all those Bola house girls, maybe), and will have the roof of the *haus Kiap* repaired for us. R. (the transferred CPO) has gone on leave, and the friendly schoolteacher has also been transferred.

The enclosed picture [of one of us swimming in the Ason] applies more to you than to me. Presumably you took it anyway? The hair and the pallor of the figure in the water look more like me than you. I got detailed instructions on photographing the cave, but even if I had the time, which I don't, I don't have the flashbulbs.

No great news on the ethnographic front. Good all round crisis because it's been suggested openly that Pangsili is pregnant (there've been mutterings for a long time, and I suspect they're correct). She's the object of Kasup's affections.

Sorry there are so many newspapers, but from all accounts the Kiaps were in a temper on Monday morning, so it's probably as well that we didn't put them to any more trouble sorting. The *Pix* was addressed to me (I also got 2 of

Dave's *Times* and I'm damned well keeping them). Have they put up the Kanda (vine across the river)? Love, Ann

Umbi Tuesday, July 7
Dear Ann,

A just-in-case note: Nothing is going on at the moment as usual. We had a very wet trip back [from the *singsing*], due, I am told, to Telbudli's making rain (magically) to wash his sacrificed pig's tracks away so he wouldn't be reminded of him!

The rain hit just as we approached the Silop cut-off and true to his nature Debli sped ahead. When we, the boys and I reached the first [descending] mountain slope on the Hulem-Umbi Road, it was a veritable stream itself and we rushed ahead. I fell twice, Iamopli once and when we reached the Ason, we found it in raging flood. We held hands and foolishly attempted the crossing and were turned back with (the youngest lads) Idpo and Iamopli in tears.

We sang out [shouted] hoping to be heard in Umbi, and debated where we would retreat to for a cold and hungry night. Debli appeared (on the opposite bank coming from Umbi) and contemplated the sight for 5 minutes, then set out for us with the water up to his armpits and rising visibly. On reaching our side he, without a word, cut a stick and then called to Idpo to climb up on his shoulders, and he struggled across, to return for Iamopli and again for Lita. [These three lads were under 12 years old and did not swim well.] The water was up to his neck at this point and Naingli [an older lad] said, "did I think I could swim it?" As he seemed willing, I said "yes" (preferable to being carried over) and we went up the bank as far as possible. Naingli went first and made it and I followed. It was not a pleasure swim—a strong undercurrent pulled Naingli under (once) and I found it a fight to stay on top. Debli went back once more for my camera bag, leaving shoes, bananas, stick and canteen for the next day and we shivered our way up, to find that Kilok had produced a son (one only), born that A.M. on my bed, and found by Ningbi as he swept the house. It's name—Abed—given by Ningbi. (Debli says its name is Sambo.) Kilok is proving a very good mother. They are now in a far corner of the cargo room. The puppy is adorable.

Kasli hasn't turned up at all and on Sunday, Kahame said he was off to Kandrian to collect Soksili, Kaliam and Ligiok to come back and carry cargo for us. So I had him collect tobacco for me, a tin of tea and £10 in shillings— just to be on the safe side, but no mail as I assume Ngolu has collected it.

Saw the ritual singsing over tying a rope on a new young pig. They blow sung-over [bespelled] lime into the pig's nostrils and ears and mouth and down the chest first. Then sing as they tie the rope on. This particular pig is black and called Dakso! As far as I can gather the grandmother (of the pig) was a white pig from Vunapope called "Dakso" and all issue carry the same name. Similarly for pigs named "Suksuk" and "Muk." (Big pigs, particularly tuskers, get individual names.) Nothing much of ethnographic importance. I've been trying to get answers to some questions, but it's slow going.

Thurs—Thanks for mail. My pictures from the NGS were so stuck together most of the comments were lost in prying them apart! But the letter sounds as if they haven't quite given us up! By the way, I've found four small boxes of flashbulbs—to use in Kandrian? Don't know what I can do with the suggestions what with the weather. I shall make a concerted effort to get a *kanda* [vine] across (the river) on the 19th or 20th. My initial efforts produced *"Em i no taim bilong ren. Oli mekim nabaut tasol"* [It isn't rainy season yet. Everyone is making rain magic all about here, that's all]. Love, Jane

Umbi, July, Tues.
Dear Ann,

Just had a long talk with Kahame re: cargo. It seems he has just come through Arihi and that "all" men there are "strong" to carry cargo for us [on our exit trip], and I'm to send a note to them saying how many and when. In back of all this is the food question. Kahame is crying "famine" again and says that your carriers will go hungry and they should bring their own food to Umbi. I've strongly suggested that it would be nice if Umbi-ites would feed their "brothers," but I have the suspicion that Kahame is saying this because of pressure put on him by the Arihi group, and what the ramifications will be in Arihi, I don't know. Anyway, I think I can count on four certainties (carriers) from here and am willing to write to Arihi for four more and can ask for 8 if you think it would be safer—re your cargo (see PS). I have a feeling that we may end up with far more than needed, but better this than not enough. I have offered the case-carriers £1 @, if they go straight through, but if they change (off with others), I've marked 6/ to Arihi, 4/ to Lapalam and 4/ to Kandrian. I've asked Kahame to talk the whole situation over with you. (I've decided not to ask him to talk to potential carriers in Yambon as who knows what he'll say.)

I will have rice enough for your household and mine here and on the road. Tin meat for me and my boys. Plenty of biscuits and peanut butter, jam and butter for us, but have decided the flour will just be too much bother. Plenty tea, but questionable on coffee.

This whole business, may be just Kahame's usual tricks, i.e. crying hunger and lack of carriers is something he always does, and as I said he's just had pressure put on him by Arihi relatives. Quite a number of people have said they were going to carry cargo for me, and I haven't turned any away, but this "refusal" to feed your people is a new one.

For reasons known only to him, Debli harvested a garden yesterday—true lack of foresight. I went up to the garden for exercise only and for my efforts have: 1) a blister from trying one of the 1st pair of boots because the upper is intact—so it's the broken down ones I'll have to wear, and 2) a very painful upper rib-cage where my fist was driven against it in a spectacular fall flat on my face (and ribs). I can just breathe and move with great caution and stiffness, but as it's wearing off slowly, I diagnose bruising, not fracturing, and 3) real bites from two leeches! and 4) a broken pair of shorts from getting hung-up on a fence post, and 5) no additional information.

My 2nd lamp is breathing its last so do not expect illumination on your last night here aside from candles and flashlights. More talk of getting a *kanda* [vine] over the river. I said if they did put it up it wouldn't rain, that this was *our* fashion and great interest was shown. I've also composed a Kaulong version of "rain, rain go away and don't come back, for Ann and Jane are going to Kandrian" and it rhymes (in Kaulong)!

The Mission Brothers have offered to look after Sungek and I've told Ningbi and Debli to start thinking about who's going to look after *their* dogs [Kilok and Abed, and Belo] while they are in Kandrian. That's about all the activity since last note. See you soon, Love Jane

Wednesday—P.S. Kahame says now he knows of only four Arihi men expecting to carry, and that Yambon carriers will probably not go hungry in Arihi.

PSS. Last night (Tuesday) they tried to marry off Debli and Tihime. Tihime broke the wall of one house escaping and no one knows where Debli is this a.m.!

Dulago, Thurs.
Dear Jane,
Kahamei apparently recanted when faced with the question on the spot. Apparently most if not all of those planning to accompany me are from Yambon and Koyok is here at the moment. He and Kasup certainly seem to think it's worth their taking the chance, so I guess we'll just have to play it by ear; assume I can get people from here (certainly I'll be able to get to Umbi—river permitting) and cope in Umbi if something ghastly goes wrong. Glad to have your information on payments; it seems reasonable to me.

I feel terribly frustrated, being as I have 18 pages of this [steno-pad] size paper with unanswered questions and my success at getting them answered is minimal. Things are going better than they were a few days ago, but I'm really looking forward to getting in a position in which I won't have to worry about it anymore, beyond Kandrian that is.

Have you heard about Piakagit's elopement with Makbili? I was surprised at the ruckus, which is said to be partly because she's a widow (but Plakli is married, just now, to a widow), and partly because she's a true sister of his first wife (but she was also a true sister of her first husband's first wife). Her first husband was Kasup's true mother's brother).

Two threatened singsings with fights, but I imagine you've heard about both of them. I thought I'd told you about the pig-naming business (concerning "dakso" etc. pigs), but it's nice to know your information agrees with mine.

I'll bring coffee and meat for us. With your biscuits, etc., I see no reason to bother with the flour. I think there'll just be enough. I found Kasup was making my coffee extra-strong and using it up at a fearful rate, but I've stepped on him. I think candles for the road will be a Good Thing. Congratulations on the addition to your household. Your trip home is a real horror story. I'll be chewing my nails till we get across the stream.

What the NGS wanted me to do was to go back and photograph the cave again. Even if I had the time and energy to organize an expedition, I don't want to use up all my flashbulbs. I'd like to take a few pictures on the way down, a few in Kandrian, and some in Lakalai. Hope you've recovered from your accident. This is a splendid time to get a blister (bet you, I have one by Arihi, no matter what, same business—old strong shoes). Love, Ann

[In the village neither of us wore shoes and we were not sure whether our boots and/or our feet would last out the final trek.

Ann made it across the Ason and we had a sleepless night before our departure due to the Umbi locals holding an all-night singsing.

The trip to Arihi, the first stop, took me twelve hours, even longer than it had on my first trek over this bush track. This time an attack of "weak knees" hit me shortly after leaving Umbi. Every step took enormous effort and I was forced to stop and rest frequently. After about nine hours, Ann went ahead to Arihi in order to negotiate for a house for us and to make it ready, as it was growing quite dark. Little by little the cargo carriers abandoned me and went on to Arihi where each reported to Ann that *Dion em i dai long rot* (Jane is dying on the road). As long as they didn't report me *dai pinis* (completely dead), she knew I was making my very weary way.]

Kandrian, July 25
Dear Family,

As you can see we are successfully out! We left Umbi on Wednesday with plenty of carriers, one of which was our local good weather magician and for three days not a drop of rain fell! This (three days of sun) is totally unheard of at this time of year. When Ann and I commentated on our good luck with (the lack of) rain, we were told that luck nothing!—the weather magician had been hired and paid for by our carriers to stop the rain.

It was a long trip to Arihi, our first stop, but no particular problems! [One doesn't write everything to already worried parents.] The next day we ran into Bruce (the Agricultural Officer) halfway and enjoyed his company until Lapalam where we stopped for the night, while he continued on to Kandrian. Our carriers decided we had to sleep at Lapalam so they could get fed. We offered to buy food for them from the local headman who first said he didn't have any and then produced over 240 pounds of taro, sweet potatoes and tapiok and greens and we bought all 240 pounds and resisted the Luluai's pleas that we should buy everything else they brought in because we had asked for food.

[In retrospect we should not have asked for food in the manner of Kiaps. Rather, we should have learned enough to have waited for the Luluai (a man with extraordinary political power and influence) to *offer* us food. It was politically typical for him then to embarrass us by offering us far more than we could eat, and for which we *must* pay.]

Yesterday we had a short two hour walk to the main (only) vehicle road where we found the Patrol Officer, Algy, waiting for us in his "new" (2 day old) landrover—Bruce having been able to set up the transportation for us. What a blessed sight as the 8 mile hike on the open road under the cloudless sky is killing. So we arrived in Kandrian at 11 a.m., almost as fresh as daisies, at least comparatively speaking. Sylvia and Bruce McLean (malaria) are on leave, but they left their house for us to use with the beds made up and all facilities and Ann and I are now eating breakfast gazing over the blue sea, and doing our best to ignore "our" people hanging about. Our houseboys will stay with us until the Aztec picks us up on Monday to fly us to Hoskins. We hope all the others will leave today. Now all we have to do is sort and repack things to—ship home, mail home, carry home, and junk—and to take pictures of Kandrian while the sun shines.

The singsing at Dulago was terrific. A beautiful moonlight night and over 200 people and with shields and spears and the dancing fight between villages—which often becomes a real fight, but didn't that night, although it came pretty close to it—close enough to make it quite thrilling for us. We also had a singsing at Umbi for three nights preceding our departure, so we feel the "session" ended with a bang, and not just a fizzle.

Love Jane

[We flew to Lakalai and spent a week on the north coast visiting the village where Ann had worked before. The thing which impressed me most about this village was that there were always people doing things there, for me to watch and to photograph, in contrast to Umbi and Dulago. We then made exit visits to colleagues and officials in Rabaul, Moresby, Canberra, and Sydney. Although our travel funds did not catch up with us until we were leaving Hong Kong, we managed on extremely limited funds to take a much needed vacation, sightseeing our way home via Alice Springs, Bangkok, Singapore, Hongkong, Manila, and Hawaii. Along the way we searched museum collections in vain for chert tools similar to those we had found.]

Postscript

In leaving Umbi and Dulago we had very mixed feelings. On the one hand information was pouring in on all topics and as our language had improved considerably, our understanding and informed questioning were at the highest level. On the other hand we were very tired mentally and physically, and needed a break from those who had been our constant companions throughout. Our money was near its end, and finally we were scheduled to begin teaching in a month. However, both of us knew that our study had just begun and we would have to return and continue fieldwork among the Kaulong and Sengseng, perhaps in other communities.

I have always found it very hard to leave field-friends, with whom I have shared a life, particularly when the likelihood of seeing them again is remote. I had grown very fond of the people of Umbi even as I found them to be unpredictable, due to my lack of cultural knowledge, and therefore exasperating at times. The feeling of emptiness after leaving a field site is similar to the one I have when closing the cover of a really good but "too short" novel. Life in the village, or novel, goes on of course without me, but I may never know how the plots play out.

Because my involvement has been, by design, emotionally intense, I also find it very hard to return to my own world directly. For me the trip to Lakalai on the north coast, where Ann had lived in 1954 (and revisited for five weeks in 1962), was a terrific break. Ann was royally welcomed, and this welcome extended to me. Life in Galilo village was a complete contrast from that in Umbi. The 300+ inhabitants were always doing something I could observe—and I didn't have to ask any questions!

Always having to ask questions is perhaps the most tedious aspect of participant-observation. I remember sometimes being so very exhausted I knew I was too tired to write down, or remember, any answer even if I got one, so in the end I chose not to ask, and immediately felt enormously guilty.

I never returned to Umbi, although Ann returned to Dulago in 1966 and briefly in 1981 while based in other Sengseng communities. While I was in Angelek (my second Kaulong community) in 1967 and 1968, Ningbi came to visit but refused my invitation to stay overnight with me. He was too afraid of sorcerers in a place where he had no kin or trade relationships. He reported that Debli had married Tihime, that the twins were fine and driving everyone crazy because they had the same "face," and they all were sorry I didn't come back. I was and still am also sorry, but with very good reasons decided to follow up on what I learned in Umbi in a second Kaulong-speaking community, and one which was closer to the coast. Here, in 1967 and 1968 and again in 1974, I conducted a study equally as long as that in Umbi and polished up my knowledge and understanding of many of the aspects covered in this volume, but that is another story (one which has already been published as *To Sing with Pigs is Human: Concepts of Person in Papua New Guinea;* see Goodale 1995).

Chapter 9

The Final Postscript

This book has as its focus the fieldwork of two anthropologists carried out in the 1960s; with the publication of the book delayed, however, to the latter half of the 1990s. In view of these two facts, we must ask whether the work has any relevance to questions being asked by contemporary readers at the dawn of the twenty-first century. Two questions that are of current interest (at least to the author) will be addressed here. The first: because the fieldwork was carried out according to a holistic and largely inductive research plan, is it reflective of "old-fashioned" and/or "obsolete" ethnographic methodology? The second: because these letters relate the fieldwork experience of women, does the publication reflect a gendered approach?

Fashion "Old" and "New" in Ethnography

Although in the 1990s we are used to "instant publication" of first-person narratives from individuals caught up in the popular media, most scholarly publications have a long gestation period. This work was longer than most to reach publication. The letters were written more than 30 years ago and cover only a brief phase in the writers' commitment to long-term fieldwork in the same and different regions. Since the writing of the letters, the people we wrote about, the people we were, and anthropology itself have all matured and altered in many ways. In seeking to understand the processes involved in this maturation and alteration, the data gathered at the beginning of understanding are, perhaps, the most difficult to describe through retrospective analysis, having long ago sunk into the unconscious regions of the mind. Therefore, at the most obvious level, I believe that these letters, written more than thirty years ago, can provide a data *base* from which to approach the problem of *process* in ethnographic understanding, while the analysis, thirty-plus years later, can be done with a more mature understanding of the nature of ethnographic description.

An annotated bibliography of our publications on Kaulong/Sengseng can be found following this chapter, and should be referred to by anyone who wishes to use our gathered data on the Kaulong/Sengseng culture in a *comparative* way, rather than rely solely on this early "understanding-in-progress" for ethnographic data.

Cultural anthropology is perhaps the most widely misunderstood subfield of anthropology. This is due, in a large measure, to the difficulty that cultural anthropologists themselves have in defining what they do in the field. Although the cornerstone of ethnographic study of culture is "participant-observation," few but the practitioners have any understanding of this type of *inductive* methodology, which is uniquely anthropological in origin.

Field studies of *nonhuman* behavior (ethology) must involve participant-observation, as the researcher patiently spends as much time as possible in the company of a representative group of the nonhuman species, observing and recording everything she or he sees that is humanly possible to do, and for as long a period of time as permitted by personal endurance and financial support.

Ethnography is the field study of a particular variety of *human* social and cultural life with a single difference—the use of language. When the language of the observed is unwritten and there is little knowledge of a common language between observer and observed, the obvious first step is to learn a language by means of which communication (participation) can begin to take place. This was my first objective among the Kaulong. Ann's goal was more specialized than mine for she was both trained in comparative linguistics, and had previously learned to speak Tok Pisin fluently as well as two other Austronesian languages. It does not follow, however, that one can learn another culture through the spoken language alone. For the observer to assume that she knows anything about the culture of the "other," she has to "experience" that culture even after learning the language spoken by members of the other culture. This is true, I believe, even when researching one's own culture, and sharing a language with one's host community from birth.

Significant aspects of all cultures, including one's own, are learned through experience supplemented in humans, through verbal and nonverbal communication. To learn a different version of one's own culture, or that of another, the observer must first depend on the *inductive* (participant-observation) methodology, and learn to look and see, to listen, and eventually to question (using increasingly a *deductive* methodology) before "understanding" is approached. Agar (1980) calls this progressive methodology the "funnel" approach—characterized by starting with a broad view and then later focusing more narrowly on key topics of interest.

Although both Ann and I had acquired knowledge of Melanesian cultures through the literature, (and for Ann through prior experience), there was little specifically pertinent literature concerning the Kaulong and Sengseng that would have allowed us to use anything but an *inductive* methodology during the initial period in the field which is covered here by our correspondence.

Ann and I, working in separate language groups, could not assume the two cultures were closely similar in any way until it could be demonstrated and checked. Checking data (using *deductive* methodology) was accomplished both through posing specific questions in the field to determine how many people in the community shared the behavioral or belief trait, and through comparison with the data of the other observer.

We set up the whole project in order to provide just such a comparative test of the data we sought. Much of the "chit-chat" in the letters is aimed at provoking a comparative response. The Kaulong and Sengseng themselves joined into the comparative aspect of our field research. They competed with each other to see who could teach us various aspects of their language and culture first. And they proudly displayed their success to visitors from other communities, asking us to "show off what we had learned."

I think that these letters make it obvious that Ann and I used the competitive attitude of Umbi and Dulago as a very useful ploy in our search of understanding. For example, for me to say to my Kaulong assistants that "The Sengseng told Ann thus and so" would always provoke a response confirming, denying, or amplifying. Such responses were of course based on *their* knowledge of the culture at Dulago and usually included the information that they at Umbi also did, or did not do, the same. Comparison then became a vital part of our data gathering and allowed us to formulate (*deduce*) hypotheses to test. Being able to make this comparison in the fieldwork *process* itself was of great help in our own progress in understanding.

When I moved to Angelek in 1967 for my continued research among the Kaulong (deliberately choosing a community a great deal more influenced by outside missions and governments), I had to begin my *comparative* study there by assuming I knew nothing about this new variety of Kaulong culture. I learned this within the first few days in Angelek when I realized that constant references to what I had learned in Umbi were not only of *no* interest to the Angelek inhabitants, but were, in fact, a very off-putting method of inquiry.

This account of the beginning period of Ann's and my fieldwork in Kaulong/Sengseng communities is illustrative of a rather elusive initial phase of the study of any "other" culture. That the Kaulong/Sengseng culture was quite unknown to us initially, and significantly different from known Melanesian cultures, and one in which the people spoke an aberrant form of Austronesian language, were all factors which made the study easier for us in some ways. At the same time, these were factors which provided extreme stress, as the people's values were unexpected and frequently in conflict with our own culturally constructed sense of appropriateness in human behavior.

If there was one single facet of their way of life that made our study unusually difficult, it was the Kaulong/Sengseng sense of privacy which dictated that married couples (and children) must live separate from each other, and separate from the unmarried men. This meant that each family lived near their own gardens (an obvious convenience too), leaving the hamlet and village men's house as permanent quarters for single men and visiting males, and occasionally for the extremely aged affiliates, who were expected to die soon and would be buried therein. For these reasons, we found we were unable to reside in the household of any community member, but rather, had to occupy a somewhat marginal position in a haus kiap (Ann) or one especially built for the anthropologist (me) located in the village. With the already small population so widely scattered throughout the forest, we frequently had only one or two (or, some days, no) people to observe or talk to in the villages in which we were based. To go to the gardens, scattered as they were, provided just about the same limited opportunities. With the exception of the occasional gathering of a greater number of people at singsings, and on the weekly Government-imposed workdays (Monday), there were very few days with activities in which we could participate, observe, or conduct interviews. Therefore, we were unusually lonely, frequently bored, and professionally frustrated most of the time.

The physical separation of the Kaulong/Sengseng and their observers was compounded by their perception of a vast social distance that existed between themselves and us. They had little experience with "others" of any culture (including Kiaps and missionaries) and had learned little in the way of accommodation of the different ways of behavior. By the time we left, we had made some intercultural relationships, which permitted both parties to relax somewhat with each other, as friends learn to do. They learned to predict our behavior as indeed we learned to predict theirs (although we continued to "surprise" each other to the very end—as the Luluai of Lapalam did by responding to our inappropriate request for food with an overabundance for which we had to pay!).

Because we both wanted to study pre-Christian ways of life and belief, we deliberately chose to work in a remote region, only recently contacted by colonial outsiders (Kiaps and missionaries), and geographically and physically very difficult. Can this be interpreted to mean that our work is "old-fashioned"? I believe that it can be so considered only in the sense that some anthropologists consider there are no such anthropologically "pristine" regions left in the world today to study. They may be right.

Women's Voices

"Yes, Virginia, there is a 'feminist' voice in anthropology" writes Bell (1993: 29-43), but I for one, have never felt that my voice was anything more than that of an anthropologist who is also female. Ann and I both trained in the nongendered "prefeminist" era in anthropology as were many of our female predecessors in oceanic ethnography (e.g., Catherine Berndt, Beatrice Blackwood, Phyllis Kaberry, Margaret Mead, Hortense Powdermaker, Marie Reay, and Camilla Wedgewood, to mention only a few). While Ann had taken undergraduate courses with a female anthropologist (Frederica de Laguna) at Bryn Mawr, I had no such experience throughout my undergraduate anthropology at Radcliffe (in the 1940s), nor did either of us have any female professors while in graduate school at the University of Pennsylvania (in the 1950s).

In writing up our first field data as Ph.D. dissertations in the late 1950s, we included data that we had collected from and about men as well as women (Goodale 1959, Chowning 1958), and discussed how, in some areas, the views of women differed from those of men. In addition, I chose to chronicle the life course of Tiwi females as the frame for my dissertation (Goodale 1959), as had Kaberry two decades earlier (1939). In writing *Tiwi Wives* (1971) I included *male* as well as *female* voices in my discussion of Tiwi culture and society.

One need only skim through the biographies and bibliographies of fifty-eight female anthropologists who were born before 1925, covered in Gacs *et al.* (1988), to find that not one of them is labeled as "feminist," nor (I would venture to guess) would any of them so label themselves as a "feminist." This term has only appeared post-1970, writes di Leonardo (1991: 1), who uses the term "prefeminist" for ethnography written by women prior to 1970.

Since 1970 there have been quite a number of books concerned with field methodology. If one looks for techniques of fieldwork, the greater number of them have been written by men: Adams 1960, Epstein 1967 (who includes two chapters written by women), Pelto 1970, Maranda 1972, Agar 1980, and Ellen 1984, to mention a few. Few women have written such technical texts. Some women like Greta Pelto have teamed up with a male author: Pelto and Pelto 1978, Crane and Angrosino 1984, and Denzin and Lincoln 1994. Is there a gender issue here? Judith Oakley writes, "Where fact is equated with 'vulgar empiricism' and its opposite is theory, women are seen to be the fact gatherers and men the theoreticians" (quoted by Lutz 1995: 256). Lutz goes on to add, "When the question of theory is not at issue, fieldwork can be coded masculine, heroic, adventurous" (1995: 256).

Theory is not at issue in *The Two-Party Line.* This is not a textbook of ethnographic technique, although it illustrates participant-observation quite well. Can our fieldwork be coded "masculine, heroic, and adventurous"? Ann and I were not the first women anthropologists to work in remote and difficult regions. We had plenty of female models (see Gacs 1988). Although these pioneers (circa 1850-1950) often downplayed the field conditions and their reactions to them, their experiences could easily be considered adventurous, and heroic, but were they also gendered (masculine or feminine) in any way?

Personal accounts of field experience seem to be written by women first (Bowen [Laura Bohannon] 1954) and continue since that date to be written as frequently by men and women. Women as well as men have also edited books in which ethnographers have described and commented upon their field experience. (See chapter 1 for citations of pertinent accounts.)

In a book published in 1967, edited and written by two men (Jongmans and Gutkind), and called *Anthropologists in the Field,* the gender of the fieldworker is simply not considered. One of the first to consider the question of gender is *Women in the Field,* edited by Golde (1970). In this book she asks her contributors to discuss the particular aspects of fieldwork faced by women anthropologists which distinguishes their experience from that related by men. Golde's recent revised edition (1986) enlarges this discussion as does Bell,

Caplan, and Karim's edited book *Gendered Fields: Women, Men and Ethnography* (1993). Refreshingly, this volume contains chapters written by men as well as women (see also Whitehead and Conaway 1986). The topic of gendered fieldwork now includes both a discussion of the voices of female and male anthropologists as well as that of their male and female cultural guides (friends, assistants, consultants, and informants). How, then, may *The Two-Party Line* be read as contributing to the current discussion concerning gendered fieldwork?

In formulating research plans for our joint Kaulong/Sengseng project, our interests were primarily derived from the dominant anthropological questions of the time: language classification, kinship and social organization, non-Christian religious beliefs, and human sexual behavior. And since much of the interior of Papua New Guinea had been ethnographically *unknown* prior to World War II, holistic and comparative Melanesian studies were considered both urgent and important.

In *Sex and Temperament in Three Primitive Societies* Mead (1935) led the way pointing out that Melanesian cultures vary in both belief and practice in how they handle human sexuality. Since the late 1960s this topic has become one of the prime topics for investigation in Papua New Guinea, as well as elsewhere. I think any ethnographer, male or female, would have discovered as quickly as we did that male and female Kaulong/Sengseng differ in *some* ways from other Melanesians in their view of sex and marriage. While the dangerous sexuality of mature women is a shared belief with many highland New Guinea groups, young single Kaulong/Sengseng men seemed to us to be *unusally* afraid of sex (and marriage), whereas women rarely commented on their own powers of pollution, and frequently chose to ignore them. The casual attitude of the Kaulong/Sengseng women toward their sexual power was recognized by the men and probably contributed to their heightened fear. But while the male attitude was expressed to us almost daily, the female attitude was more difficult to learn and was made primarily by observation.

Macintyre (1993) noticed that Tubetube (Papua New Guinea) women used the *inclusive* "we" to *her* whereas men used the *exclusive* form. I cannot recall which form the Kaulong or Sengseng used with Ann and me, but we were both aware of the difficulty our hosts had in classifying us as women. With little experience with any women other than those of the interior with whom they traded, the Kaulong of Umbi decided that I was essentially ungendered: they initially incorporated me in the sexually mature generation of women, but uniquely unable *to pollute* (men) and to *be polluted* (by women). Because I was a woman, I was well aware of the problem I *could* cause for Kaulong males, but I consciously sought to remain passively neutral in asserting any gender identity, allowing the men and women to accommodate my presence in the least intrusive manner. Ann, too, was considered to be a woman, but nonpolluting to the men who cooked food underneath her house.

As my study proceeded, and my hosts grew familiar with my presence, I found that Kaulong men seemed more concerned to keep me in an ambiguous category than did the women, often warning me of pollution dangers while the women never did. But when I uncharacteristically pushed for my inclusion with women to the fullest in Umbi, by asking my female friends for data concerning sexual intercourse and conception, Umbi women could not bring themselves to bridge the conceptual distance and accept me in *their* gendered category. It is, of course, reasonable to consider that my exclusion from sharing in this data was in part due to my single and childless state. But I believe it is more likely that they, like the men, did not see me as being the same kind of human as them, particularly regarding gender distinction. When the twins were born in Umbi, a man commented that *their* women didn't produce multiple births like *natapela meri* (other women). Significantly, Umbi women, did not comment this way on the occurrence of multiple births. Rather, they said that when a woman has a second child too close to the former, the new infant is "thrown away," occasionally to be rescued and reared by another woman. "Too close" could mean twins or any child born before the previous child has been weaned, which sometimes was not for three or four years. For Kaulong men, the essence of this question resolves to one of inclusion in the category of human, rather than one of gender designation (see Goodale [1995] for a fuller discussion of Kaulong concepts of being human and Chowning [1984] for the biological implications of their sexual beliefs and practices).

Our gender ambiguity and placement may be related to our frequent frustration in being "understood" by our hosts and to a question we frequently asked each other: Why is it that neither the Kaulong or Sengseng ever really showed interest in us as people from another culture? We probably could have been from Mars (we said to each other) and have been as little understood. But then how would *you* begin to ask a Martian about her(?) life at home? They had no problem in considering us as *waitpela* (European) because we arrived in their world escorted by white Kiaps (and indigenous police), lived in houses whose style was dictated by Kiaps, and had "cargo" of European origin, and so on. But our hosts, not without cause, quickly became confused as almost immediately we both went about dispelling their initial belief that we were "kin" in *any* way to the Kiaps—most certainly not to be called *misis*, Tok Pisin for European women—but to be addressed by name.

We told them repeatedly that we were not Australians but Americans. This meant little, as our hosts had almost no contact with any Europeans other than Australians. While we managed, finally, to convince our hosts that we were "Americans" (or at least, non-Australian), they continued to believed that America was a "place" close to Rabaul. On our return from our post-Christmas holiday, they asked about our families who they assumed we had just seen. In addition to our negotiation of gender, and interest in cross-sex relationships, there are probably other reflections of our gender in this account.

Bell (1993: 1–18) talks about a number of gender distinctive aspects in what she calls "feminist" ethnography: (1) women anthropologists more often than men cite data as coming from specific and gendered individuals rather than inferring a generalized nongendered source, (2) women more frequently than men experiment in the writing of ethnography, and (3) women more easily than men reveal the emotional impact on themselves of the stresses of cross-cultural understanding. I think these letters richly illustrate the validity of all these aspects which Bell considers characterize women's ethnographic research and writing.

Ann and I talk about people by name and particularly as sources of information (and misinformation). We also talk constantly about our own emotional states, and we choose to publish these letters in a form which we believe is very experimental, accepting that some critics will say (because the letters are so revealing of our ourselves, although thirty-plus years younger) it is foolhardy for scholars to do—even mature (and retired) ones!

Some gender-related questions remain. To understand other cultures one must not only listen to the native voice, but also to the voice of the ethnographer but, as is well known there are some aspects of culture that cannot be put easily into the written word. "Listening" to Ann's and my representations of the fieldwork experience must also include the reader paying attention to nonverbal expressions of our gender and our culture found in this account—not just what we wrote to each other but where, when, how, and why.

Where, when, and how are quite explicit in this account. Why we chose to do fieldwork together is not so obvious. While some of the answer to this question may have more to do with friendship and little to do with gender, it is true that having experienced mixed gendered fieldwork previously, we were deliberate in seeking a situation which would not involve male colleagues. And in order to remain friends, we chose to do fieldwork in two separate communities sharing information rather than competing for it. By working in two communities we could compare the similarities and differences in a friendly mode without evaluation. Working in separate communities also resolved any potential problems that might arise with the slight variations in *style* of fieldwork we each practiced.

I was the *constant spectator type* frequently unwilling to discontinue any observation, however boring, in the firm belief that *something interesting* or *significant* might happen and I would miss it. Ann was more of a *focused observer type*, recording an event in meticulous detail until repetition became boring when she turned to other matters (such as typing notes) unrelated to the ongoing activity. When we read each other's notebooks we admired what the other included in her notes, some attributable to differences in style: I frequently took the time while still observing to reflect (in writing) on the interpretations and meanings of what was going on, while Ann had many more details of the exact movements of all involved individuals and this resulted in her filling stenographic notepads at twice the rate I did.

Our relationships with our hired assistants also varied. Each of us found a mode of operation with which we were personally comfortable. Ann had one young male assistant working in the house, and hired additional people to cut firewood and collect drinking water. My two male assistants did the housework, washing, and cooking, while I only "hired" the very young to collect water and paid them in hard candy. (The fact that these assistants were male relates to the expectation of our hosts that allowed males to work for Europeans and not females.) Ann imported food especially for her assistant and distinct from her own, while I and my assistants ate together the same imported and locally obtained food. And I frequently fed others as well. These relationships were difficult for both of us at times, but we avoided any possible conflict between ourselves caused by these stylistic differences, by maintaining two households in two places. We laughed when we realized that the only time our dishes were washed in *both* hot water and soap was on our trips out of the field when the households were combined.

I believe that our decision to go together into the field was motivated by a recognition of the need for emotional support—support such as I had not received from my male companions in previous fieldwork. Certainly as these letters attest, we "needed to communicate" with each other to an unusual degree. How great the need was can be seen in the frequency with which we wrote notes to each other, compared to the rare frequency with which we communicate with each other when out of the field situation (reduced to perhaps a few times a year). Neither of us is by nature much of a correspondent!

I cannot help but wonder whether men in our places (in the study of Kaulong and Sengseng) would have felt a similar need to share experiences with each other. Would their letters (if indeed they felt the need to write them) have included more or less personal and emotional content in relation to ethnographic data? In reviewing the content of these letters, full of accounts of our relationships with particular Kaulong/Sengseng individuals, can we say that we were more sensitive than a male colleague would have been to *Kaulong/Sengseng* expressions of emotions, both personally and academically? Whether male anthropologists would be sensitive to the *same* stimuli and to the *same* extent as we were must await comparative empirical data to answer. As far as I am aware, these data do not exist today.

Whatever the case concerning emotions, these letters are certainly revealing about the cultural load (often termed "baggage") that Ann and I carried into the field. Mead (1976) and Powdermaker (1966) both felt that the ethnographer should know herself before she could effectively study of the "other." In retrospect, I believe that the study of ethnography (whether of one's own or another's culture both in the field and in the analysis) requires the ethnographer to continually reflect on her own cultural assumptions. Powdermaker underwent psychoanalysis before embarking on her first ethnographic project.

I feel I have gained a similar in-depth understanding of who I am *culturally* through the challenge of all my field projects and in the writing of the culture of other people. One value in particular which was challenged by the Kaulong was the (European) assumption that one's word, once given, should not be questioned. This one was battered about almost daily by the Kaulong, who, with rare exceptions, use bluff, ambiguity, and outright lies as accepted means of social and political discourse.

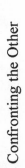

Confronting the Other

The Kaulong/Sengseng acceptance of violence in courtship and marriage, as well as in intercommunity singsings was somehow easier to take (although based on distinctive values of proper cross-sex behavior and proper host/guest attitudes) than their somewhat inefficient manner of spearing pigs, resulting in long delays and agonizing cries of the victim, which have bothered most Europeans. Fortunately, we never witnessed the strangulation of widows, which would have tested our tolerance for differing values while forcing us to become even more self-aware of our own cultural values.

One final value which gave me trouble was that for the Kaulong it is better to steal than ask for something, particularly, but not exclusively, food. It took me a long time to learn that offering food is a political put-down for the receiver, and a mark of honorable generosity for the giver.

Being self-aware (the mark of postmodernism), does it follow that we (male or female) are less able to offer valid representations of the "other," less able to extrapolate from the particular to the general? The answer to this question in regard to us lies in the papers and books we have written on the Kaulong/Sengseng (see bibliography).

What Impact Did Our Sojourn Have?

When we left we had few illusions concerning our "impact" on the indigenous culture. Our respective Kaulong/Sengseng friends made it quite clear by constantly asking us, "Who will replace (*senis* in Tok Pisin) you?" and adding, "Without you here our children will die and we won't be able to find (European) money." Providing medical aid, superior to that available at the aid posts, was the act through which we probably gained most of their respect. At the same time this did little to encourage them to seek western medical help elsewhere after we left.

By bringing in European "money" we made possible an alternative monetized exchange pattern to exist alongside with the previously valued one based on gold-lip pearl shells. This had an effect of permitting a limited amount of nonpersonalized exchange transactions and relationships, and also allowed more individuals (including women and children) to enlarge their exchange network to include people in the "outside" world.

And finally, even as we learned Kaulong and Sengseng, they became more fluent in Tok Pisin. By ourselves often speaking in Tok Pisin, initially to the few males who knew this *lingua franca*, we encouraged others including women and children, to learn how to communicate with others like ourselves who belonged to the "outside" world.

Process in Ethnographic Understanding

I believe that any cross-cultural experience should provide both parties with a chance to learn about the other. That curiosity about the other is *learned* behavior became apparent when I contrasted the interaction I had in Umbi (shown in these letters) with that I experienced in Angelek.

In Angelek, in contrast to Umbi, the people had earlier and more extensive contact with Europeans and Asians dating from the turn of the century. They communicated with these "others" using Tok Pisin often, it seemed, asking for explanation. However, they were more often ordered by the Europeans to change their own behavior, even as they also observed the different behavior of the European. Even if they were given explanation, they frequently could not understand the answers as they were often given in terms to which they could not relate.

In Angelek, I found that I was constantly being asked questions about "my" culture (and that of other outsiders with whom they were in contact), even as I was asking them about theirs. Just answering these questions became a test of my knowledge of their "world" as I sought to find valid comparisons and metaphors through which they could grasp meaning and understanding. The questions I was asked in turn, were a lens through which I could see my own culture as *they* perceived it. Thus it was in Angelek that I was able to set up a reciprocal "two-party line" relationship with many members of the community. We became, over time, able to *compare* and *share* values, behaviors, and indeed emotions as we explored each other's culture. This more than anything else illustrates the reciprocal process of ethnography as one of gradual acquisition of the knowledge necessary for both observer and observed to translate between cultures.

This reciprocal learning process is a lengthy one. Indeed, as ethnographers who have been engaged in long-term research in the *same* culture know, it is a process without end. In that both the observed and observer are undergoing constant change, long-term researchers are less concerned with the superficial changes that increased contact with outsiders bring, but become more concerned with persistence and change in the core values of the culture, and in tracking the choices and interpretations individuals have and are making.

But in any study of change one has to set an arbitrary beginning, and for the ethnographer this is the period of first contact she or he makes with the particular others selected. While this is the beginning for the ethnographer, today it is rarely considered as a beginning by the observed. But in 1962 we came close to being the first *waitskin* some of our informants had seen, certainly the first to have extensive and intensive contact. Thus *The Two-Party Line* documents this fleeting moment in time as people of two cultures try to understand each other's different ways of life.

Glossary of Terms

E (English), K (Kaulong), S (Sengseng), TP (Tok Pisin)

ADO—Assistant district officer (colonial government).

amok—A type of temporary insanity.

ANZAAS—Australian New Zealand Association for Advancement of Science.

banis (TP)—Fence.

betel (E)—Areca palm nut; commonly chewed together with betel pepper (leaf, bark, or peppercorn) and crushed lime—produces a mildly stimulating effect.

big man/woman (E)—Man/woman with influence; an adult male or female.

bilas (TP)—Decorative items.

bisnis (TP)—Kin group, those with whom one trades.

BP—Burns Philip, a major trading and general merchandise establishment with stores throughout Papua New Guinea and other South Pacific locations.

cargo, *kago* (TP)—Any material goods. Usually applied to imported goods.

cargo cult—a nativistic, millenarian or religious movement, appearing fairly commonly among people of coastal Melanesia. Leaders often proclaim the ritual means by which followers can gain quick (often magical) access to European material wealth ('kago').

cognatic kin groups—A descent group traced through both parents. See also kindreds.

cognates—Members of a cognatic kin group.

cross-cousins—Children whose parents are siblings of opposite sex (MB/FZ children); second cross-cousin—children whose grandparents are siblings of opposite sex.

CPO—Cadet patrol officer (colonial government). The lowest Kiap level.

diwai (TP)—Tree; wood.

dinau (TP)—Debt.

DO—District officer (colonial government).

enu (K)—Soul.

FZ (E)—Father's sister.

expatriates —Any nonnative resident in Papua New Guinea.

haus boi (TP)—Men's house (see also *mang*).

haus kiap (TP)—Village house built for government officers (Kiaps) on patrol.

haus kuk (TP)—Kitchen or separate house used for cooking.

haus waswas (TP)—Bath/shower room/house.

kaikai (TP)—To eat (v); a meal; a feast (n).

kalabus (TP) Calaboose —to jail (v); a jail (n).

kaukau (TP)—Sweet potato.

Kiap (TP)—Colonial government administrators (often used collectively for all ranks).

kindreds—A group of kin traced bilaterally from and through both parents.

kivung (TP)—A meeting, a gathering of people; cargo-cult.

kros (TP)—Cross, angry (v); an argument (n).

kundu (TP)—Drum, hour-glass shaped.

lain (TP)—To reside officially for census purposes (v); a group of kin descended from a common ancestor/ancestress(n).

laplap (TP)—Strip of cloth, worn overlapping and fastened at the waist or sometimes at the neck.

limbum (TP)—Type of palm, used for house floors.

longlong (TP)—Crazy, insane.

lotu (TP)—Church meeting, *haus lotu* a church.

Luluai (TP)—Top village official appointed by colonial government.

mang (K)—Main hamlet house; men's house; used for all village houses.

manki (TP)—Young lad; boy.

masalai (TP)—A spirit being, usually inhabiting the bush or rivers.

masang (K)—Man; men's house (S).

matmat (TP)—Graveyard, place of burials; also used for hamlet by Kaulong and Sengseng.

matrilateral—On the mother's side.

menge (K/S)—Type of temporary mental state (insane), similar to amok.

midan (K), *mihidan* (S)—hamlet leader, see big man.

mok (K/S)—Lean-to shelters in hamlets, women's houses, most garden huts; married couple's houses in village.

muli (TP)—Lime/lemon.

MZ (E)—Mother's sister.

NGS —National Geographic Society.

paper, *peipa* (TP)—Newspaper; used to roll tobacco into small cigar-shaped "smokes."

parallel cousins—Children of siblings of the same sex (MZ/FB children).

pass, *pas* (TP)—A letter or note.

patrilateral—On the father's side.

patrol box (E)—A small aluminum trunk, made to be waterproof and lockable and with two long looped metal handles at each end through which a single strong pole could be inserted, enabling two men to carry it slung between them with the pole on their shoulders.

Pidgin—See Tok Pisin.

pinatang (TP)—insect.

ples (TP)—Hamlet.

PO—Patrol officer (see Kiap).

polamit (K)—Big woman, any adult female.

pomasang (K)—People.

pomidan (K)—Big man, any adult male.

potunus (K/S)—Human.

purpur (TP)—Skirts made from leaves and other fibers; ornamental plants (introduced).

rite-of-passage—Rituals which mark culturally significant transitions in a person's life, such as at birth, maturity, marriage, and death.

scale, *skel* (TP)—A measured amount; e.g. pay, rations, etc.

small house (*smolhaus* in TP)—Pit latrine.

singsing (TP)—A song "fest"(n); to sing (v), for ceremonial and other social occasions.

tamberan (TP)—Ghost.

tapiok (TP)—Sweet manioc, an introduced root cultigen.

taro—Staple root crop for Kaulong and Sengseng.

Tok Pisin (TP)—A trade language developed and spoken throughout areas of contact in the former Territory of New Guinea, and today one of three official languages of the Nation of Papua New Guinea.

tobacco sticks—Tobacco pressed into sticks each measuring approximately. 8 in. by 0.5 in. by 0.25 in. Equivalent to one shilling (in 1964 worth approximately 20 U.S. cents).

Tultul (TP)—Colonial government appointed number 2 village official.

tusker (E)—A large male boar with protruding and curving tusks.

ulu (K)—A type of mental illness; temporary fit.

ulal (K/S)—Courtship fighting initiated by females.

unilineal descent—Tracing descent through either males or females but not both.

BIBLIOGRAPHY

The bibliography has been divided into two sections. Part I contains the pertinent writings by Ann Chowning primarily on the Sengseng and Jane Goodale on the Kaulong, while Part II contains works cited. Since Ann's titles are quite descriptive, her entries have not been annotated but rather *starred to indicate significant information on the Sengseng; those left unstarred, are more widely comparative with other areas of Melanesia, but include some information on the Kaulong/Sengseng groups. I have added some brief annotations to my bibliography since I tend to use less descriptive titles. Those marked # are more readily available.

SENGSENG

Chowning, Ann. "Acculturation and the Role of Spirits in the Passismanua." Paper read at The Annual Meeting of the American Anthropological Association, 1964.

——.* "The Languages of Southwest New Britain," Paper read at 11th Pacific Science Congress, Tokyo, 1966.

——.* "The Austronesian Languages of New Britain." Papers in Linguistics of Melanesia no. 2. *Pacific Linguistics* A-21 (1969):17–45.

——."Recent Acculturation between Tribes in Papua-New Guinea." *Journal of Pacific History* 4. (1969): 27–40.

——."Child Rearing and Socialization." *Encylcopedia of Papua New Guinea.* Melbourne: University of Melbourne Press, 1972.

——."Child Rearing and Socialization" (revised and expanded). *Anthropology in Papua New Guinea.* Edited by Ian Hogbin. Melbourne: Melbourne University Press, 1973: 61–79.

——. *An Introduction to the Peoples and Cultures of Melanesia.* Addison-Wesley Modules in Anthropology, 1973.

————. "The Recognition and Treatment of Abnormal Mental States in Several New Guinea Societies." *Psychology in Papua New Guinea 1972.* Edited by M. A. Hutton *et al.* Australian Psychological Society, Papua New Guinea Branch, 1973.

————.* "Disputing in Two West New Britain Societies: Similarities and Differences," *Contention and Dispute: Aspects of Law and Social Control in Melanesia.* Edited by A. L. Epstein. Canberra: Australian National University, 1974: 152–197.

————. * "History of Research in Austronesian languages: New Britain" and "Austronesian Languages." *New Guinea Area Languages and Language Study,* vol. 2. Edited by S. A. Wurm. *Pacific Linguistics* C-39, 1976.

————. *An Introduction to the Peoples and Cultures of Melanesia,* 2d ed. Menlo Park: Calif. Cummings, 1977.

————. * "Changes in West New Britain Trading Systems in the Twentieth Century." *Mankind* 11 (1978): 296–307.

————."Comparative Grammars of Five New Britain Languages." Second International Conference on Austronesian Linguistics: Proceedings, Fascicle 2. *Pacific Linguistics* C-61 (1978): 1129–1157.

————."Changes in Staple Crops in West New Britain." Paper read at ANZAAS, Auckland, 1979.

————."Leadership in Melanesia." *Journal of Pacific History,* vol. 20 (1979), pts. 1 and 2: 66–84.

————.* "Culture and Biology Among the Sengseng." *Journal of the Polynesian Society* 89(1) (1980): 7–31.

————."Physical Anthropology, Linguistics, and Ethnology." *Biogeography and Ecology of New Guinea.* Edited by J. L. Gressitt. Junk, 1 (1982): 131–168.

————.* "Interaction Between Pidgin and Three West New Britain Languages." *Pacific Linguistics* A-65 (1983): 169–198.

————.* "Rapid Lexical Change and Aberrant Melanesian Languages: *Pacific Linguistics* C-88 (1985): 169–198.

————."Melanesian Religions: An Overview." *The Encyclopedia of Religion,* Macmillan, 9 (1986): 349–359.

————."The Development of Ethnic Identity and Ethnic Stereotypes on Papua New Guinea Plantations." *Journal de la Societe des Oceanistes* 42 82-86 (1986): 153–162.

————. "A Note on Underestimating Female Age in Lowland Papua New Guinea." *The Survey under Difficult Conditions: Population Data Collection and Analysis in Papua New Guinea.* Edited by T. McDevitt. New Haven, HRAFlex Publications, 2: 239–242.

————.* "Sengseng." *Encyclopedia of World Cultures,* vol. 2. Edited by Terence E. Hays, Boston: G.K. Hall and Co. (1991): 295–298.

————.* "Relations Among Languages of West New Britain." *Pacific Linguistics.* In press.

KAULONG

Goodale, Jane C. "Blowgun Hunters of the South Pacific." *National Geographic Magazine* 129, vol. 6 (1966): 793–817.
[The article which resulted from the National Geographic Society's involvement in the photographic aspect of our 1963–1964 trip.]
———. "Imlohe and the Mysteries of the Passismanua, Southwest New Britain." *Expedition*, Philadelphia, University Museum, 8: no. 3 (1966): 20–31.
[A discussion of finding and collecting the chipped stone tools (*imlo*) and the associated myth.]
———. "The Kaulong Gender." Paper presented at the Association of Social Anthropology in Oceania, Orcus Island. Washington, 1973.
———. "The Rape of the Men and Seduction of Women among the Kaulong and Sengseng of New Britain." Paper presented at Association of Social Anthropology in Oceania, Orcus Island. Washington, 1973.
[These two papers both written in 1973 were my first efforts in explaining the Kaulong concepts of gender difference. See Goodale 1995.]
———. "Big Men and Big Women: The Elite in Melanesian Society." Paper read at American Anthropological Association Annual Meeting, Washington, D.C., 1976 (see Goodale 1995).
———. "The Management of Knowledge among the Kaulong." Paper presented at Association of Social Anthropology in Oceania. Monterey, Calif., 1977.
———. "Saying It with Shells in Southwest New Britain." Paper presented at American Anthropological Association Annual Meeting, Los Angeles, Calif., 1978.
[A discussion of the Gold-lip Pearl shell valuable in trade and transactions. An enhanced discussion appears in Goodale 1995.]
———.# "Gender, Sexuality and Marriage: A Kaulong Model of Nature and Culture." *Nature Culture and Gender*. Edited by Carol MacCormack and Marilyn Strathern. Cambridge: Cambridge University Press, 1980: 119–142.
———.# "Siblings as Spouse: The Reproduction and Replacement of Kaulong Society." *Siblingship in Oceania: Studies in the Meaning of Kin Relations*. Edited by Mac Marshall. ASAO Monograph no. 8 Ann Arbor: University of Michigan Press, 1981: 375–405.
[A discussion of the classification of siblings, the relation-ship roles between same- and opposite-sex siblings, and explanation of how it is that Kaulong marry those who are (also) called sibling.]

————.# "Pig's Teeth and Skull Cycles: Both Sides of the Face of Humanity."
American Ethnologist, 12, No. 2 (1985): 228–244.
> [On the importance and meaning of song and song
> performances (singsings), in particular those involving
> mortuary rituals in which the skull is featured.]

————.# *To Sing with Pigs Is Human: Concepts of Person in Papua New
Guinea.* Seattle, Wash. University of Washington Press. 1995.
> [A final integration of many of the ideas in the above papers
> (unpublished and published); a more complete description
> and interpretation, utilizing more of collected data and a fresh
> analysis of many of the topics.]

————."The Music of Southern West New Britain: The Kaulong."
Encyclopedia of World Music. Washington, D.C.: Smithsonian Institu-
tion. In press.

Chowning, Ann and Jane C. Goodale. "The Passismanua Census Division,
West New Britain Open Electorate." *The Papua New Guinea Elections
1964.* Edited by David G. Bettison, Colin. A. Hughes, and Paul. W. van
de Veur. Canberra: Australian National University Press, 1965: 264–278.

————.# "A Flint Industry from Southwest New Britain, Territory of Papua
New Guinea." *Asian Perspectives.* 9 (1966): 150–153. (See also Pavlides
1993.)

————.# "The Contaminating Women." Paper presented at the American
Anthropological Meeting, Washington, DC 1971 (See Goodale 1995).

Chowning, Ann, Jane C. Goodale, T. Scarlett Epstein, and Ian Grosart.
"Under the Volcano." *The Politics of Independence, Papua New Guinea
1968.* Edited by A. L. Epstein, R. S. Parker, Marie Reay. Canberra:
Australian National University Press, 1971: 48–90.

BIBLIOGRAPHY OF WORKS CITED

Abramson, Allen. "Between autobiography and method: being male, seeing
myth and the analysis of structures of gender and sexuality in the eastern
interior of Fiji." *Gendered Fields: Women, Men and Ethnography.* Edited
by Diane Bell, Pat Caplan, and Wazir Jahan Karim. London: Routledge,
1993.

Adams, Richard A., and Jack J. Preiss, eds. *Human Organization Research,
Field Relations and Techniques.* Homeward, Ill.: Dorsey Press, 1960.

Agar, Michael H. *The Professional Stranger: An Informal Introduction to
Ethnography.* New York: Academic Press, 1980.

Appadurai, Arjun. "Dust jacket review" of *Fictions of Feminist Ethnography* by
Kamala Visweswaran. Minneapolis, Minn: University of Minnesota Press,
1994.

Bateson, Gregory. *Naven: A Survey of the Problems Suggested by a Composite Picture of the Culture of a New Guinea Tribe Drawn from Three Points of View.* Cambridge: Cambridge University Press, 1936.

Bell, Diane. "Introduction 1: The Context." *Gendered Fields: Women, Men and Ethnography.* Edited by Diane Bell, Pat Caplan, and Wazir Jahan Karim. London: Routledge, 1993.

Bell, Diane, Pat Caplan and Jahan Karim., eds. *Gendered Fields: Women, Men and Ethnography.* London: Routledge, 1993.

Blackwood, Beatrice. *Both Sides of Buka Passage: An Ethnographic Study of Social, Sexual and Economic Questions in the North-Western Solomon Islands.* Oxford: Oxford University Press, 1935.

Bowen, Elenore Smith (pseudonym). *Return to Laughter.* New York: Harper and Bros., 1954.

Briggs, Jean. *Never in Anger.* Cambridge, Mass: Harvard University Press, 1970.

Chinnery, E. W. P. "Certain Natives of South New Britain and Dampier Straits." *Territory of New Guinea Anthropological Report No. 3.* Melbourne, Australia: Government Printer, 1928.

Chowning, Ann. *Lakalai Society,* Ph.D. dissertation, University of Pennsylvania. Ann Arbor Mich.: University microfilm, 1958. (See also above for Sengseng Bibliography.)

Clifford, James, and George E. Marcus, eds. *Writing Culture: The Poetics and the Politics of Ethnography.* Berkeley: University of California Press, 1986.

Coon, Carleton Stevens. *The Tribes of the Rif.* Harvard African Series Vol. 4. Cambridge Mass: Peabody Museum of Harvard University, 1931.

Crane Julia G., and Michael V. Angrosino. *Field Projects in Anthropology, a Student Handbook.* Morristown, N. J.: General Learning Press, 1974.

de Laguna, Frederica. *Voyage to Greenland: A Personal Initiation into Anthropology.* New York: W. W. Norton and Co., 1977. (Reprinted, Prospect Heights Ill.: Waveland Press, 1995.)

di Leonardo, Micaela, ed. "Introduction: Gender, Culture, and Political Economy. Feminist Anthropology in Historical Perspective" In *Gender at the Crossroads of Knowledge: Feminist Anthropology in the Postmodern Era.* Berkeley: University of California Press, 1991.

Denzin, Norman K., and Yvonna S. Lincoln eds. *Handbook of Qualitative Research.* Thousand Oaks, Calif: Sage, 1994.

DeVita, Philip R. *The Humbled Anthropologist: Tales from the Pacific.* Belmont, Calif.: Wadsworth Publishing Co., 1990.

Douglas, Mary. "Deciphering a Meal." Clifford Geertz, ed. *Myth, Symbol, and Culture.* New York: W.W. Norton and Co. Inc., 1971.

Dumont, Louis. *The Headman and I.* Austin: University of Texas Press, 1978.

Ellen, R. F. *Ethnographic Research: A Guide to General Conduct.* London: Academic Press, 1984.

Epstein, A. L. *The Craft of Social Anthropology*. London: Tavistock Press, 1967.

Evans-Pritchard, E. E. *The Nuer*. Clarendon: Oxford University Press, 1940.

Farb, Peter, and George Armalegos. *Consuming Passions: The Anthropology of Eating*. Boston: Houghton Mifflin, 1980.

Gacs, Ute, Aisha Khan, Jerrie McIntyre, and Ruth Weinberg. *Women Anthropologists: A Biographical Dictionary*. Westport, Conn.: Greenwood, 1988.

Geertz, Clifford. *The Interpretation of Cultures*. New York: Basic Books, 1973.

Gilliard, Thomas. "Exploring New Britain's Land of Fire." *National Geographic Magazine*. Vol. 119, No. 2 (1961).

Golde, Peggy. *Women in the Field: Anthropological Experiences*. Chicago: Aldine, 1970. (Revised: 1986.)

Goodale, Jane C. *Tiwi Women*. Ph.D. dissertation. University of Pennsylvania. Ann Arbor Mich.: University microfilm, 1959.

—. *Tiwi Wives: A Study of the Women of Melville Island, North Australia*, Seattle: University of Washington Press, 1971. (Reprinted Prospect Ill. Waveland Press, 1995 (See also above for Kaulong bibliography.)

Goodenough, Ward Hunt. *Language, Culture and Society*, 2d ed. Menlo Park, Calif.: Cummings, 1981.

Hayano, David M. *Road Through the Rain Forest: Living Anthropology in Highland Papua New Guinea*. Prospect Heights, Ill: Waveland Press, Inc., 1990.

Hays, Terrance E., ed. *Ethnographic Presents: Pioneering Anthropologists in the Papua New Guinea Highlands*. Berkeley: University of California Press, 1992.

Jongmans, D. G., and Gutkind, P. C. W., eds. *Anthropologists in the Field*. Assen, The Netherlands: Van Gorcum and Co. N.V, 1967.

Kaberry, Phyllis M. *Aboriginal Women, Sacred and Profane*. London: Routledge, 1939.

Kilbride, Philip L., Jane C. Goodale, and Elizabeth Ameisen. *Encounters with American Ethnic Cultures*. Tuscaloosa, Ala.: University of Alabama Press, 1990.

Kilbride Philip L., and Janet Kilbride. *Changing Family Life in East Africa: Children and Women at Risk*. University Park: Pennsylvania State University Press, 1990.

Leahy, Michael. *New Guinea Probes into New Areas 1930-34*. Tuscaloosa, Ala: University of Alabama Press, 1991.

LeClair, Edward E. "Problems of Large-scale Anthropological Research." Adams, Richard A., and Jack J. Preiss, eds. *Human Organization Research, Field Relations and Techniques*. Homeward, Ill., Dorsey Press, 1960.

Levi-Strauss, Claude. *Structural Anthropology*. New York : Basic Books Inc., 1963.

Lowie, Robert H. *The Crow Indians*. New York: Farrar and Rinehart, 1935.

Lutz, Catherine A. "The Theory of Gender." *Women Writing Culture/Culture Writing Women.* Ruth Behar and Deborah Gordon, eds. Berkeley, Calif.: University of California Press, 1995.

Macintyre, Martha. "Fictive Kinship or Mistaken Identity." *Gendered Fields: Women, Men and Ethnography.* Diane Bell, Pat Caplan and Wizir Jahan Karim, eds. London: Routledge, 1993.

Malinowski, Bronislaw. *Argonauts of the Western Pacific.* London: Routledge, 1922.

———. *A Diary in the Strict Sense of the Term.* New York: Harcourt, Brace, and World, 1967.

Maranda, Pierre. *Introduction to Anthropology: A Self-Guide.* Englewood Cliffs, N.J.: Prentice-Hall, 1972.

Maschio, Thomas. *To Remember the Faces of the Dead: The Plenitude of Memory in Southwestern New Britain.* Madison, Wis.: University of Wisconsin Press, 1994.

Maybury-Lewis, David. *The Savage and the Innocent.* London: Evans, 1965.

Mead, Margaret. *Sex and Temperament in Three Primitive Societies.* New York: William Morrow, 1935.

———. *Letters from the Field: 1925-1975.* New York: Harper and Row, 1977.

Morgan, Lewis Henry. *League of the Ho-de-no-sau-nee or Iroquois.* Rochester, New York: Sage and Broa, 1851.

Pavlides, Christina. "New archaeological research at Yombon, West New Britain, Papua New Guinea. *Archaeology in Oceania* 28 (1993):55–59.

Pelto, Pertti J. *Anthropological Research: The Structure of Inquiry.* New York: Harper and Row, 1970.

Pelto, Pertti J., and Gretel H. Pelto. *Anthropological Research: The Structure of Inquiry,* 2d ed. New York: Cambridge University Press, 1978.

Powdermaker, Hortense. *Stranger and Friend: The Way of an Anthropologist.* New York: W. Norton and Co., 1966.

Rabinow, Paul. *Reflections on Fieldwork in Morocco.* Berkeley: University of California Press, 1977.

Radcliffe-Brown, Alfred Reginald. *The Andaman Islanders.* New York: Free Press, 1964 [originally published 1922].

Read, Kenneth. *The High Valley.* New York: Scribner's, 1965.

Riesman, Paul. *Freedom in Fulani Social Life.* Chicago: University of Chicago Press, 1977.

Sanjek, Roger, ed. *Fieldnotes: The Makings of Anthropology.* Ithica: Cornell University Press, 1990.

Schebesta, Paul. *Among Congo Pigmies.* Trans. from German by Gerald Griffin. London: Hutchinson and Co., Ltd., 1933.

Schneider, David M. *American Kinship: A Cultural Account,* 2d ed. Chicago: University of Chicago Press, 1980.

Spencer, Baldwin, Sir and F. J. Gillen. *The Arunta. A Study of Stone Age People.* 2 vols. London: Macmillan, 1927.

Specht, Jim, I. Lilley and J. Norman. "More on Radiocarbon Dates from West New Britain, Papua New Guinea. *Australian Archaeology* 16 (1983) : 92–95.

Todd, J. A. "Report on Research Work in S. W. New Britain, Territory of New Guinea." *Oceania* 5 (1934-35): 193–213.

———. "Native Offenses and European Law in S. W. New Britain." *Oceania* 5 (1934-35): 437–461.

———. "Redress of Wrongs in S. W. New Britain." *Oceania* 6 (1935): 401–440.

Whitehead, Tony Larry, and Mary Ellen Conaway. *Self, Sex, and Gender in Cross-Cultural Fieldwork.* Urbana Ill: University of Illinois Press, 1986.

Index

ABOUT THE AUTHORS

Jane C. Goodale is Professor Emeritus at Bryn Mawr College where she has been a member of the Anthropology Department since 1960, retiring in 1995. In addition to the research among the Kaulong of New Britain, Papua New Guinea, she has continued long-term research in North Australia among the Tiwi of Melville Island beginning in 1954 and extending into the 1990s. She has published monographs on both Kaulong and Tiwi.

Ann Chowning recently retired as Professor of Anthropology at Victoria University of Wellington, New Zealand. Earlier she taught at Bryn Mawr and Barnard Colleges and the University of Papua New Guinea, and was a Senior Research Fellow at the Australian National University. Between 1954 and 1992 she carried out long-term fieldwork in four Papua New Guinea societies. She has published extensively on the cultures and languages of Melanesia.